Psychotherapy of Psychosis

Edited by
CHRIS MACE
FRANK MARGISON

Psychotherapy of Psychosis

GASKELL

Gaskell is an imprint of the Royal College of Psychiatrists,
17 Belgrave Square, London SW1X 8PG

British Library Cataloguing-in-Publication Data
A catalogue record for this book is available from
the British Library.
ISBN 0-901242-048

Distributed in North America
by American Psychiatric Press, Inc.
ISBN 0-88048-579-5

Printed by Bell & Bain Ltd, Glasgow

Contents

List of contributors   vii
Foreword   *Andrew Powell*   ix
Acknowledgements   xii

1   Psychosis and psychotherapy: elements for integration
    Frank Margison and Chris Mace   1

**Part I. Psychodynamic and psychoanalytic approaches
    to psychosis**   11

2   Psychoanalytic and psychodynamic approaches
    to psychosis: an overview   *Stephen P. Reilly*   13
3   The great feast of languages: passwords to the
    psychotic's inner world   *Murray Cox*   31
4   The psychoanalytic approach to psychotic aspects
    of the personality: its relevance to psychotherapy
    in the National Health Service   *David Taylor*   49
5   Psychosis and groups   *John Walshe*   63
6   Borderline phenomena in analytic groups   *Malcolm Pines*   77

Part II. Behavioural and cognitive approaches to psychosis   89

7   Cognitive–behavioural approaches to psychosis:
    an overview   *Lynne M. Drummond and Anita Duggal*   93
8   Cognitive therapy of schizophrenia: collaborative
    and integrated approaches   *David Kingdon and
    Douglas Turkington*   115
9   The use of coping skills in the treatment of
    hallucinations and delusions in schizophrenia
    *Nicholas Tarrier, Lawrence Yusupoff, Caroline Kinney
    and Eilis McCarthy*   130

Part III. Systemic and family therapies   149

10 Family and systemic approaches to psychosis:
    an overview   *Chris Evans*   152
11 Psychosis and treatment of the whole family
    Roger Kennedy   169
12 Behavioural family therapy approaches to the
    treatment of schizophrenia   *Graínne Fadden*   181

Part IV. Integrative approaches to psychosis   197

13 Integration and psychosis   *Frank Margison and
    Chris Mace*   199
14 Pathological interactions between psychosis and
    childhood sexual abuse in in-patient settings:
    their dynamics, consequences and management
    Sarah Davenport   205
15 The Hawthorn Project. A group psychotherapy
    project with chronically psychotic in-patients
    Dianne Campbell LeFevre and Frank Morrison   220
16 The Finnish National Schizophrenia Project:
    a strategy for psychotherapeutic treatment and
    balanced deinstitutionalisation   *Kari Pylkkanen*   238
17 Meaning and madness. A narrative approach to
    psychopathology and treatment   *Glenn A. Roberts*   255

    Afterword   *Chris Mace and Frank Margison*   272

Contributors

Dr Murray Cox, Consultant Psychotherapist, Broadmoor Hospital, Crowthorne, Berkshire RG45 7EG, and Honorary Research Fellow, Shakespeare Institute, University of Birmingham

Dr Sarah Davenport, Consultant Psychiatrist, Department of Rehabilitation, Mental Health Services of Salford NHS Trust, Salford

Dr Lynne M. Drummond, Senior Lecturer and Consultant Psychiatrist, St George's Hospital Medical School, Cranmer Terrace, London SW17 0RE

Dr Anita Duggal, Senior Registrar, Central Wandsworth CMHT, Garratt Court, Furmage Street, London SW18 4DF

Dr Chris Evans, Senior Lecturer in Psychotherapy, St George's Hospital, London, and Locum Consultant to Prudence Skinner Family Therapy Clinic

Ms Gráinne Fadden, Consultant Clinical Psychologist, Buckingham Mental Health Service, 22 High Street, Buckingham MK18 1NU

Dr Roger Kennedy, Consultant Psychotherapist, Cassel Hospital, Richmond, Surrey TW10 7JF

Dr David Kingdon, Medical Director, Nottingham Healthcare Trust, Nottingham NG3 6AA

Ms Caroline Kinney, Research Assistant, Department of Clinical Psychology, University of Manchester, Withington Hospital, Manchester

Dr Dianne LeFevre, Consultant Psychotherapist, Mental Health Unit, Basildon Hospital, Basildon

Dr Chris Mace, Senior Lecturer in Psychotherapy, University of Warwick and Consultant Psychotherapist, South Warwickshire Mental Health Services Trust

Dr Frank Margison, Consultant Psychotherapist, Manchester Royal Infirmary

Ms Eilis McCarthy, Research Assistant, Department of Clinical Psychology, University of Manchester, Withington Hospital, Manchester

Mr Frank Morrison, Formerly Project Manager, Hawthorn Project

Dr Malcolm Pines, Consultant Psychotherapist, Group Analytic Practice, 88 Montagu Mansions, London W1H 1LF

Dr Andrew Powell, Consultant Psychotherapist, Warneford Hospital, and Honorary Senior Lecturer, University of Oxford

Dr Kari Pylkkanen, Director of Mental Health Services, Finnish Student Health Service Foundation, Helsinki, Finland

Dr Stephen P. Reilly, Consultant Psychiatrist with Special Responsibility for Psychotherapy, Bootham Park Hospital, York YO3 7BY

Dr Glenn Roberts, Consultant Psychiatrist, North Devon District Hospital, Barnstable

Professor Nick Tarrier, Professor of Clinical Psychology, Department of Clinical Psychology, University of Manchester, Withington Hospital, Manchester

Dr David Taylor, Consultant Psychotherapist, Adult Department, Tavistock Clinic, London NW3 5BA

Dr Douglas Turkington, Consultant Psychiatrist, St Nicholas' Hospital, Newcastle upon Tyne

Dr John Walshe, Consultant Psychotherapist and Honorary Fellow of Essex University, North East Essex Mental Health Services Trust, Psychotherapy Department, 1 Hospital Road, Colchester, Essex CO3 3HJ

Dr Lawrence Yusupoff, Senior Psychologist and Senior Fellow, Department of Clinical Psychology, University of Manchester, Withington Hospital, Manchester

Foreword

ANDREW POWELL

This book brings to a wider audience papers that were presented at the first joint conference of the Association of University Teachers of Psychiatry (AUTP) and the Psychotherapy Section of the Royal College of Psychiatrists at the University of York in 1994.

'The Psychotherpy of Psychosis' followed a series of biennial residential conferences, organised by the AUTP since 1982, which had served to bring together psychiatrists and psychotherapists from all parts of the UK. These had provided a forum for discussion of academic aspects of psychotherapy and an important opportunity for networking among specialists, who were often working in isolation. The 1992 conference 'Psychotherapy in the Marketplace: Responding to the NHS Reforms' explored the prblems and challenges confronting psychotherapy in a rapidly changing social and political climate.

That these conferences flourished for more than a decade was largely due to the personal efforts of Dr Sidney Bloch and Dr Mark Aveline. Their success prompted the Psychotherapy Section of the Royal College of Psychiatrists to establish its own biennial psychotherapy conferences in the intervening years. These had a more experiential and less academic bias, and began in 1989 when Dr Jon Sklar and I convened a conference entitled 'Trauma and its Aftermath'. This was followed by 'Understanding Prejudice' (1991), 'Destruction – the Psychological, Social and Psychodynamic Aspects' (1993) and, in 1995, 'Intimacy – an Exploration of Love and Hate in the Couple, the Family and the Group'.

The AUTP and the Royal College then joined forces in 1994 to share in this focus on the contribution of psychotherapy to the management of the severely mentally ill. In the UK there has been a striking lack of integration in this area. Until recently, psychotherapy had been driven by the psychoanalytical approach which, with a few notable exceptions, has largely concentrated on neurotic conditions and mild to moderate disorders of personality. At the same time, the thrust of biological psychiatry in the UK has been extraordinarily denying, and sometimes downright intolerant, of the psychodynamic contribution, which in many other countries is taken for granted.

The need for a more integrated approach has been sharpened by political developments in the National Health Service over the last few years. 'Purchasers' in the form of government-funded health authorities are now free to select the treatments to be bought for their captive populations, often as many as a million prospective patients. The 'providers' of the service are issued with business contracts, the commodity is 'health' and in this marketplace National Health Service trusts must compete with the private sector. The cost-effectiveness of treatments are monitored closely and 'audit' is the buzzword of our times.

Dynamic psychotherapy, which addresses personality development and maturational change, is disadvantaged in comparison with treatments for the acutely mentally ill which, in line with the medical model, can be counted in terms of episodes of patient care for which few would question the need. Family therapy has aligned itself vigorously with general psychiatry, although family interventions are not always welcomed. Behavioural and cognitive therapies are more at home in the new climate, although their practitioners still do not always enjoy genuine recognition within the speciality of psycho-therapy, with the associated need for a strong base for medical specialist training.

This has all led to a shake-up in thinking, old barriers and differences having to be challenged, and for ideologies, however lofty, having had to show themselves to be commercially viable. In all this, the needs of individual patients have to be remembered.

Medical psychotherapists, like most other practitioners, have been deeply divided about the true nature of the Health Service reforms. But the spur is there to review and revise what we do, and can do. On the positive side, the profession of psychotherapy is impelled to enter into a new kind of dialogue, both inwardly among its members, and outwardly towards psychiatric colleagues managing the acute services.

For a three-day conference, this focus had to be narrowed and the organising committee settled on the topic of psychosis. Even so, it was felt that no more than an assortment of key areas could be selected. By complementing plenary presentations with sessions of eight parallel workshops, repeated morning and afternoon, delegates were offered as wide a choice as seemed possible in a two-day event. In both the workshops and lectures, a rich mixture of presentations from the cognitive–behavioural, family and psychodynamic approaches was attempted.

Our objectives at the time could be listed as follows: to overcome some of the stereotypes within the different branches of psycho-therapy; to draw together colleagues of different persuasions and to find strands of common meaning and concern; to provide continuing professional development and up-to-date information across a range of treatments; and, lastly, as always, to mix and meet with friends and colleagues in the field, renewing old friendships and making new ones. In the National Health Service of tomorrow, there will be a need as never before to maintain that sense of community that serves to remind us that although health has now become a business, people must never become mere commodities.

Acknowledgements

We are indebted to Jean Wales and her staff at the Royal College of Psychiatrists. The conference on which the book is based owes a great deal of its success to their expert administration. We are also grateful for the helpful assistance of Dave Jago at Gaskell, and for advice received from Professor Richard Bentall, Professor Digby Tantam, and an anonymous reviewer.

The text of Chapter 6 is an edited version of Chapter 6 of *Ring of Fire*, edited by Victor L. Shermer and Malcolm Pines and published by Routledge & Co. (1994). It is reproduced here by kind permission of the publisher and the author.

1 Psychosis and psychotherapy: elements for integration

FRANK MARGISON and CHRIS MACE

Psychosis: fact or fiction?

The conference on which this book is based presented, through a series of contrasting lectures and parallel workshops, several different perspectives on psychosis and its psychotherapy. Participants were encouraged to sample work with which they were less familiar, and not simply consolidate ground they already knew well. It had been assumed that everybody there would use the word 'psychosis' in a broadly similar way. This appeared to be so, most of the patients discussed seeming to be easily classifiable within the framework of the 10th edition of the *International Classification of Diseases* (World Health Organization, 1992). Although 'psychosis' is not used there as a formal category, the term is sprinkled liberally throughout. Patients discussed at the conference would come under rubrics in the chapter on schizophrenia, schizotypal and delusional disorders or one of the affective disorders 'with psychotic symptoms'. A few inevitably fall into the confusing territory of 'emotionally unstable personality disorder – borderline type'. International consensus about terminology is relatively recent, however, and not necessarily fixed in its present form. In examining some trends in the psychotherapy of psychosis, it is helpful to appreciate some of the different ways in which the term 'psychosis' has been used.

Sir Aubrey Lewis (1946) has been credited with saying that psychosis is nothing more than "the doctor's word for 'mad'". However, it has not been doctors', or anybody else's, word for 'mad' for very long. It was introduced during the last century, once 'madness' was already a medical concern. After dignifying this state of affairs with more technical terminology, 'psychosis' has been used with more specific, and changing, connotations.

At the middle of the 19th century, 'psychosis' was a very broad term encompassing what we would now refer to as personality disorders, organic and functional states and neuroses. Its wide reference reflected belief in theories of hereditary degeneration, which led authors to expect that the many manifestations of mental disorder might be traced to one underlying 'unitary psychosis' (*Einheitpsychose*). Griesinger developed a unifying theory that different levels of cerebral excitation or retardation could account for the varied presentations of this unitary psychosis (Scharfetter, 1983). The tendency to define psychosis in terms of an assumed underlying physical cause is maintained in modern psychiatry by those, such as Schneider, who would reserve the term 'psychosis' for illnesses with an underlying physical cause (Schneider, 1967).

Even in the early 19th century, the appropriation of psychosis as a concept inextricably linked with physical disorder of the brain had been challenged. Heinroth maintained the German Romantic view of the soul (*Seele*), which overlaps with our modern concepts of both mind and character, and whose disturbance led to a variety of mental disorders. By the middle of that century there were competing classifications of psychosis that often reflected national differences. The French term *démence* covered some of the territory of organic states and also of functional and reactive psychoses. In Germany, where isolated syndromes were described in considerable detail, psychosis became an umbrella term (embracing dementia praecox, manic–depressive psychosis and epileptic psychosis (Kraepelin, 1899, 1920), which effectively detached it from any one specific cause.

From the late 19th century there has been relative stability around the classification of the psychoses, but significant distinctions continued to be made on the basis of the *course* of the illness, as in the opposition between Falret's *folie circulaire* and Kraepelin's *dementia praecox*. When other subsidiary categories were proposed, such as Kleist's schizoaffective and cycloid psychoses, these were seen as anomalies which did not disturb this general pattern of a deteriorating (schizophrenic) psychosis and an episodic (manic–depressive) version.

Despite subsequent changes in nomenclature, this diagnostic system has endured. Its apparent stability, however, masks the extent to which a descriptive classification system is a relatively primitive form of nosology, based on the (descriptive) syndrome rather than the (pathological or aetiological) disease level. At a practical level, classification by syndromes has been fruitful in developing a common language to describe abnormal states, but the specificity of the language and descriptions used hides the extent of ignorance concerning the pathology underlying the descriptive categories. The alignment of descriptions to underlying pathology remains the dream of a truly aetiological classification system. A recurrent aspect of this dream has been the distinction between illnesses that are constitutionally based and those that arise from effects of the environment. The confusion that arises when aetiology is spuriously linked with description has been widely examined in relation to reactive and endogenous depression (e.g. Paykel, 1974) but it applies equally to the psychoses.

Traditionally there have been psychotic illnesses that are seen as a direct consequence of a *physical* illness classified elsewhere in medicine. Examples include the separation of psychoses attributed to syphilis, myxoedema and porphyria. Attempts were also made to distinguish a group of illnesses that have a specific relation to *psychological* stress. Gaupp (1938), in describing the case of Wagner, identifies the specific 'sensitive' experience which brings on the psychosis. This theme was elaborated in greater detail by Kretschmer (1927), who clarified the relationship between underlying constitution that led to a biological vulnerability, and triggering events, often occurring at times of 'exhaustion', in those exhibiting '*Beziehungswahn*'. Strömgren (1968) went on to delineate the logical requirements for an illness to be classified as 'psychogenic' in summarising a substantial Scandinavian tradition of attention to these illnesses. He drew on Jaspers (1913) in stating that there is a precipitating factor closely related in time and in content to an illness with a short course. Quoting Wimmer (1916), Strömgren defines "clinically independent (psychogenic) psychoses" that:

(a) usually have a predisposition;
(b) are caused by mental agents or 'traumata' which determine the start, fluctuations and remissions;
(c) have a form and content that are 'comprehensibly' determined by the causal agent;
(d) tend to recovery.

He classifies the traumata into:

(a) impersonal catastrophes;
(b) more personal social disasters;
(c) family conflicts;
(d) isolation and disrupted communication;
(e) inner conflicts between different aspects of the personality, conscience and blows to self-esteem.

The concept of the understandability of trauma and its relation to psychosis has led to dispute about the cultural knowledge of psychiatrists and the limits this imposes on their ability to empathise with a diverse range of experiences. But Jaspers' notion of a non-understandable 'break' in development as a distinguishing feature of 'endogenous' psychoses has been influential in the way in which a history is taken by a psychiatrist. Rather than concentrating on the narrative coherence hidden within psychotic speech (an approach illustrated at length in the chapters by Cox and Roberts in this volume), the psychiatrist became drawn by training to notice and explore inconsistencies rather like a detective testing an alibi.

Between the extremes represented by organic and psychogenic psychoses lies a muddled grouping of so-called 'functional' psychoses. This, for some, is a hunting ground for syndromes to be attached to newly defined pathology discovered by gene probes, virology, and neuroimaging. For others, it is the area of psychiatry summarised loosely as severe, enduring mental illness.

Birnbaum's (1923) attempt to provide a structure to the "making of a psychosis" goes some way to resolving the confusion. He commented that a psychosis is not a fixed nosological entity, but "a highly intricate, discrete, animate, functional complex which originates in the dynamic interaction and counteraction of different forces, biological and psychological, normal and pathological, organic and functional". In distinguishing pathogenic from pathoplastic, Birnbaum assumed that the "biological" or organic factors determine why the psychosis is "thus and no other", while leaving space for those pathoplastic factors that "shape the disorder in that they give content, colouring and contour to individual illnesses whose basic form and character have already been biologically established". Birnbaum also delineated predisposing and provoking factors in the environment and thereby provided a coherent and plausible structure that has been enormously influential in European psychiatry.

With such a definitive framework, Birnbaum generated, in effect, a hierarchy of causation. By analogy, organic factors are the defining elements of the picture while other factors are essential to the picture as a whole as they supply light, shade, colour and contour to the pre-existing design. This view of psychosis remains so influential that it stands as an unchallenged truth in modern psychiatry. The implications of accepting this plausible structure are profound for psychotherapy. Pathoplastic factors are never seen as primary causes, and inevitably psychology takes second place to that claimed by the physical sciences in the development of treatments.

Psychotherapy for psychosis: (a) development

It might be argued that psychotherapy for psychosis enjoyed its heyday before the medicalisation of madness led to the introduction of 'psychosis'. Ellenberger (1970) has chronicled the continuities between modern 'dynamic psychiatry' and the charismatic efforts of shamans and priests to relieve madness by various means of ritual and persuasion rather than physical treatments. Once treatments for psychosis became a medical preserve, ideas of what was therapeutically possible were heavily conditioned by prevailing views concerning the pathogenesis of the psychosis. The subsequent history of psychotherapy for psychosis represents a dialectical movement between novel views on its pathogenesis and new treatments.

As the asylums and mad houses of the late 18th century grew, remarkable psychotherapeutic initiatives developed alongside far more nihilistic attitudes. The progressive 'mad doctors' of the time espoused therapy in the form of 'moral management' – a direct appeal to the mind and character over the body, rather than the conscience alone (Porter, 1987). They were indebted to Locke's doctrine that man was essentially malleable. They believed that madness arose as a result of a disturbance in life rather than a constitutional fault, and that direct engagement between the will of the physician and that of the patient was essential to break the mental habits and associations wherein the madness lay. The way in which the mad doctor conducted himself was tactical and opportunistic, placing great emphasis on the initial meeting. He would use eye-to-eye contact and a minimum of physical coercion as the patient's attention and respect were won and a personal battle was fought so that the patient's highly disordered will might be supplanted by that of the physician.

As enlightenment associationism became overshadowed by materialism in psychiatric thinking, psychotherapeutic manoeuvres were believed to have less potential to touch the core of psychosis and lead to cure. It is interesting, as Reilly notes in Chapter 2, that the revolutionary principles of psychoanalytic thinking were incubated at several removes from asylum psychiatry. Indeed, Freud, a former neurologist who based his psychoanalytic practice on the treatment of neurosis, even compiled his famous commentary on Schreber's paranoid illness at second hand. Others were then in a position to introduce psychoanalysis to the asylum and its largely psychotic population, notably Jung and Ferenczi among Freud's immediate contemporaries.

Jung's attitudes to the scope of psychotherapy for schizophrenia are of special historical significance because of his close early association with Eugen Bleuler at the Burghölzli Hospital. Bleuler had invented 'schizophrenia', a syndrome that superseded dementia praecox, by describing some core psychological processes that patients with very different symptoms had in common. These centred on a breakdown in internal associations. It is remarkable how consistent Jung's own descriptions of the relatively greater autonomy of 'complexes' among schizophrenic patients were with Bleuler's model (Barham, 1995). Jung maintained a fascination with schizophrenia throughout his life, along with a considerable psychotherapeutic optimism. He believed hospitalised schizophrenic people represented the tip of a clinical iceberg, claiming 'latent' schizophrenic illness was ten times as common in his subsequent practice. Among these cases, cure as well as amelioration was often possible through analytical psychology (Jung, 1939). However, this demanded both an unusual degree of familiarity with unconscious symbolism by analysts undertaking such work, and great personal resilience when faced with the risk of becoming psychotic themselves. At the end of a life spent defending the psychogenic nature of schizophrenia, Jung stated psychology was indispensable in accounting for its onset, although by 'psychological elimination' a metabolic factor appeared necessary to account for the characteristic form of the disturbance (Jung, 1957).

Considerable optimism concerning the scope of psychotherapy with schizophrenia was also expressed in the US, where Sullivan and Fromm-Reichman influenced the adoption of innovative analytic methods in hospital practice. Well aware of Jung's views (and critical of them), Sullivan (1974) emphasised cultural and interpersonal factors in the appearance of psychosis, to the exclusion of purely individual psychological features. He formed the view that early intervention in adolescence could be decisive, that the total therapeutic environment had to be carefully maintained to prevent lasting damage from some forms of regression, and that the early moments of therapeutic contact were critical.

Freeing psychopathology from an individual base paved the way for systemic concepts of pathogenesis that emphasise the injurious impact of schizophrenic communication patterns through concepts such as the double bind (Bateson *et al*, 1956; cf. Chapter 10 this volume). While these analyses provide rationales for potentially well-constructed interventions, they remain vulnerable to criticism through a lack of consistent evidence of improvement or cure arising from them.

One further psychotherapeutic tradition has remained relatively aloof from debate about causation. Behavioural psychotherapy, through its original associations with learning theory, justified its use in the treatment of neurotic and behavioural problems by attributing these developments to faulty learning. In approaching patients with psychosis it has tended to be more circumspect about the illness itself. Initial work on behaviour modification was neutral as to whether the institutionalised patterns of passive behaviour were the result of disease or social influence. At the same time, pragmatism has led to less emphasis being placed on symptom-focused interventions for psychosis than on treatments for neurosis, through an emphasis on the importance of educating relatives and on the enhancement of general coping skills (cf. Chapters 12 and 9, this volume). Although identified with the cognitive–behavioural tradition within the categories of modern psychotherapy, it can be argued that these initiatives extend management practices of previous eras in a way that recalls Ackernkneckt's dictum "theories come and go, but practices, good or bad, have a surprising way of surviving and of being rationalised differently according to the fashionable theories of the day" (Rippere, 1980). If this loss of conceptual specificity (despite impressive methodological precision) reflects a greater neutrality concerning the pathogenesis of psychotic illnesses, it is also a clue to the acceptability of cognitive–behavioural methods and their practical success.

Psychotherapy for psychosis: (b) current views and practice

The material in this book represents a snapshot of some of the approaches making up recent and current practice. Contributions representative of the analytic/dynamic, behavioural/cognitive and family/systemic approaches are presented in turn. All are based on presentations at the York conference and, given the inevitable lack of breadth and depth that such a sample can offer, each of these sections is preceded by a commissioned survey of developments in these three principal traditions. They provide helpful illustrations of current trends.

Reilly (Chapter 2) comments further on the theoretical developments that have accompanied the post-Freudian return of psychoanalysis to the study of psychosis. There is evidence from his account of further progress occurring through a kind of dual movement: internally as work with psychosis continues to illuminate and deepen understanding of the countertransference and its clinical uses, and externally with a more refined understanding of the place of education and collaboration alongside analytic therapies with psychotic patients.

Drummond and Dugal (Chapter 7) present a full menu of the behavioural and cognitive interventions that have contributed to the treatment of psychosis within mental illness services. While they stress the need for flexible treatment in response to formulation, the earlier achievements of behaviour modification in treating and rehabilitating hospitalised patients appear to have lost the limelight to family/behavioural and cognitive approaches that lend themselves to individualised treatment in the community.

Evans (Chapter 10) presents systemic treatment as a model that appears to be rarely achieved in pure form. He illustrates its considerable historical importance as a critical force in arguments about mental illness, presenting a radical model that has at times been linked to therapeutic evangelism rather than mere optimism. He concedes some of the resistance this has incurred in the evaluation of its claims, as well as the recent tide of interest in making therapy systemic through greater integration with other approaches rather than striving after methodological purity.

These traditions present contrasting responses to the madness that the concept of 'psychosis' originally attempted to fix or isolate. While they may sometimes converge as sources of therapeutic ideas, they do not necessarily agree as to what 'psychosis' is. As Evans makes clear, the systematist can see talk of 'psychosis' as the consequence of communicative closure that leads to a shared disturbance being displaced towards one individual. The cognitive–behavioural philosophy has been eloquently summarised by Aaron Beck. In welcoming a clear distinction between "the diagnosis of 'schizophrenia' and the label of 'insanity'" he states "the fact that patients diagnosed as 'schizophrenic' have a circumscribed set of irrational beliefs does not mean that they are irrational individuals" (Beck, 1994). This refusal to equate even psychotic illnesses with madness is in clear opposition to the underlying supposition of many approaches acknowledging a dynamic unconscious in which, in the terms of Walshe's quotation from Samuel Beckett (Chapter 5), "we are all mad: some of us remain so". The theoretical contributions of British object-relations thinking on the dynamics of psychosis elaborate on its regressive aspects: brief summaries can be found in Chapters 2 and 4. The idea that a fundamental stratum of unconscious activity becomes exposed in psychosis, despite differences in the way this has been portrayed by the analytic schools of Zurich, Washington or London, is undoubtedly at odds with cognitivists' insistence on a basic rationalism. Nevertheless, analytic/dynamic and behavioural/cognitive approaches all minimise differences and emphasise continuities between psychotic and non-psychotic individuals. In its first three parts the book presents contributions from each of the three main approaches to the psychotherapy of psychosis in more detail. Their relative strengths and shortcomings should become more evident from this material. The final section of the book looks more directly towards the future, illustrating ways in which constantly shifting needs can demand new solutions that require familiar elements to be reintegrated in novel ways.

References

BARHAM, P. (1995) Manfred Bleuler and the understanding of Psychosis. In *Psychosis: Understanding and Treatment* (ed. J. Ellwood), pp. 23–33. London: Jessica Kingsley.

BATESON, G., JACKSON, D., HALEY, J., *et al* (1956) Towards a theory of schizophrenia. *Behavioural Science*, 1, 251–264.

BECK, A. T. (1994) Foreword. In *Cognitve–Behavioural Therapy of Schizophrenia* (eds D. G. Kingdon & D. Turkington). Hove: Lawrence Erlbaum.

BIRNBAUM, K. (1923) The making of a psychosis: principles of structural analysis in psychiatry (transl. H. Marshall). In *Themes and Variations in European Psychiatry* (eds S. Hirsch & M. Shepherd, 1974), pp. 197–238. Bristol: John Wright.

ELLENBERGER, H. (1970) *The Discovery of the Unconscious*. New York: Basic Books.

GAUPP, R. (1938) The illness and death of the paranoid mass murderer, schoolmaster Wagner: a case history (transl. by H. Marshall). In *Themes and Variations in European Psychiatry* (eds S. Hirsch & M. Shepherd, 1974), pp. 134–152. Bristol: John Wright.

JASPERS, K. (1913) Causal and meaningful connections between life history and psychosis (transl. by H. Marshall). In *Themes and Variations in European Psychiatry* (eds S. Hirsch & M. Shepherd, 1974), pp. 81–96. Bristol: John Wright.

JUNG, C. G. (1939) On the psychogenesis of schizophrenia. In *Collected Works, Vol. 3* (eds H. Read, M. Fordham & G. Adler, 1960), pp. 233–249. London: Routledge and Kegan Paul.

—— (1957) Schizophrenia. In *Collected Works, Vol. 3* (eds H. Read, M. Fordham & G. Adler, 1960), pp. 256–273. London: Routledge and Kegan Paul.

KRAEPELIN, E. (1899) *Psychiatrie* (6th edn). Leipzig: Barth.

—— (1920) Patterns of mental disorder (transl. by H. Marshall). In *Themes and Variations in European Psychiatry* (eds S. Hirsch & M. Shepherd, 1974), pp. 7–30. Bristol: John Wright.

KRETSCHMER, E. (1927) The sensitive delusion of reference (Der sensitive Beziehungswahn) (translated and annotated by J. Candy). In *Themes and Variations in European Psychiatry* (eds S. Hirsch & M. Shepherd, 1974), pp. 153–196. Bristol: John Wright.

LEWIS, A. (1946) Psychological medicine. In *A Textbook of the Practice of Medicine* (ed. F. W. Price), pp. 845–878. Oxford: Oxford Medical Publications.

PAYKEL, E. S. (1974) Life stress and psychiatric disorder. In *Stressful Life Events: Their Nature and Effects* (eds B. S. Dohrenwend & B. P. Dohrenwend), pp. 135–149. Chichester: Wiley.

PORTER, R. (1987) The making of psychiatry. In *Mind Forg'd Manacles*, pp. 206–228. London: The Athlone Press.

RIPPERE, V. (1980) Behavioural treatment of depression in historical perspective. In *Contributions to Medical Psychology, Vol. 2* (ed. S. Rachman), pp. 31–54. London: Pergamon.

SCHARFETTER, C. (1983) The evolution of some basic concepts: psychosis. In *Handbook of Psychiatry* (eds M. Shepherd & O. Zangwill), pp. 39–40. Cambridge: Cambridge University Press.

SCHNEIDER, K. (1967) *Klinische Psychopathologie* (8th edn). Stuttgart: Thieme.

STRÖMGREN, E. (1968) Psychogenic psychosis. In *Themes and Variations in European Psychiatry* (eds S. Hirsch & M. Shepherd, 1974), pp. 97–117. Bristol: John Wright.

SULLIVAN, H. S. (1974) *Schizophrenia as a Human Process.* New York: Norton.
WIMMER, A. (1916) *Psychogenic Varieties of Mental Diseases* (St Hans Jubilee Publication). Copenhagen: Gad.
WORLD HEALTH ORGANIZATION (1992) *The Tenth Edition of the International Classification of Diseases* (ICD–10). Geneva: WHO.

Part I. Psychodynamic and psychoanalytic approaches to psychosis

The historical importance of psychodynamic views of psychosis has been stated in the previous chapter. The tradition continues to generate important initiatives in the understanding of psychotic illness within psychoanalytic practice as well as the wider tradition of psychodynamic psychotherapy. Psychoanalytic ideas are usually developed and refined through clinical consultations, an emphasis that will be evident throughout this section of the book. Experiences from both individual and group practice have been important in the development of thinking about psychosis in this tradition. The major landmarks in the development of ideas from individual practice are charted in Stephen Reilly's overview, which concentrates on the contributions deriving from psychoanalysis on either side of the Atlantic. Readers can observe how increasing sophistication in subjective understanding of the dynamics activated in work with psychotic people has been accompanied by development of models of the pathology of psychosis that are potentially more amenable to 'scientific' investigation. Reilly also raises the important issue of 'borderline' pathology, which straddles psychosis and more tradition-al forms of personality disorder. This topic is pursued in the helpful illustrations of David Taylor, a Kleinian psychoanalyst working within the National Health Service, who is well aware of its potential significance in determining the future role played by psychoanalytic therapies within this state-funded system.

Group perspectives on psychosis and borderline phenomena are presented here by John Walshe, who introduces some key theories concerning psychotic phenomena in groups and discusses their practical implications across a range of settings. Malcolm Pines complements that discussion, which owes a good deal to the work of

Wilfrid Bion, with one indebted to the group analysis of S. H. Foulkes. Pines' discussion highlights some of the hazards of working with borderline patients in groups, as well as offering considered practical advice for the group therapist in this situation.

As each of the illustrations in this section illustrates, psychodynamic therapists of all persuasions place great significance on the way words are used to communicate latent as well as consciously intended meanings. Murray Cox, whose presentation launched the conference on which this book is based, has studied the nuances of speech inside and outside psychotherapy as attentively as anybody. The talk that is fully reproduced here embodies a strand of linguistic insight and interpretation of psychotic experiences that, like poetry, is likely to continue to carry its own standards of value and truth, irrespective of how trends in theory and practice develop in the future.

2 Psychoanalytic and psychodynamic approaches to psychosis: an overview

STEPHEN P. REILLY

Psychosis, psychoanalysis and psychiatry

From its earliest days, psychoanalysis has included psychosis within its field of study (Freud, 1896, 1911). However, the uneasy and often hostile relationship between psychoanalysis and psychiatry (which retains the principal role in the diagnosis and treatment of psychosis) has meant that psychoanalytic and psychodynamic ideas have tended to infiltrate psychiatric thinking about the understanding and management of psychotic disorders in a slow and haphazard fashion.

Pines (1991) traces the recognition of shell shock in the First World War, the identification of a range of psychological disorders in traumatised soldiers in the Second World War, and the consequent need to establish effective individual and group psychotherapies as important factors in anchoring the psychodynamic understanding and treatment of neuroses within British psychiatry.

Freeman (1989) describes how subsequent development was slowed by the introduction of antidepressant and anxiolytic drug treatments for neurotic disorders which brought about rapid improvement and appeared to make psychotherapy redundant. The introduction of chlorpromazine in the 1950s probably had a similar, and more severe, retardant effect on the development of the psychodynamic understanding and treatment of psychosis. Nevertheless, the erudite and popular work of R. D. Laing and colleagues in the 'anti-psychiatry' movement (1960, 1961, 1964) helped to bring psychoanalytic debate back into the mainstream. Interest may be fuelled by a more recent realisation among mental health professionals and the general public that pharmacotherapy is largely ineffective for a substantial subgroup of psychotic and non-psychotic patients (Freeman, 1989), coupled with current concerns about the long-term and irreversible side-effects of neuroleptic drugs (Silver & Yudofsky, 1988). This has rekindled an increasingly vigorous interest in psychological treatments, including psychoanalysis and psychodynamic psychotherapy.

Other factors within psychiatry include the wide acceptance of the work of Brown *et al* (1972) and Vaughn & Leff (1976) on the influence of family dynamics on the course of schizophrenia and the need to address quality-of-life issues of patients with chronic schizophrenia who are now grappling with the challenges of living in the community. The relatively recent recognition of borderline personality disorder (Gunderson & Singer, 1975) and the opportunities that the disorder provides for the study of developmentally early psychological processes and mental states also found in frank psychoses have probably contributed to this renewed interest.

There are distinct national differences in the attention paid to psychodynamic issues in psychosis. Interest in the psychoanalytic and psychodynamic understanding and treatment of schizophrenia (Searles, 1965; Sullivan, 1974) and borderline personality disorder (Kernberg, 1975) has been long-standing in the US. In a number of Scandinavian countries psychoanalytic and psychodynamic approaches are well established within a broad-based and integrated psychiatry, and psychodynamic psychotherapy is often included as part of an individually tailored treatment package (Jackson, 1993*a*; see also Pylkkanen, Chapter 16 in this volume). In the UK, the psychodynamic approach continues to inform psychiatric practice in a local and haphazard manner. A small number of specialist centres, for example the Cassel Hospital (see Kennedy, 1992; and Chapter 11 in this volume), provide residential, intensive, psychoanalytically oriented treatment for a range of psychiatric disorders.

Schizophrenia

Freud (e.g. 1896, 1911, 1914, 1915, 1917, 1940) made a number of important contributions to the psychoanalytic understanding of schizophrenia. He categorised it as a narcissistic psychoneurosis, elaborating on key dynamics once he had developed his tripartite structural theory of the mind. According to his model, the fragile ego is overwhelmed in psychosis by conflicting demands from the id and superego with resulting impairment of its ability to function. Ego boundaries are lost, reality testing is faulty and the primary process thinking characteristic of the id predominates. Here psychosis is a waking dream, a severely regressed state of objectless narcissism in which the schizophrenic patient is incapable of forming a transference with the analyst.

Jung, whose considerable interest and views on the psychogenesis of schizophrenia were noted in Chapter 1, offered a very different dynamic model to Freud. In his view the ego fragments into a number of experiencing subjects and the schizophrenic patient is flooded with imagery from the collective unconscious (Jung, 1928, 1927/31). Whereas the apparent lack of transference had rendered the schizophrenic patient beyond the reach of treatment in Freud's view, Jung defended the importance of psychotherapy in the treatment of mild forms of schizophrenia (Jung, 1939).

Klein's theory of the psychological development of the infant from the paranoid-schizoid position to the depressive position provides a comprehensive basis for the psychodynamic understanding and treatment of psychotic states. The paranoid-schizoid position (Klein, 1946) characterises the first few months of life in which the early ego defends against psychotic anxieties and manages intense and conflicting instinctual drives by utilising a range of psychological mechanisms, including splitting, projective identification and idealisation. Serious difficulties arising during this period result in failure of the infant to negotiate this position satisfactorily, so that primitive mental mechanisms continue to predominate. Paranoid anxiety and schizoid mechanisms of defence are evident in schizophrenia which, in Kleinian terms, is associated with regression to paranoid-schizoid functioning. The identification of the psychotic transference (when the 'as if' quality of the transference is absent) and the understanding of early object relations were important in stimulating the further development of psychotherapy with psychotic patients (Segal, 1979).

Subsequent analytic contributions can be seen as further variations on the themes sketched out by these pioneers.

Winnicott (1988) viewed psychosis as a deficiency state brought about by environmental failure and lack of secure holding. The environment refers to the early mother–infant relationship and secure holding is an aspect of 'good-enough mothering'. Important within this theoretical framework are Winnicott's ideas of un-integration (the postulated starting point of the infant) and disintegration. This is the loss of integration caused by the mother's inability to intuit and satisfy her baby's needs appropriately, time her involvement accurately and contain the baby's anxieties adequately. Sometimes, when a baby is 'difficult', it contributes significantly to this environmental failure. In all cases, psychosis involves a regression to the early phase of development at which the failure occurred. This represents an unconscious returning to the point at which a more normal psychological development might follow – a search for a 'facilitating environment' that was originally absent.

According to Balint (1968), even the most regressed schizophrenic patient is capable of responding to the environment and is, therefore, potentially accessible to analysis. This is difficult to pursue in practice, however, because of the tenuous nature of the patient's response and the severe narcissistic withdrawal.

Bion made many important contributions to the psychoanalytic understanding of psychosis in papers such as: 'The differentiation of the psychotic from the non-psychotic personalities' (1957), 'Attacks on linking' (1959), and 'A theory of thinking' (1962*a*). His concepts of pathological projective identification (e.g. 1962*a*) (which accounts for the severe depletion and fragmentation of the psyche) and 'the container and the contained' (1962*b*) (which account for how the infant's mother, or the analyst, may render unmanageable experiences manageable) are especially useful to the psychotherapist in helping to understand and manage powerful interactions within the psychotic transference.

Rosenfeld (1965, 1987) made an extensive study of transference psychosis in a variety of psychotic conditions. He stressed the importance of adhering strictly to the psychoanalytic method in order to allow the psychotic transference to develop unhindered. He states that in schizophrenia the ego is weakened by the use of schizoid mechanisms of defence, and a preponderance of persecutory impulses in early life leads to the development of a very primitive superego.

In the US, Sullivan (1974) described his theories of schizophrenia in a series of papers written in the 1920s, '30s and '40s. He saw schizophrenia was meaningful only when considered within its interpersonal context. To understand it he combined psychoanalytic theory with ideas from social psychology, cultural anthropology and philosophy. His treatment approach was highly practical, advocating early admission to a hospital ward with a milieu orientation, treatment of the patient as a person among persons, an emphasis on helping the patient tell (and so put together) his/her story and attending to abnormal personality development in psychotherapy. Schizophrenia is described as an attempt, by regression to genetically older thought processes, to reintegrate successfully those masses of life experience that remain unprocessed.

Fromm-Reichmann (Arieti, 1978) emphasised schizophrenic patients' loneliness as well as their isolation and willingness to engage in interpersonal relationships if the conditions are appropriate. The therapist can foster the relationship with the patient in order that useful therapeutic work can be done.

Searles (1965) focused on the schizophrenic patient's need to project destructiveness and craziness into the therapist and, with frenetic use of aggressiveness, to destroy (psychically) the therapist.

Recent developments

Recent contributions to the literature range over theory, clinical applications, large-scale projects, outcome studies, training in psychotherapy, and quality assurance.

Theory and clinical applications

More recent writings (Freeman, 1988; Yorke *et al*, 1989) have compared the developmental accounts of schizophrenia that result when it is attributed to a specific deficiency or deficit state (the 'specific' theory; e.g. London, 1973) with explanations that account for psychoses in a similar way to neurotic illness in terms of instinctual drive and conflict (the 'unitary' theory; e.g. Rosenfeld, 1954). More elaborate modern theories have attempted to combine both these positions. Pao (1979) follows Mahler (1952) in attributing a core deficiency to an early lack of mutual cueing between mother and infant which then obliges the emerging personality to use primitive defence mechanisms in order to deal with otherwise paralysing conflictual drives. As the infant's ego struggles to survive, the increasing resort to primitive defences effects a compromise that predisposes to the emergence of schizophrenic symptoms.

In contrast to the traditional psychoanalytic emphasis on early mother–infant relationships, Alanen *et al* (1994) stress that vulnerability to schizophrenia also depends on contributions from ongoing interactional psychopathology within the family. Primitive defence mechanisms, particularly projective identification, commonly operate in the families of schizophrenic patients. The effects of (abnormal) parental personality on the vulnerable child continue throughout development while the persisting symbiotic needs of the vulnerable child continue to distort relationships within the family.

Other recent theoretical developments also have important practical consequences. Birner (1992) discusses the distortion of reality in the psychotic patient and links this with the concept of betrayal. He argues that all neurotic and psychotic patients have suffered from experiences of betrayal. Psychotic patients have been betrayed so severely that they feel there is no one left to trust in the world. Trust between therapist and patient must be built on reality, and ego mechanisms that seek to distort reality must be challenged. Giovacchini (1993), in a similar vein, says that the private, inner reality constructed by the schizophrenic patient acts as a barrier to empathy and a threat to the analyst. Stein (1993) and Volkan (1994) stress that therapeutic work with the psychotic transference is possible and can facilitate movement towards personality integration and more mature ego functioning. Steiner (1989) had earlier highlighted an important aspect of this work when he stated that acceptance of the theory of projective identification leads to a radical change in the aim of therapy, namely helping the patient to regain lost parts of the self.

Stanton (1984) argues that normal ego activity in the psychotic patient and its role in therapy are often neglected by the therapist. Schultz (1983) highlights the importance of listening to the patient and coming to some agreement about the goals of therapy, particularly in the long-term therapy of the schizophrenic patient. He also stresses the need for educational interventions alongside the establishment of a therapeutic relationship. Psychotic patients will seek out a compatible therapist, changing from one to another if necessary, and will take an active part in negotiating the aims of therapy (Gilbert & Ugelstad, 1994).

A robust sense of trust between patient and therapist is necessary if useful work is to be done. Karon (1988) states, unambiguously, that it is up to the therapist to create the therapeutic alliance with the schizophrenic patient. He goes on to say that the therapist should be strong enough to act as a protective object and 'auxiliary ego' for the patient. Telephone contact with the therapist should be possible if necessary and a care network for the patient outside sessions is vital. Karon prefers to work with patients who are not taking antipsychotic medication but others (e.g. Greenfeld, 1985; Alanen *et al*, 1991; Jackson & Cauley, 1992) state the need sometimes to combine pharmacological and psychotherapeutic approaches.

As is evident from much of the above, working with schizophrenic patients in psychotherapy is difficult. Frey-Wehrlin *et al* (1978) bring into focus the therapist's meeting with the incurably sick part of him/herself, which occurs in therapy with the chronic schizophrenic patient. The painful acceptance of this dimension of psychological reality can ease the pressure on psychotherapist and patient alike. Paradoxically, through accepting that the condition is incurable and that change is not possible, it sometimes happens that improvements occur. Therapy with the chronic psychotic patient is described as a process of waiting: waiting for a moment of transformation that might never come.

Moving from the activity of 'waiting with' to the activity of 'warring with', Redfearn (1978) examines the difficulties the therapist might have in coping with the powerful, opposing psychic forces within the psychotic patient, and in managing the psychotic aspect of him/ herself. Countertransference phenomena and the therapist's struggle to contain and work with the patient's intense and disturbing projections are graphically described from a Jungian perspective. Jung had frequently used alchemical images to refer to psychological qualities; Redfearn refers to the alchemical vessel as a container in which substances come into contact and are changed, using this as a model for understanding psychotic processes in patients, the holding capacity of their ego and the containing function of the therapist. This view upholds the successfully treated patient as one who has introjected the holding/containing function of the therapist, translating ideas familiar from Bion, Balint and Winnicott to a contemporary Jungian framework.

In a seminal paper, Jackson & Cawley (1992) describe the work of an experimental unit at the Maudsley Hospital, London, between 1975 and 1988. The unit ran on psychodynamic principles and was set up to treat general psychiatric patients. Assumptions underlying patient care centred on the need for in-depth psychodynamic exploration of the patient's problems and the incorporation of individual psychodynamic psychotherapy in the treatment plan unless contraindicated. The psychotherapeutic milieu provided a safe, containing environment in which staff and patients could work together in coming to some understanding of the patient's illness. Medication was used, where appropriate, alongside psychotherapeutic interventions. Despite the problems of limited psychotherapy resources, inevitable staff changes (particularly nurses and junior doctors) and the increased stresses inherent in this way of working, the unit proved to be effective. About 150 patients were treated over 13 years. Of the first 112 patients, 27 had a diagnosis of schizophrenia. The average length of stay was nine months in the latter years. Psychotherapy continued after discharge if indicated. It is stated that many psychotic patients can be helped in such units and many more treatment facilities run on psychodynamic lines should be established.

In the Scandinavian countries there is an integration of biological and psychoanalytical orientations within psychiatry (Jackson, 1993a). This has facilitated the development of a comprehensive and balanced treatment approach to schizophrenia that incorporates pharmacological, psychological and social therapies.

Failure and suicide

In discussing factors associated with success and failure in psychotherapy, Ugelstad (1985) picks out the importance of the quality of early attachment/care-giving interaction, non-psychotic components of the personality and the actual life situation. Cullberg (1991) attributes the failure of a group of schizophrenic patients to improve in psychotherapy to the possibility that they are suffering from a schizophrenia related to a 'brain lesion', rather than a schizophrenia of the 'genetic vulnerability with disordered personality growth' type. It is argued that only the latter is amenable to psychodynamic psychotherapy.

The characteristics of schizophrenic patients who committed suicide and various aspects of their treatment were examined by Cotton *et al* (1985). They stress that therapy should be supportive, protective and not overambitious. The need for an active stance on the part of the therapist is emphasised by Benedetti *et al* (1993) if the suicidal patient is to be saved (e.g. arranging admission to hospital).

Large-scale projects

Large-scale projects researching the implementation and efficacy of psychotherapeutically oriented treatment programmes for schizophrenic patients include the Nordic Investigation of Psychotherapeutically Oriented Treatment for New Schizophrenics (NIPS ; Alanen *et al*, 1994), the Turku Project (Alanen *et al*, 1991) and the Finnish National Schizophrenia Project (FNSP; Alanen *et al*, 1990). Pylkkanen (Chapter 16, this volume) describes the FNSP. Key features include the concept of the needs-adapted treatment approach to schizophrenia, the acute psychosis team (APT), which goes out to assess the patient in his/her own environment and plans the treatment strategy, the provision of psychodynamic psychotherapy training to an adequate level for large numbers of mental health staff, and the organisational complexity of the task, which require government, mental health and welfare services, local communities and individuals to work together towards a common goal.

Outcome

The FNSP has undoubtedly improved the quality of treatment and rehabilitation for schizophrenic patients, but the need for ongoing treatment and care was not reduced to the extent that was hoped for: 80% of schizophrenic patients still required some kind of treatment five years after initial contact with the services (Salokangas, 1994).

The Chestnut Lodge Follow-Up Study in the US (McGlashan, 1984), which assessed patients, on average, some 15 years after discharge (after intensive psychoanalytic psychotherapy within a milieu setting), had noted that schizophrenic patients tended not to do well, with 67% either chronically ill or functioning only marginally. It is interesting to note, however, that some of the schizophrenic patients in the 33% who did well were among the most chronic and 'hopeless' patients treated.

Training and quality assurance

Pylkkanen (1989, 1993) and Jackson (1993a) stress the need for more psychodynamic training opportunities for mental health staff, and a further plea will be found in David Taylor's chapter in this volume. Freeman (1989) laments the passing of 'hands-on' psychoanalytically trained psychiatrists and their replacement by the consultant psychotherapist who has largely relinquished the territory of psychosis to general psychiatry colleagues. It should be noted, though, that the psychodynamically oriented psychiatrist is far from extinct (Holmes, 1991).

The role of the consultant psychotherapist in providing training in psychodynamic understanding for National Health Service staff is the subject of a paper by Sklar (1985). The specific role of a consultant psychotherapist acting as a resource for staff of in-patient units in facilitating psychodynamic understanding and acting as a container for intolerable anxieties is described by Hobbs (1990). A comprehensive psychotherapy service would include provision for treatment of psychotic patients and support and supervision for staff (Holmes & Mitchison, 1995). A quality assurance programme for psychotherapy has been outlined by Pylkkanen (1989).

Manic–depressive psychosis

Freud, in 'Mourning and melancholia' (1917), described similarities and differences between grieving and depression, in terms of their symptomatic features, and the dynamic processes he felt each reflected. He also pointed out the common clinical linkage of manic and depressive states, arguing that any psychoanalytic explanation of depression must logically be extended to mania. In contrast to schizophrenia, he regarded manic–depressive disorder as treatable by psychoanalysis and indicated his awareness of several cases in which therapeutic improvements had occurred.

In Freud's model, depression is regarded it as a pathological form of mourning in which the ego becomes identified with a loved, lost object. Ambivalent and conflicting wishes of the ego towards the lost object come to operate instead between the ego and a part of the ego that has become identified with the lost object. The incorporation of this conflict, and the turning of aggression originally associated with the object against the self, is the basis for the psychoanalytic understanding of depression. In depressive psychosis, the capacity for reality testing is lost as normal ego functions are impaired by the severe internal conflict. Suicide occurs when the hostile impulses prove more powerful than the protective self-love of the ego. If in depression the ego is diminished as it succumbs to loss, in mania it appears to triumph over it by a compensatory retraction and expansive regrouping. Libido is liberated and becomes available for new object cathexes. In 'The ego and the id' (1923), melancholia, or depression, is viewed as one of a number of disorders involving conflict between superego and ego.

Abraham (1911, 1924) used the psychoanalytic method to treat manic–depressive patients. In the depressed patient he found that violent anger denied access to consciousness turned against the self. He hypothesised a state of 'primary depression' that the depressed person (and the bereaved) regresses to in response to loss and locates the developmental fixation point as late oral–early anal (Segal, 1979). He understood mania as a failure of repression in which normal restraints on thinking, feeling and behaviour are lacking.

Jung hypothesised a damming up of psychic energy in depression. In a regressed state in which regenerative possibilities exist, the release of this energy assists in the resolution of the depression (Samuels *et al*, 1986).

Klein (1935, 1940, 1946; and Mitchell, 1986) builds on the work of Freud, Abraham and others, but not without significant departures from Freudian theory. In Klein's theory of psychological development the paranoid–schizoid position is followed by the depressive position. This period is characterised by the emergence of new defences and is associated with a process of integration in which the infant begins to experience the mother as a whole object rather than as good and bad part objects. The objects of the infant's love and hate are all aspects of the one whole. Manic defences are utilised to combat feelings of guilt, loss and pining. Infants are hypothesised to feel concern for the mother and wish to make reparation for the damage they imagine their hate has inflicted on her. The strength of the postulated death instinct and innate envy are key factors in determining whether or not the infant will successfully negotiate the depressive position. The infant has succeeded when the secure establishment of a good internal object has been achieved (Segal, 1979). Failure to work through the depressive position adequately leaves the person vulnerable to the development of mental illness in later life. Loss reactivates the conflicts of the depressive position. The manic–depressive patient and the person who cannot mourn normally have in common their past failure to establish good internal objects and a sense of security in the world in the depressive position.

Klein stressed that movements between paranoid–schizoid and depressive positions are a part of normal development and that aspects of the two positions can intermingle and interact (more so in abnormal development). This interaction could influence the clinical picture of some forms of schizophrenia and manic–depressive disorder and account for the not infrequent difficulty in distinguishing them diagnostically.

Winnicott (1988) talked of the feeling of wholeness of the self, referring to both body and psyche, which occurs in the depressive position. Alongside this there develops a sense of continuity of self over time. The infant's ability to have new experiences and be altered by them while retaining a sense of self greatly enriches both relationships and the inner world. The capacity for concern for the loved object as a structured and valued person grows as the infant's own structure and inner richness develop. Depressed mood is caused by 'loss of vitality' or a defensive 'damping down' of the activities of the inner world. In mania, the expansiveness and activity of manic defences cover the deadness of the inner world and the pain of knowing that death is inevitable.

Recent developments

There are relatively few references to manic–depressive psychosis in the recent psychoanalytic and psychodynamic literature.

Theory and clinical applications

The concept of developmental disharmony is used to extend psycho-analytic models of affective psychoses by Yorke *et al* (1989). They examined childhood prototypes of mania and hypomania for clues as to how the disorder might arise. The hyperactivity of children living in an environment of deprivation is seen in terms of developing drives outstripping the development of ego. Acquisition of speech is retarded, as are regulation and coordination of motor activity.

This uncoordinated progress causes conflict for the child and carers. Such children tend to live unhappy and frustrating lives and have periods when they are withdrawn and apathetic as well as periods when they are overactive and intrusive.

Federn (1953) hypothesises the emergence of a pathological ego state which is associated with drive discharge predominantly through the motor system uninhibited by the delaying function of thought. The ego is considered to be more permeable to primary process functioning, with resulting loss of contact with external reality. This abnormal ego development could be exposed in adolescence or adult life in response to feared or actual object loss. Katan (1953) suggests that the underlying conflict in mania and depression might well be the same. In the depressed phase the conflict between the wish to retain the object and the desire to destroy it is resolved by turning the aggressive feelings towards the self (which is identified with the lost object). In the manic phase psychic structures are largely dissolved and one pole of the conflict is then externalised. Destructive wishes are then experienced as arising from the external object.

Jacobson (1954) describes how mania following object loss expresses a primitive merging of self and love object, a psychotic identification which relieves the pain of intolerable loss. Pathological identification with a powerful, idealised object allows the manic patient to feel full of life and power and gives him/her a sense of triumph over the needed object which becomes the target of aggressive discharges (Jackson, 1991).

Rosenfeld (1987) outlines contributions to the psychoanalytic understanding and treatment of manic–depressive psychosis and is referred to by Jackson (1991). He describes the intense, unstable transference that develops between patient and therapist and the powerful, destructive impulses that must be contained and dealt with in the therapy.

Redfearn (1978) states that depressed patients feel devoured by the self while manic patients feel they have devoured the self. The therapist's main task with the manic patient is to avoid being taken over and swallowed up by asserting him/herself and maintaining a sense of his/her own identity. With depressed patients the therapist must help them to protect themselves from their own self-destructiveness and help them to express anger towards the loved (and lost) object.

The psychoanalytic psychotherapy of a patient with manic–depressive psychosis admitted to a psychiatric ward run on psychodynamic principles is described by Jackson (1993*b*). The use of psychodynamic psychotherapy in the treatment of manic–depressive disorder is described by Kahn (1993). Loeb & Loeb (1987) describe how psychotherapy helped three manic–depressive patients to identify a periodic increase in what they term phallic imagery and symbolism which precedes a manic episode. Increasing the dosage of lithium at these times helped them to avoid manic episodes. It is postulated that mania occurs when the ego defences are overwhelmed by an increase in the strength of the phallic instinctual drive.

In a survey of 19 university-affiliated lithium clinics, Gitlin & Jamison (1984) found that 18 offered psychotherapy; there were 45% of unipolar patients and 36% of bipolar patients in individual or group therapy. Teixeira (1992) considers the role of psychoanalytic psychotherapy in manic–depressive psychosis in the context of growing concern surrounding the possible long-term side-effects of lithium.

Outcome

The Chestnut Lodge Follow-Up Study (McGlashan, 1984) included 19 bipolar and 44 unipolar patients assessed, on average, 15 years after discharge (after intensive psychoanalytic psychotherapy within a milieu setting). Patients tended to be chronically ill before admission and bipolar patients had tended to leave treatment against medical advice. At follow-up 63% of bipolar patients and 42% of unipolar patients were receiving some form of treatment. The suicide rate in the unipolar group was 16% whereas there were no suicides in the bipolar group.

Borderline personality and psychosis

The term 'borderline' is used to include those with a diagnosis of borderline personality disorder (BPD; Gunderson & Singer, 1975) and/or those who exhibit a predominantly borderline personality organisation (BPO), whatever the primary psychiatric diagnosis (Kernberg, 1975). The validity of the concept and the differentiation of borderline personality from schizophrenia, manic–depressive disorder and other personality disorders were reviewed by Tarnopolsky & Berelowitz (1987). The generally accepted view is that the psychopathology of borderline patients places them most appropriately in the category of personality disorder, but lively debate continues (Paris, 1993). Although listings of the component features vary widely, Higgitt & Fonagy (1992) suggest that the combination of numerous psychiatric diagnoses, predictably varying intensity and major interpersonal difficulties identifies a specific group of patients in psychotherapeutic practice "for which the term 'borderline' will do".

Bateman (1991) considers the development of the concept of BPD and its treatment and suggests that psychotic symptoms are common. He notes that psychotic episodes are typically brief, unsystematised and stress related. The pathology of borderline patients is proposed to occupy a 'borderline position' (Steiner, 1979) between Klein's two infantile positions. It provides a refuge from the psychic fragmentation and psychotic anxiety of the paranoid–schizoid position and the unbearable pain of the depressive position. In response to unmanageable stress the patient shifts from the borderline position to the paranoid–schizoid position and psychotic symptoms manifest over a short period until the pathological organisation re-establishes its fragile equilibrium.

Kernberg's (1975) concept of BPO embraced the whole of character pathology, having three defining characteristics: identity diffusion; dominance of primitive defence mechanisms; alongside maintenance of the capacity for reality testing. He allowed that brief losses of reality testing could occur in response to overwhelming anxiety, leaving the borderline patient vulnerable to the development of sudden psychotic episodes. While Kernberg felt a capacity to recover a sense of self (however fragmented) and to reassert a boundary between inside and outside protected the patient from extended psychotic episodes, Porder (1993) has suggested enduring as opposed to brief failures of reality testing can occur, particularly with reference to the transference with the analyst.

With so many borders for the concept of 'borderline' to refer to, Pines (1989) concurs with Frosch (1988) before him that the term borderline is unhelpful and suggests that the concept of 'psychotic character' would be preferable. The views of Higgitt & Fonagy (1992) are consistent with this, and the continuing arguments between psychodynamic theorists are likely to fuel further reforms in the diagnosis and classification of the complex (or 'cluster B') personality disorders.

References

ABRAHAM, K. (1911) Notes on the psycho-analytical investigation and treatment of manic–depressive insanity and allied conditions. In *Selected Papers* (1927). London: Hogarth Press.
—— (1924) A short study of the development of the libido, viewed in the light of mental disorders. In *Selected Papers* (1927). London: Hogarth Press.
ALANEN, Y. O., SALOKANGAS, R. K. R., OJANEN, M., *et al* (1990) Tertiary prevention: treatment and rehabilitation of schizophrenic patients – results of the Finnish National Programme. In *Public Health Impact on Mental Disorder* (eds D. P. Goldberg & D. Tantam), pp. 176–187. Toronto: Hogrefe and Hubert.

——, LEHTINEN, K., RAKKOLAINEN, V., *et al* (1991) Need-adapted treatment of new schizophrenic patients: experiences and results of the Turku Project. *Acta Psychiatrica Scandinavica*, **83**, 363–372.

——, UGELSTAD, E., ARMELIUS, B-A., *et al* (1994) *Early Treatment for Schizophrenic Patients. Scandinavian Psychotherapeutic Approaches.* Oslo: Scandinavian University Press.

ARIETI, S. (1978) *On Schizophrenia, Phobias, Depression, Psychotherapy, and the Farther Shores of Psychiatry.* New York: Bruner/Mazel.

BALINT, M. (1968) Schizophrenia, addiction and other narcissistic conditions. In *The Basic Fault*, pp. 52–58. London: Tavistock.

BATEMAN, A. (1991) Borderline personality disorder. In *Textbook of Psychotherapy in Psychiatric Practice* (ed. J. Holmes), 335–357. Edinburgh: Churchill Livingstone.

BENEDETTI, G., FURLAN, P. M. & PECICCIA, M. (1993) Emergency interventions and direct interventions in psychotic crises during psychotherapy. World Psychiatric Association Regional Symposium: new models in psychiatry (1992, Palermo, Italy). *International Forum of Psychoanalysis*, **2**, 226–236.

BION, W.R. (1957) The differentiation of the psychotic from the non-psychotic personalities. *International Journal of Psycho-Analysis*, **38**, 266–275. Also in *Second Thoughts* (1967), London: Heinemann; and in *Melanie Klein Today, Volume 1, Mainly Theory* (ed. E. Bott Spillius, 1988), London: Routledge.

—— (1959) Attacks on linking. *International Journal of Psycho-Analysis*, **40**, 308–315. Also in *Second Thoughts* (1967), London: Heinemann; and in *Melanie Klein Today, Volume 1, Mainly Theory* (ed. E. Bott Spillius, 1988), London: Routledge.

—— (1962*a*) A theory of thinking. *International Journal of Psycho-Analysis*, **43**, 306–310. Also in *Second Thoughts* (1967), London: Heinemann; and in *Melanie Klein Today, Volume 1, Mainly Theory* (ed. E. Bott Spillius, 1988), London: Routledge.

—— (1962*b*) *Learning from Experience.* London: Heinemann.

BIRNER, L. (1992) Betrayal: a major psychological problem of our time. *Psychotherapy Patient*, **8**, 41–52.

BROWN, G. W., BIRLEY, J. L. T. & WING, J. K. (1972) Influence of family life on the course of schizophrenic disorders: a replication. *British Journal of Psychiatry*, **121**, 241–258.

COTTON, P. G., DRAKE, R. E. & GATES, C. (1985) Critical treatment issues in suicide among schizophrenics. *Hospital and Community Psychiatry*, **36**, 534–536.

CULLBERG, J. (1991) Recovered versus nonrecovered schizophrenic patients among those who have had intensive psychotherapy. *Acta Psychiatrica Scandinavica*, **84**, 242–245.

FEDERN, P. (1953) Manic–depressive psychosis. In *Ego Psychology and the Psychoses.* London: Imago.

FREEMAN, T. (1988) *The Psychoanalyst in Psychiatry.* London: Karnac.

—— (1989) Psychotherapy within general psychiatry. *Psychiatric Bulletin of the Royal College of Psychiatrists*, **13**, 593–596.

FREUD, S. (1896) Analysis of a case of chronic paranoia. *Standard Edition of the Complete Psychological Works of Sigmund Freud, Volume 3.* London: Hogarth Press.

—— (1911) Psychoanalytic notes on an autobiographical account of a case of paranoia (dementia paranoides). *Standard Edition, Volume 12.* London: Hogarth Press.

—— (1914) On narcissism: an introduction. *Standard Edition, Volume 14.* London: Hogarth Press.

—— (1915) The unconscious: vii, assessment of the unconscious. *Standard Edition, Volume 14.* London: Hogarth Press.

—— (1917) Mourning and melancholia. *Standard Edition, Volume 14.* London: Hogarth Press.

—— (1923) The ego and the id. *Standard Edition, Volume 19.* London: Hogarth Press.

—— (1940) *An Outline of Psychoanalysis* (ed. J. Strachey, 1979). London: Hogarth Press.

FREY-WEHRLIN, C. T., BOSNAK, R., LANGEGGER, F., *et al* (1978) The treatment of chronic psychoses. *Journal of Analytical Psychology*, **23**. Also in *Psychopathology – Contemporary Jungian Perspectives* (ed. A. Samuels, 1989), pp. 205–212. London: Karnac.

28   Reilly

FROSCH, J. (1988) Psychotic character versus borderline. Part I. *International Journal of Psychoanalysis*, **69**, 347–358.

GILBERT, S. & UGELSTAD, E. (1994) Patients' own contributions to long-term supportive psychotherapy in schizophrenic disorders. *British Journal of Psychiatry*, **164** (suppl. 23), 84–88.

GIOVACCHINI, P. L. (1993) Schizophrenia, the pervasive psychosis: paradoxes and empathy. 36th Annual Meeting of the American Academy of Psychoanalysis (1992, Washington DC). *Journal of the American Academy of Psychoanalysis*, **21**, 549–565.

GITLIN, M. J. & JAMISON, K. R. (1984) Lithium clinics: theory and practice. *Hospital and Community Psychiatry*, **35**, 363–368.

GREENFELD, D. (1985) *The Psychotic Patient: Medication and Psychotherapy*. New York: Free Press.

GUNDERSON, J. G. & SINGER, M. T. (1975) Defining borderline patients: an overview. *American Journal of Psychiatry*, **132**, 1–10.

HIGGITT, A. & FONAGY, P. (1992) Psychotherapy in borderline and narcissistic personality disorder. *British Journal of Psychiatry*, **161**, 23–43.

HOBBS, M. (1990) The role of the psychotherapist as consultant to in-patient psychiatric units. *Psychiatric Bulletin of the Royal College of Psychiatrists*, **14**, 8–12.

HOLMES, J. (ed.) (1991) *Textbook of Psychotherapy in Psychiatric Practice*. Edinburgh: Churchill Livingstone.

—— & Mitchison, S. (1995) A model for an integrated psychotherapy service. *Psychiatric Bulletin of the Royal College of Psychiatrists*, **19**, 209–213.

JACKSON, M. (1991) Psychotic disorders. In *Textbook of Psychotherapy in Psychiatric Practice* (ed. J. Holmes), pp. 307–334. Edinburgh: Churchill Livingstone.

—— (1993a) Integration of psychodynamics in Scandinavian psychiatry. *British Journal of Psychiatry*, **163**, 125–126.

—— (1993b) Manic–depressive psychosis: psychopathology and individual psychotherapy within a psychodynamic milieu. *Psychoanalytic Psychotherapy*, **7**, 103–133.

—— & CAWLEY, R. (1992) Psychodynamics and psychotherapy on an acute psychiatric ward. The story of an experimental unit. *British Journal of Psychiatry*, **160**, 41–50.

JACOBSON, E. (1954) On psychotic identifications. *International Journal of Psychoanalysis*, **35**, 102–108.

JUNG, C. G. (1927/31) The structure of the psyche. In *Jung: Selected Writings* (ed. A. Storr, 1983), pp. 66–67. London: Fontana.

—— (1928) Mental disease and the psyche. In *Jung: Selected Writings* (ed. A. Storr, 1983), pp. 40–43. London: Fontana.

—— (1939) On the psychogenesis of schizophrenia. In *Jung: Selected Writings* (ed. A. Storr, 1983), pp. 43–44. London: Fontana.

KAHN, D. A. (1993) The use of psychodynamic psychotherapy in manic–depressive illness. *Journal of the American Academy of Psychoanalysis*, **21**, 441–455.

KARON, B. P. (1988) The treatment of acute schizophrenic patients in private practice. *British Journal of Psychotherapy*, **4**, 135–140.

KATAN, M. (1953) Mania and the pleasure principle. In *Affective Disorders* (ed. P. Greenacre). New York: International Universities Press.

KENNEDY, R. (1992) Inpatient treatment of the psychotic adolescent: the Cassel Hospital's psychoanalytic approach. In *International Annals of Adolescent Psychiatry, Volume 2* (eds A. Z. Schwartzberg, A. H. Esman, S. C. Feinstein, *et al*), pp. 193–196. Chicago: University of Chicago Press.

KERNBERG, O. F. (1975) *Borderline Conditions and Pathological Narcissism*. New York: Jason Aronson.

KLEIN, M. (1935) A contribution to the psychogenesis of manic–depressive states. In *The Writings of Melanie Klein, Volume 1*. London: Hogarth Press (1975). Also in *The Selected Melanie Klein* (ed J. Mitchell, 1986). Harmondsworth: Penguin.

—— (1940) Mourning and its relation to manic–depressive states. In *The Writings of Melanie Klein, Volume 1*. London: Hogarth Press (1975). Also in *The Selected Melanie Klein* (ed. J. Mitchell, 1986). Harmondsworth: Penguin

—— (1946) Notes on some schizoid mechanisms. In *The Writings of Melanie Klein, Volume 3*. London: Hogarth Press (1975). Also in *The Selected Melanie Klein* (ed. J. Mitchell, 1986). Harmondsworth: Penguin.

LAING, R. D. (1960) *The Divided Self*. London: Tavistock.

—— (1961) *Self and Others*. London: Tavistock.

—— & ESTERSON, A. (1964) *Sanity, Madness and the Family*. London: Tavistock.

LOEB, F. F. & LOEB, L. R. (1987) Psychoanalytic observations on the effect of lithium on manic attacks. *Journal of the American Psychoanalytic Association*, **35**, 877–902.

LONDON, N. J. (1973) An essay on psychoanalytic theory: two theories of schizophrenia. Part 1: Review and critical assessment of the development of the two theories. Part II: Discussion and restatement of the specific theory of schizophrenia. *International Journal of Psycho-Analysis*, **54**, 169–193.

MAHLER, M. (1952) On child psychosis and schizophrenia: autistic and symbiotic infantile psychoses. *Psychoanalytic Study of the Child*, **7**, 286–305.

McGLASHAN, T. H. (1984) The Chestnut Lodge Follow-up Study. I. Follow-up methodology and study sample. II. Long-term outcome of schizophrenia and the affective disorders. *Archives of General Psychiatry*, **41**, 573–601.

MITCHELL, J. (1986) *The Selected Melanie Klein*. Harmondsworth: Penguin.

PAO, P.-N. (1979) *Schizophrenic Disorders*. New York: International Universities Press.

PARIS, J. (ed.) (1993) *Borderline Personality Disorder: Etiology and Treatment*. Washington, DC: American Psychiatric Press.

PINES, M. (1989) Borderline personality disorders and its treatment. *Current Opinion in Psychiatry*, **2**, 362–367.

—— (1991) A history of psychodynamic psychiatry in Britain. In *Textbook of Psychotherapy in Psychiatric Practice* (ed. J. Holmes), pp. 31–55. Edinburgh: Churchill Livingstone.

PORDER, M. (1993) An ego psychological view of the borderline patient. In *Borderline Personality Disorder: Etiology and Treatment* (ed. J. Paris). Washington, DC: American Psychiatric Press.

PYLKKANEN, K. (1989) A quality assurance programme for psychotherapy: the Finnish experience. *Psychoanalytic Psychotherapy*, **4**, 13–22.

—— (1993) Promoting commitment for psychotherapeutic treatment approach. Experience of the Finnish National Schizophrenia programme 1981–1991. In *Crossing the Borders* (eds S. Haugsgjerd, B. Sandin, K. Pylkkanen, *et al*), pp. 82–89. Ludwika: Nordic Association for Psychotherapy of Psychoses.

REDFEARN, J. (1978) The energy of warring and combining opposites: problems for the psychotic patient and the therapist in achieving the symbolic situation. *Journal of Analytical Psychology*, **23**(3). Also in *Psychopathology – Contemporary Jungian Perspectives* (ed. A. Samuels, 1989), pp. 213–227. London: Karnac.

ROSENFELD, H. A. (1965) *Psychotic States: A Psychoanalytical Approach*. London: Hogarth Press.

—— (1987) *Impasse and Interpretation*. London: Tavistock.

SALOKANGAS, R. K. R. (1994) Community care and need for treatment of schizophrenic patients in Finland. *British Journal of Psychiatry*, **164** (suppl. 23), 115–120.

SAMUELS, A., SHORTER, B. & PLAUT, F. (1986) *A Critical Dictionary of Jungian Analysis*. London: Routledge and Kegan Paul.

SCHULZ, C. G. (1983) Technique with schizophrenic patients. *Psychoanalytic Inquiry*, **3**, 105–124.

SEARLES, H. F. (1965) *Collected Papers on Schizophrenia and Related Subjects*. London: Hogarth Press.

SEGAL, H. (1979) *Klein*. Glasgow: Fontana.

SILVER, J. M. & YUDOFSKY, S. C. (1988) Psychopharmacology and electroconvulsive therapy. In *Textbook of Psychiatry* (eds J. A. Talbott, R. E. Hales & S. C. Yudofsky), pp. 781–783. Washington, DC: American Psychiatric Press.

SKLAR, J. (1985) Some uses of the psychoanalyst in the NHS. *Psychoanalytic Psychotherapy*, 1, 45–53.

STANTON, A. H. (1984) Some implications of the complexities of ego-functioning and of self-representation for psychotherapy with psychotic patients. 28th Annual Chestnut Lodge Symposium in Memory of Dexter Means Bullard, Sr., 1898–1981 (1982, Rockville, MD). *Psychiatry*, 47, 11–17.

STEIN, G. S. (1993) A transference psychosis. *Journal of Clinical Psychoanalysis*, 2, 245–262.

STEINER, J. (1979) The border between the paranoid–schizoid and the depressive positions in the borderline patient. *British Journal of Medical Psychology*, 52, 385–391.

—— (1989) The aim of psychoanalysis. Freud Memorial Lecture (1987, London, England). *Psychoanalytic Psychotherapy*, 4, 109–120.

SULLIVAN, H. S. (1974) *Schizophrenia as a Human Process*. New York: W. W. Norton.

TARNOPOLSKY, A. & BERELOWITZ, M. (1987) Borderline personality: a review of recent research. *British Journal of Psychiatry*, 151, 724–734.

TEIXEIRA, M. A. (1992) Psychoanalytic theory and therapy in the treatment of manic-depressive disorders. 98th Annual Convention of the American Psychological Association (1990, Boston, Massachusetts). *Psychoanalysis and Psychotherapy*, 10, 162–177.

UGELSTAD, E. (1985) Success and failure in individual psychotherapy with psychotic patients: some follow-up considerations. *Nordisk Psykiatrisk Tidsskrift*, 39, 279–284.

VAUGHN, C. E. & LEFF, J. P. (1976) The influence of family and social factors on the course of psychiatric illness. *British Journal of Psychiatry*, 129, 125–137.

VOLKAN, V. D. (1994) Identification with the therapist's functions and ego-building in the treatment of schizophrenia. *British Journal of Psychiatry*, 164 (suppl. 23), 77–82.

WINNICOTT, D. W. (1988) *Human Nature*. London: Free Association Books.

YORKE, G., WISEBERG, S. & FREEMAN, T. (1989) *Development and Psychopathology: Studies in Psychoanalytic Psychiatry*. London: Yale.

3 The great feast of languages: passwords to the psychotic's inner world

MURRAY COX

The title of this chapter, apart from the substitution of the definite article, comes from *Love's Labour's Lost* (V.1.35):

> "They have been at A Great Feast of Languages, and stolen the scraps."

To this we might add Macbeth's injunction to Banquo – although not, I hope, his malignant intent:

> "Fail not our feast." (*Macbeth* III.1.27)

This is what our psychotic patients may, through word, gesture and posture, require of us.

Murray (1994, p. 6) writes "It is now clear, as Ron & Harvey (1990) have pointed out, that 'to have forgotten that schizophrenia is a brain disease will go down as one of the great aberrations of 20th century medicine'". By the same token, we might say that to assume that psychotics are, by definition, empathy resistant, because they are currently unable to trust, and that they must therefore be dynamically treatment resistant, could go down as an aberration of early 20th-century psychodynamic psychology.

The focal purpose of this chapter

When dealing with a subject as potentially diffuse as that suggested by the "Great Feast of Languages", it is necessary from the outset to be as precise as possible about the particular aim of the chapter. It is not about the wider theme of dynamic psychotherapy with the psychotic patient. Neither does it deal with the complex ramifications of the development and resolution of psychotic transference, or the ominous complication of psychotic countertransference should this spectre appear. On the contrary, it sets out to give an account of a particular mode of approach that frequently (although not always) enables empathic contact to be established with patients hitherto regarded as empathy resistant. Empathy resistance is related to the inability to trust, although it is not identical. No attempt will be made to describe the subsequent dynamic processes, which are initially dependent upon precarious mutuality and fragile trust. In many ways this is a hazardous undertaking, but it can suggest a *via therapeutica* with patients for whom dynamic engagement is rarely attempted. Axiomatic to this agenda is the patient's awareness that the therapist can appreciate a thread of meaning, albeit disguised, in fragmentary utterances. It is the patient's cautiously trusting response to being understood that facilitates the onset of dynamic movement in the direction of integration. Frosch (1983, p. 468) writes:

> "With few exceptions [therapists] do not try to attack the delusional system through interpretations. Yet it is psychoanalytic understanding of the nature of the psychotic process and all its components that enables one to grasp and respond meaningfully to the patient, at whatever stage of the illness whether acute or more chronic. With this understanding, decisions can be made about the feasibility of management and treatment programs."

This chapter offers a way of enhancing psychodynamic work with severely disturbed patients under the rubric of passwords to the psychotic's inner world.

Our attention will be upon ways of discerning and deciphering disguised meanings in fragmentary psychotic utterance. This is inevitably closely linked to the establishment of a good-enough empathic contact, *pace* Winnicott, which is made, or unmade, by the patient's awareness that his/her words have been received – not just heard or recorded, but received at a depth commensurate with that at which they were uttered. One of the risks for clinicians is that they may concentrate so hard upon assessing, formulating and formally presenting the mental state, that the actual words of the patient – their content, their cadence and their connotation – together with their intonational surge and idiosyncratic syntax, are ignored. For this reason, the plea "Fail not our feast" is not inappropriate at the outset of this exploration.

The ensuing suggestions have gradually taken shape during 25 years' experience of working with psychotic patients in Broadmoor

Hospital. Indeed, through adoption, the words of a poorly educated, psychotic arsonist have become a personal 'signature tune':

> "I'm blind because I see too much, so I study by a dark lamp."
> (Cox, 1978, p. xv)

The translocation of content and context

There is a paradoxical theoretical strand in these deliberations. It has acquired working value during the 'without limit of time' possibility of limit testing offered by psychotherapy conducted in a secure forensic setting. It can be stated succinctly as follows. When seeking to understand the *inner* world and the *content* of disclosure, particular attention is paid to the *outer* world and *context* of disclosure. Focus reversal of this kind and dislocation of attention can be a manifestation of anxiety and may therefore be evident in the clinical presentation of patients from any diagnostic category. Thus, a middle-class administrator described in detail the rotten floor, the leaking spouts and drains, and the general decay of the whole (hole) of her recently acquired summer house. She was sub-audibly also just not talking about her pressing need for a pelvic floor repair, incontinence and the fear of irreversible genital atrophy. The psychotic patient, however, may have a more concrete sense of the translocation of inner and outer world objects. There is the equation of object loss and dissolution of the self. Had the administrator been psychotic, she might have feared that the floor of her very life was rotten and beyond repair so that she did not know where she stood, had lost any sense of standing and could not detect how things stood for her. Whether men, and/or their penises, would 'stand' in her presence or stand up for her when threatened, could all be interwoven in a semantic matrix.

A further manifestation of the transient reversibility of content and context is always at the back of my mind when asked to give a lecture like the one that formed the basis of this chapter. I invariably study invitational material in great detail, wondering what the contextual setting may have to say about the theme under consideration. There may be a clue, a text or a subtext in the very context where lecturer and audience encounter each other. On such occasions I have been rewarded by finding that I was speaking in a music room or adjacent to a demonstration of fossils! The setting for this study of the great feast of languages was no exception. I was scheduled to speak in the lecture theatre of the Chemistry Department. This gave rise to numerous potential associations as I started collecting my thoughts. What kind of empathic 'chemistry' needs to exist if patients are to allow a stranger into their fragile inner world, where defences are crumbling and contents dispersing even to the point of dissolution. I wondered whether the chemistry lecture theatre would resemble those of my school days, where the 'fume cupboard' provided an incessantly unpleasant leak, or whether there would be evidence of incomplete experiments or displays of crystals. It seemed a lifetime ago since I had last been present in a lecture theatre with a gigantic table of elements displayed on the wall. In my inner world, at least, King Lear was comfortingly present to greet me. This was something I could not withhold from the audience.

"I tax you not, you elements, with unkindness." (*King Lear* III.2.16)

I have given this example in order to defend it! At first sight, it sounds like a klang association, an incidental happening, which might at best be considered an example of synchronicity. But it opens a door upon extensive ramifications which we shall subsequently consider in depth. Once again, we are approaching an already familiar theme from an unusual angle, because the customary reference to 'klang associations' is usually stigmatic and derogatory. Here it is constructively linked to the interesting work by Kugler (1982), whose studies show that as the level of consciousness lowers, so semantic significance tends to be replaced by phonetic resonance. It thus comes close to *phatic* language – so vital a bond between mother and infant. It also assumes crucial relevance when empathic contact with the schizophrenic patient is under consideration and is therefore central to this review of passwords to the psychotic's inner world. Such associative linking, hitherto trivialised as capricious and 'klang', assumes a new measure of meaning through the process of phonetic mutation. Similarly, playing with words is often dismissed as being nothing other than 'punning'. Once the nature of *paronomasia* has been understood, it carries a rich investment of relevance 'beyond the meaning'. We are then into a deeper configurational network, where bondings can take place which, to the uninitiated, seem to offer no possibility of semantic purchase. This process is not new, but it has been ignored in recent times, as the following quotation demonstrates: "It is interesting to note that in 1890 the *Saturday Review* refers to 'the Playful Paronomasia method of the Poet'" (Cox & Theilgaard, 1987, p. 114).

King Lear's inner turmoil and the table of the elements simultaneously available for all to see in the chemistry lecture theatre, yet not to be "taxed with unkindness", was an unexpected mutative opportunity which made the point of detecting disguised meaning *in vivo* in the presence of the audience.

In this search for the developing matrix of meaning, had we but world enough and time, we could follow several inviting associative pathways initiated by the theme of the great feast of languages: feast – festal – sacramental feast – *O Sacrum Convivium,* implying an incorporation of satisfying introjects (see Kilgour, 1990, subtitled *An Anatomy of Metaphors of Incorporation*). But we return to the words that have been adopted as the psychotic's cautionary reminder to those who would discern meaning in fragmentary utterance:

"Fail not our feast."

This could be taken to be saying fail not to attend (be there) and attend to (witness, concentrate upon, discern) the great feast (many ingredients, preparation processes and a selection of courses) of potential linguistic nourishment which we shall both enjoy. The anxiety evident in the eyes of psychotic people often reflects a concern that we are not fully concentrating upon the content of what they are saying, other than for the purposes of assessing their mental state and monitoring the efficacy of their medication. Before leaving this introductory theme of 'the feast' we cannot help observing how different is the analytical, logical, linear, 'left-brain' thinking of the word-processor from the illogical, capricious, iconic, associative, tangential, 'right-brain' thinking of the psychotic patient. Yet, in terms of 'the feast' the metaphor of the appropriate *menu* is at home in both modes. It seems that human kind cannot do without a nourishment option, always needing a menu from which to make a selection.

Passwords

And what of the password? It is described in the *Oxford English Dictionary* as "a word authorizing the utterer to pass: watchword: secret of admittance". Does the subtitle "passwords to the psychotic's inner world" imply a "secret of admittance"? If so, there could be an implicit stigma of devious, circuitous 'manipulation' (Cox, 1994), by which the primed therapist is able to gain privileged access to the patient's inner world, from which the uninitiated are excluded. Should this prove to be the case, such an approach flies in the face of all that has been written of the necessity of *authenticity* when effectively engaging at depth with patients of any diagnostic category, perhaps chiefly so when attempting therapeutic contact with those presenting clinically with psychopathic or psychotic features. Both groups have usually experienced unreliability in others and in themselves, because they lack 'gyroscopic introjects' – to use Stierlin's (1970, p. 321) useful term – which can keep them 'on course' when seeking and maintaining appropriate relationships. Was it an intuitive guess by Shakespeare, or had he recalled a useful tip from an apothecary, when he wrote the following passage?

> "Lear: Give the word [password].
> Edgar: Sweet marjoram.
> Lear: Pass.
> Gloucester: I know that voice."
> (*King Lear* IV.6.92)

The Arden edition footnote (1978, p. 164) *re* "Sweet marjoram" suggests that "This was a remedy for diseases of the brain". So that we have here an instance of a password being requested by the man 'on the gate' of access to himself, even at the height of intrapsychic disorganisation. Yet admission to his company and his chaos depended upon the awareness of mutual understanding of that which could heal. It was the mention of medication that constituted the password, to which Lear said "Pass", not to his doctor, but to the companion and fellow traveller who was there. Edgar had already been with Lear on the heath. It is characteristic of the extremity of psychic dispersal that encounters are punctuated by checks on authenticity – such as asking for the password.

An emphasis on phenomenology rather than interpretation

When searching for disguised meaning in fragmentary psychotic speech, it is beneficial to concentrate on phenomenology rather than potential interpretive mutation of meaning. Interpretation runs the risk of intensifying the patient's sense of psychological distance from the therapist, except when the interpretation itself is an intrinsic part of dynamic psychotherapy, so that the language has an inherent momentum and buoyancy of its own. But in early therapeutic encounters, psychotic patients fear that their words are not being taken at face value. An interpretive receptive set always implies that 'this means that', rather than 'this means this'. Yet the classical therapeutic interpretational constellation necessitates that, when the timing is right for a mutative interpretation, then, 'this means this *and* that'.

Paradoxically enough, psychotic patients are often desperate to ensure that they are heard as meaning what they say (this means this). But when we place such a psychophilosophical claim alongside a disclosure characteristic of many forensic psychotic utterances, we are aware of the enormity of the claim. There is a many layered mantle of meaning, rich in nuance and allusive inference, which often invests psychotic language. Consider, for example, this comment on decapitation:

> "I've been decapitated to death ... ([*whispered*] And death sometimes kills.)"

What does the patient intend to convey, as her jerky gaze pattern conveys concern that the therapist might not be taking in what she needs to say? Our focus is the great feast of languages, to which the psychotic invites us. When emphasis is placed upon phenomenology rather than interpretation, the patient is more likely to sense that we "fail not [his/her] feast". Thinking intellectually about *synchronic* (non-historical simultaneities) and *diachronic* (historical successions) aspects of language, and their relevance to the therapist's perception of the optimal moment for making a *mutative interpretation*, may be appropriate in some settings. But it is not in the spirit of the occasion, when an invitation to a great feast of languages has been received – and such preoccupation might well block the enjoyment thereof.

Aesthetic access to the hidden psychotic part

Rosenfeld (1992), a pioneer in the psychotherapy of the psychoses, writes "We understand some things about the psychotic patient thanks to the healthier part with which he can verbalize and conceptualize. *We do not know the hidden part directly:* it is a model that *we must create as we work*" (p. 4 – emphasis added). He then quotes Freud (1925) "since the analysts have never relaxed their efforts to come to an understanding of the psychosis ... they have managed now in this phase and now in that, *to get a glimpse beyond the wall*" (p. 60 – original emphasis). Both citations take us directly to the fulcrum of this chapter, which is the significance of *aesthetic access* to the personality of that group of patients often regarded as being empathy resistant and therefore treatment resistant. This is closely linked to the phenomenon of poetic precision which, in turn, is interwoven with the *aesthetic imperative* (Cox & Theilgaard, 1987, 1994). It cannot be repeated too often that the use of the word 'aesthetic' in this context adopts Bateson's connotation: "By aesthetic I mean responsive to the pattern which connects" (1979, p. 17). In other words, it implies a multimodal, cross-disciplinary, integrated approach that augments the textured 'grain' of therapeutic listening. It does not necessarily imply the conventional connotation of appreciation and creativity activated by poetry, painting, music and every other wavelength set resonating by 'aesthetic' stimuli. It has to do with the penumbra of heightened attunement. Thus, in the example just given, "I've been decapitated to death", the patient might sense that the therapist could 'receive' such a disclosure because he had already heard of those who "die many times before their deaths" (*Julius Caesar* II.2.32). "Heaven knows! I die often enough!" (therapeutic space).

Previous aesthetic experience might just have primed the therapist's attunement so that, alongside his clinically perceived perception of thought disorder, his associative aesthetic reservoir had been activated and set resonating by the awareness that if parting is to die a little, then devastating, climactic parting must be to die a lot. Thus the patient, who felt not only abandoned, but also *very* abandoned, described her awareness of repeated banishment and diminishment in these memorable, illogical, but indubitably expressive, words: "Heaven knows! I die often enough!"

In my view, this facility of gaining aesthetic access to the personality of patients, hitherto regarded as being empathy resistant, is of such prime importance that it has been emphasised in several recent publications (Cox, 1995, 1997). This is because once empathic engagement and adequate emotional contact have been made with such patients, then all kinds of therapeutic initiatives and life-story trajectories can unfold, which would have been impossible had adequate bonding between therapist and patient not taken place.

In this short chapter we can only touch on a few of these provocative and stimulating facets of the great feast of languages to which the psychotic patient extends a continuous and open invitation to those whom they sense share the same tastes. Nevertheless, we now need to concentrate upon the process of *poiesis* and its vital derivative, namely *poetry* itself. We shall try to set poetic parameters alongside clinical categories. When doing so, it seems appropriate to start with an indubitably organic clinical presentation of a patient of 37 who had an intracranial tumour. I have a vivid recollection of an elegant man from Romford who ran a dancing school and was organising a dinner dance for the Latin American section which was to celebrate the rumba, the samba and the conga. Before the dessert, he stood up and said "Please take your partners for a peach melba!". All laughed at this apposite turn of phrase – except his wife, who realised that the patient himself had not intended this *double-entendre*. It was in fact the first manifestation of a meningioma in the speech area.

Coherence between clinical categories and poetic parameters: descriptive phenomenology, psychodynamics and poiesis

We now need to refer to the link between traditional descriptive phenomenological psychiatry, psychodynamic appraisal of the patient's personality structure and defensive organisation, together with the patient's mode of being with the other. Countertransference contours, coloured by the presence of the patient, activate responsive *poiesis* within the therapist. The constraints of time and space impose the necessity of excessive condensation of material, which thus appears to be unduly dogmatic and stated as 'given'. Nevertheless, within the more capacious compass of separate volumes it has already been presented and illustrated step by step (Cox & Theilgaard, 1987, 1994).

Seen from a traditional psychodynamic vantage point, psychotic language can be construed in terms of defensive organisation, object relationships, ego functions and the like. It also needs to be studied in terms of conventional descriptive phenomenological psychiatry. Such appraisal is necessary when assessing the patient's mental state. The two approaches are complementary and have diagnostic, prognostic and therapeutic implications. Thus, they might suggest that medication and a supportive regime, rather than an analytic approach, was currently indicated.

Seen in terms of phenomenology, the presentation may include first-rank symptoms and formal thought disorder with word salad (perhaps a vegetarian's great feast of languages?), so that a particular diagnostic (DSM–IV) category placement seems appropriate. It is sometimes wrongly assumed that poetry only interprets – and we speak of poetic interpretation. But it can also endorse phenomenology, the intense essence of the thing itself.

At the same time, *poetic parameters* open other avenues of access. The same language may be heard in terms of *poiesis*, which alerts the therapist's associative attention. When aesthetic cadences are activated, the patient's inner world is 'open' in another key and an entirely different frame of reference is brought into play. This occurs because the creative quality of *poiesis* insists that there is "a calling into existence of that which was not there before" (Cox & Theilgaard,

1987, p. 21). Thus the question with which the psychotic utterance challenges the clinician takes this form:

"What are you hearing that you have not heard before?"

Needless to say, this does *not* imply a brand new, neologistic 'virgin' sequence of words! On the contrary, the words may be familiar, even commonplace, but the enunciatory emphasis, the intonational surge, the deictic stress and all the ephemeral paralinguistic overtones will colour what the patient is trying to say. And, more important, not only what he is trying to say to *you* but what he is trying to say to you *now*, that he has not said before. Has his *dialectal emphasis* regressed to the dialect of his childhood (as do all our utterances when we are emotionally disinhibited and freed by the delights of orgasm or the horrors of anxiety)? The detection of regressed dialect is indeed one of the focal dialectics of finely tuned reception implicit in fully 'hearing' what the patient is saying, as it is continually with all with whom we speak.

We return to Rosenfeld's words, "we do not know the hidden part directly ... we must create as we work" and Freud's reference to getting "a glimpse beyond the wall"; we find ourselves at the point of confluence where therapeutic listening and *poiesis* (the core of creativity) merge. Indeed, in everyday speech we say 'What did you *make* of that?' when there is something open to a variety of significances. This brings us to another pivotal point in responding to the invitation to the great feast of languages.

The dissolution of syntax

This is the question of changes in *syntax* that imply changes of feeling evident in the formulation of speech. Shakespeare is the master craftsman of such things, demonstrating how the breakdown of inner stabilities is reflected in the breakdown of closely knit syntax. Blank verse regresses into prose, or even chaotic, fragmentary, explosive non-linguistic phonation. Perhaps the best example is to be found in *King Lear*.

Space does not allow more than a glance, but a glance is sufficient to make the point. It has been suggested (Flynn, 1995) that "the rhythm and form of language of blank verse collapses under the weight of the explosive feelings. Blank verse is broken and no longer able to serve as an effective container of feelings which are too immediate, rough and uncontrollable". We have already noted Lear's demand for the password, even from a familiar companion, and it is in the same setting that his order breaks down. This speech is often referred to as the 'Let copulation thrive' speech. Commenting on the Arden editor's setting of the text, Flynn continued, "He does not set out to present the utterance in verse, with a well defined meter or a predetermined rhythm. It is entirely flexible. 'Let copulation thrive' – this is an unexpected rhythm thrusting against the form before it collapsed altogether". This comment is in itself an excellent paraphrase of the paraclinical description of sexual tumescence and detumescence – "thrusting before it collapsed". It precisely echoes the sexually laden *rhythms of ejaculation* which carry the dual referent of a figure of speech and sexual physiology.

The sexualisation of language is another theme crying out to be linked to the discernment of passwords to the great feast of languages. The 'Let copulation thrive' speech exemplifies the almost deafening subtext, which is another hallmark of psychotic language. This has been called 'double-density dialogue' by Meyer (1995), who is Ibsen's main English translator. Double-density dialogue refers to numerous passages in Ibsen where one thing is said and another is implied. But in the syntactical fragmentation that Lear exhibits, and that is particularly evident in psychotic group therapeutic space, one could refer to multiple-density dialogue. Perhaps, in order to keep an alliterative hold on the memory, we might speak of a multiple-meaning matrix.

Othello (IV.1.35) furnishes the second example of broken syntax at the point of psychic decompensation. Flynn continues, "In this passage Othello and Iago discuss in blank verse. They even complete each other's verse lines, as evidence of their shared thoughts".

> Iago: Faith that he did ... I know not what he did.
> Othello: But what?
> Iago: Lie.
> Othello: With her?
> Iago: With her, on her, what you will.

Othello then explodes – in an unmeasured kind of fragmented language, including references to body parts, handkerchiefs, housing and "such shadowing passion" before the stage direction "he falls down". (This is not the place to discuss the existence or the characteristics of the 'Othello syndrome', but this is certainly one of the key passages on which the debate usually rests.)

Poiesis, the inner world and passionate syntax

Our theme also pulls us towards the recognition of passionate syntax, which was Yeats' infallible guide to the point of greatest affect. That, too, is something we try to detect when seriously listening to psychotic speech. The peculiar syntax of passion is often evident in the precise wording and emphasis of enunciation in the psychotic's attempt to 'get through' to us. I am aware that the therapist's ears may seem to be "fortified against [their] story", to borrow words about unbelievable wording from *Hamlet*. Let us read a few psychotic utterances from therapeutic space:

> "The smell took the shape of my father."
> "I heal her with colours and images to counteract the strong smell of blood."
> "I was cutting-up inside."
> "I just went on killing him – it never occurred to me that he'd die."
> "There is something in you which is seriously unmet."
> "I'm drowning in something which wells up inside me."
> "I have met people who have walked off the edge of language – and then they DO THINGS."

We must hurry on with a regrettably brief glance at a fascinating study in which a passage by Dylan Thomas is described both by a literary critic and then in the grammar of psychopathology. Critchley (1964, p. 362) sets the twin commentaries in sequence and they must be given in full.

> "The transition from image to image is by means of the pun, the double meaning, the coined word, the composite word, the noun-verb, the pronoun with a double antecedent. And there is a larger machinery, verbal and syntactical: clauses that read both forward and backward; uneven images that are smoothed by incantatory rhythms, rhymes, word-patterns, verse-forms, by the use of commas in place of full-stop punctuation; cant, slang terms and formal, general abstract wording juxtaposed in image after image, so that the agitation of each becomes the repose of the group."

> "What does this mean? The words are metalinguistic, but the sense is not. Could the paragraph perhaps be paraphrased using the grammar of psychopathology? Thus a psychiatrist might well be tempted to speak of telescoping of ideas; agrammatism; klang-associations; idiosyncratic and obscure allusions. This is perhaps another way of expressing the same opinions. We are even reminded of Schneider's fourfold mechanisms of schizophrenic speech – fusion, derailment, omission and drivelling. And also of Piro's four fundamentals of psychotic speech, namely: semantic distortion, semantic dispersion, semantic dissolution, and enlargement of the semantic halo, whereby meaning is extended like Alice in Wonderland and language becomes ambiguous, vague and indeterminate."

In formulating our response to the psychotic's 'RSVP' to the great feast of languages, we need to remember that it is by listening to the patient as we would to the words of a poet that we shall hear what might be missed when his/her language is passed through traditional clinical, diagnostic and defence-detecting filters. Such professional activities are of course essential and must never be ignored. But, simultaneously, we need to fine-tune aesthetic receptivity, so that we can detect the patterns which connect the therapist and patient to their own deep language and thus to each other. This can be regarded as one manifestation of *the pull of the primordial* (Cox & Theilgaard, 1987, p. 147). Because readers of this chapter will be familiar with customary clinical aspects of psychotic language, but perhaps less so with dynamics linked to the poetic process, this exploration will conclude by looking at the facets of poetics that impinge upon 'reading' significance in fragmented utterance. We need to start with Kugler's (1982) thought-provoking study on *The Alchemy of Discourse: An Archetypal Approach to Language.* He writes: "An archetypal approach attempts to open the ego to the language of the imaginal, to loosen the grammar and syntax which restrict the person's 'clinical picture' to one meaning: I am only a psychotic ... etc" (p. 91). Kugler discusses the two main operational axes of language, the *metonymic* (linear chains of words according to the laws of grammar and syntax) and *metaphoric* (associating words according to some degree of phonetic and/or semantic parity) (p. 109). This is another vast theme closely related to the use of mutative metaphors in psychotherapy (Cox & Theilgaard, 1987) and the importance of *Imaginal Dialogues* (Watkins, 1986).

Kugler's reference to loosening the syntax brings us to Hussey's (1982, p. 86) study of Shakespeare's capacity to loosen the structures of language. One cannot help responding with constant amazement to Shakespeare's ability not only to 'get under the skin' of the psychotic patient, but to see the world and describe it as he does, and yet retain sufficient creative integrated skill to convey a fractured inner world. And, as a crowning glory, to set such disturbance in an extended drama within the trajectory of a complicated plot.

Critchley (1964, p. 360) observes that "written compositions ... are invaluable data for linguistic analysis. Being permanent records they lack, however, the ephemeral paralinguistic overtones which are *of such importance* in human communication but which *defy transcription*" (emphasis added).

Important issues that defy transcription

Nevertheless, it is upon such transcription-defying issues that the discernment of appropriate passwords may well depend. We therefore return to further consideration of the place of the *aesthetic imperative* in facilitating access to hitherto empathy-resistant unable-to-trust patients. The aesthetic imperative refers to an unignorable summons to active response through a heightened perception of meaning latent, or disguised, in the patient's language. This is linked to the activation of allusive bonding, which may be coloured by associative verbal resonance or focused poetic precision. But, either way, it means that the patient senses that because of linguistic resonance with the therapist, he/she is no longer solitary in a perplexed inner world. In a threatening situation, patients might sense that reinforcements have arrived. In spite of the grandiose implications, there is nevertheless an ancient symbolic parallel in answer to the astonished question "Were there not three?", which is followed by an almost incredible exclamation "Behold I see a fourth!" Such a response could easily come under the rubric of supportive or stabilising therapeutic initiatives.

Poiesis is the active process of creativity itself. Although it is the Greek word from which 'poetry' comes, it refers to the act of writing, reading, speaking and/or listening to poetry. It does not refer to the closed volume of poetry on a dusty shelf. It therefore embraces the active creation–reception of language. It colours every aspect of the spoken word and, as far as the schizophrenic person is concerned, it will influence what is concealed-yet-revealed and its dynamic reversal. It may therefore help to make a brief diversion to the poet's inner world and to hear what poets have to say about what they 'do'.

Poetic terms, energies and processes

"[A] *poem* ... may be defined as a projection, by means of compressed and patterned language, of specific qualities and intensities of emotionally and sensually charged awareness." (Rosenthal, 1987, p. 96)

We hear of *torques*, which are "sharp, unexpected shifts of perspective" (p. 67) and of "shifting tonalities and degrees of intensity, which are given structure and subtle shading through the resonance and interweaving of sounds and images and key phrases" (p. 75). When Rosenthal (p. 63) refers to "cumulative power", clinicians are persuaded to think of their patient's language in a fresh, unfettered way, so that they do not prematurely file away what they hear as clinical evidence of a certain category of thought disorder. Thus their attention to the patient and the utterance remains 'alive' for longer.

Strangely enough, one of the poems considered in the landmark lecture on psychotic speech by Critchley (1964) is by Dylan Thomas.

And it is certainly no accident that Maud (1963) wrote a book entitled *Entrances to Dylan Thomas' Poetry*. This is entirely congruous with the theme of this chapter in suggesting that aesthetic access to the psychotic's inner world is precisely homologous with the search for 'entrances' to the inner world of the poet. Commenting on Thomas' phrase "Christ-cross-row of death", Maud (p. 4) observes "There is no dislocation of syntax here" and then raises the vital question of the "validity of secondary meaning" (p. 13). The issue of the presence or absence of the dislocation of syntax and secondary meanings speaks of the 'bilingual' referents relevant to both the language of the poet and the language of the psychotic. The syntax of dislocation, a reversal of Maud's statement, is one of the more frequent components of psychotic speech and is often associated with massive metaphors of departure, sometimes with concrete correlates of departure from existence itself, by way of suicide or homicide.

Dislocation as a mode of defensive distancing touches on another aspect of mirroring between some poetry and psychosis. Hear Maud again: "The distancing is achieved ... by *using syntax as though it were a lock-gate, allowing meaning to come slowly through*" (p. 83, emphasis added). "This is the final aim of distancing: not to obscure, but to *prevent us from rushing in with the hackneyed,* with our own notions rather than the poet's" (p. 101, emphasis added). What a cautioning reminder to therapists 'rushing in' with hackneyed interpretations, too enthusiastic to suggest that 'this means that', so that they are blind to the *haecceity* – the *'thisness'* inherent in 'this means this'. There are clues to password *poiesis* here.

We have already referred to Yeats and his concept of passionate syntax. In "1916 he wrote in a manuscript: 'if a poem talks ... we have the passionate syntax, the impression of the man who speaks, the active man, no abstract poet'; and in an interview with the *Irish Times* when he was awarded the Nobel Prize in 1923, he declared that the aim of all his work had been to perfect the syntax of passionate speech" (Meir, 1974, p. 105). Knights (1992, p. 43) takes up a point originally developed by Slatoff (1970, p. 14), who says "much of our greatest literature involves a disordering as well as an ordering of experience ... subsequently referring to countercurrents, explosive tensions and precarious suspensions". I suggest that this is another example of categories of analysis and appraisal, coming from a professional field other than that of dynamic psychology, which can help the clinician to allow the language of the patient to speak for itself, before it is categorised as evidence of a knight's move or a word salad. (It must be fortuitous, and may be synchronistic, that when referring to the writing of Knights we so soon revert to clinical concepts such as knight's moves!) Slatoff's reference to "a disordering as well as an ordering of experience" also stimulates us to think about the patient's language of disclosure from a different perspective. Holding his phrase in mind, one wonders exactly what a Broadmoor patient implied when a lawyer asked him why he had taken a life. His reply took the following form:

> "I took a life because I needed one."

This was the title of a paper on forensic psychotherapy (Cox, 1982). It seemed absurd when *I* was subsequently congratulated on "Such a brilliant title!" It was nothing other than the precise language of the patient being rightly given pride of place.

An after-dinner speech

It seems appropriate that, after digesting the various courses – some of them heavy – of the great feast of languages, this chapter should conclude in the lighter mode of an after-dinner address.

Hitherto, no mention has been made of the sparkle, the fun and the numerous delights of participating in therapeutic groups with schizophrenic patients. Such enterprises often feature the playfulness of experimentation and have a 'let's have a go' quality about them which also characterises rehearsals for a play. We should close with three vignettes – all saying something about empathic contact with psychotic patients.

(1) A fragment of a brief conversation in a hospital corridor:

> Mary: "Hello, Dr Cox, I've just failed my typing exam."
> MC: "I'm sorry to hear that Mary. I wonder why that was?"
> Mary: "I did alright on speed and presentation. But I failed on accuracy."
> MC: "Oh dear. Did that mean that you got words wrong?"
> Mary: "Oh no, only the letters!"

Mary's final line was said with a warm smile, showing how much she had enjoyed the exchange.

(2) Many of the female patients in Broadmoor are excellent cooks. The Christmas party on the ward is indeed a great feast of languages in the presence of a great feast. I am approached by a group member:

> "Hello Murray, what you need is death by chocolate!"

(3) "I know what a comma is, it is a full-stop with legs!"

The enticing field of psychotic language, *per se*, is studied by Rosenbaum & Sonne (1986). The capricious instabilities of un-anchored utterance and mobile full stops which could, on a whim, dance over the page and entirely change syntax is a passionate possibility indeed. These issues are further explored in Cox & Theilgaard (1994, p. 148).

I trust that from time to time various possible avenues of access to the psychotic's inner world will have been activated in those reading this chapter, whose task it is to administer the modern equivalent of sweet marjoram, this being both a word enabling acceptable access to psychotic presence, and a prescribed 'remedy.'

References

BATESON, G. (1979) *Mind and Nature: A Necessary Unity.* London: Wildwood House.

COX, M. (1978) *Structuring the Therapeutic Process: Compromise with Chaos.* Oxford. Reprinted 1995. London: Jessica Kingsley.

—— (1982) I took a life because I needed one: psychotherapeutic possibilities with the schizophrenic offender-patient. *Psychotherapy and Psychomatics*, **37**, 96–105.

—— (1994) Manipulation (Editorial). *Journal of Forensic Psychiatry*, **5**, 9–13.

—— (1995) On not adding Hamlet to taste: a plea for the necessary distance between theatre and therapy. *British Journal of Psychodrama and Sociodrama*, **10**, 27–38.

—— (1997) On the capacity to be inside enough: some Winnicottian forensic emphases. In *The Winnicott Legacy* (ed. B. Kahr). London: Karnac Books.

—— & THEILGAARD, A. (1987) *Mutative Metaphors in Psychotherapy: The Aeolian Mode.* London: Tavistock. Republished 1997, London: Jessica Kingsley.

—— & —— (1994) *Shakespeare as Prompter: The Amending Imagination and the Therapeutic Process.* London: Jessica Kingsley.

CRITCHLEY, M. (1964) The neurology of psychotic speech. *British Journal of Psychiatry*, **110**, 353–364.

FLYNN, R. (1995) Personal communication.

FREUD, S. (1925) An autobiographical study. *Standard Edition, Volume 20*, pp. 7–74. London: Hogarth Press and the Institute of Psycho-Analysis (1959).

FROSCH, J. (1983) *The Psychotic Process.* New York: International Universities Press.

HUSSEY, S. S. (1982) *The Literary Language of Shakespeare.* London: Longman.

KILGOUR, M. (1990) *From Communication to Cannibalism: An Anatomy of Metaphors of Incorporation.* Princeton: Princeton University Press.

KNIGHTS, B. (1992) *From Reader to Reader: Theory Text and Practice in the Study Group.* London: Harvester Wheatsheaf.

KUGLER, P. (1982) *The Alchemy of Disclosure: An Archetypal Approach to Language.* London: Bucknell University Press and Associated University Presses.

MAUD, R. (1963) *Entrances to Dylan Thomas' Poetry.* Lowestoft: Scorpion Press.

MEIR, C. (1974) *The Ballads and Songs of W. B. Yeats: The Anglo-Irish Heritage in Subject and Style.* London: Macmillan.

MEYER, M. (1995) Personal communication.

MILLER, C. (1987) *Emily Dickinson: A Poet's Grammar.* Cambridge, MA: Harvard University Press.

MURRAY, R. M. (1994) Neurodevelopmental schizophrenia: the rediscovery of dementia praecox. *British Journal of Psychiatry*, **165** (suppl. 25), 6–12.

Ron, M. & Harvey, I. (1990) The brain in schizophrenias. *Journal of Neurology, Neurosurgery and Psychiatry*, **53**, 725–726.

Rosenbaum, B. & Sonne, H. (1986) *The Language of Psychosis*. New York: New York University Press.

Rosenfeld, D. (1992) *The Psychotic: Aspects of the Personality*. London: Karnac Books.

Rosenfeld, H. (1965) *Psychotic States: A Psycho-Analytical Approach*. London: Karnac Maresfield Library.

Rosenthal, M. L. (1987) *The Poet's Art*. New York: W. W. Norton.

Slatoff, W. (1970) *With Respect to Readers: Dimensions of Literary Response*. Ithaca: Cornell University Press.

Stierlin, H. (1970) The functions of inner objects. *International Journal of Psycho-Analysis*, **51**, 321–329.

Watkins, M. (1986) *Invisible Guests: The Development of Imaginal Dialogues*. Boston, MA: Sigo Press.

4 The psychoanalytic approach to psychotic aspects of the personality: its relevance to psychotherapy in the National Health Service

DAVID TAYLOR

Introduction. Diagnosis and aetiology

In psychoanalytic psychotherapy, diagnosis, while remaining important, does not have the aspect of exclusive categorisation that it tends to have in psychiatry. Psychoanalytic investigation with individual patients brings continuities in the functioning of outwardly dissimilar patients into the foreground. In the psychoanalysis of normal people, areas of functioning are regularly revealed that are not very realistic and that have some characteristics encountered in psychotic patients. On the other hand, seriously ill patients have areas of their personality that function in a normal or neurotic fashion.

Other continuities can also be discerned between patients with different diagnoses. Schizophrenic patients are often depressed and their mental states can possess configurative psychological issues that are typical of depressed patients. These include mental states of sympathetic identification with objects important to the patient and where feelings of remorse and regret for damage done in fantasy are pronounced. At a symptomatic level, manic–depressive patients often have paranoid features and, at a slightly deeper level of mental functioning, their frequent use of paranoid and schizoid mental mechanisms can be seen. Furthermore, we find that these similarities extend beyond the level of symptoms to that of basic preoccupations and characteristic ways of handling anxiety. The basic problems of life can be discerned, although in different proportions and with different relations to one another, in all personalities, irrespective of diagnosis.

It has not been left to the supposedly arcane arts of psychoanalytic investigation to observe areas of normal functioning in the more disturbed patient. The eminent psychiatrist Manfred Bleuler, when reporting his long-term study of the lives of over 200 schizophrenic patients, wrote, "behind or beside psychotic phenomena, signs of a normal intellectual and emotional life can be discovered". He continued, "research on the clinical course of the illness confirms what clinicians realised long ago; in the schizophrenic, the healthy human is hidden and remains hidden, even if the psychosis lasts long. The healthy life of the schizophrenic is never extinguished" (Bleuler, 1970).

Bleuler was an organic psychiatrist whose initial research was on the relationship between endocrine disorders and schizophrenia. But in a paper that summarises some of his work, he wrote:

> "I suffer doubts when I consider critically my impression that the disease develops clearly as the consequence or the actions and reactions of the patient's personality to his human environment. Can we explain such a tremendous disaster as becoming schizophrenic by simple psychological conclusions, just as we explain everyday experiences with our healthy acquaintances? Similar doubts lead many physicians to refuse to consider that schizophrenia could be psychogenic... I am tormented again and again with this great question: have I discovered the actual aetiology or have I imagined it? Can I deduce the causes of the psychosis from psychological principles? Is an apparent psychodynamic explanation the right one? Confronted with these questions I feel myself compelled to look for answers in every possible way." (Bleuler, 1970)

How we approach these features – firstly, the coexistence of normal or neurotic functioning along with psychotic processes, and, secondly, the preservation of the potential for normal functioning when at the same time the schizophrenic patient's capacities are so catastrophically and seemingly irrevocably damaged – will determine the kind of explanation we develop of serious functional mental illness.

The psychoanalytic theory I will be considering here ascribes psychotic states to the operation of omnipotent mental mechanisms. These are the mind's ability to act upon itself, often in a manner to produce a fundamental deterioration in the capacity to think and to process emotional information. This deterioration appears, both to the sufferer and to the objective observer, to be irrevocable, although it is psychological. The nature of the mind's ability to act upon itself and the sources of the belief in the potency of omnipotent mechanisms are key areas of future research.

Psychotic functioning compared with neurotic functioning

I will start the discussion of these ideas with a clinical example to illustrate what, in this context, is meant by psychotic functioning.

> The patient, Mrs C, was a 35-year-old woman born and brought up in France with an obsessive–compulsive condition who was preoccupied with her spectacles and tortured by anxiety when she feared damage to the set of spectacles that fitted her. The patient's ex-husband looked after their three children but she saw the children every day. However, her husband announced a plan to move away and the prospect of being parted from her children greatly distressed her. One evening, shortly afterwards, she was walking her children home. In the darkness she was abstractedly gazing into the lighted windows of the houses she was passing. In the living room window of one house an adult playing the piano could be seen and the patient imagined a youngster coming in through the living room door. This part of the room was not actually visible and the scene was imaginary. In her state of preoccupation Mrs C forgot to look where she was going and walked into a metal signpost on the pavement, breaking the one pair of glasses she could wear. This felt like a catastrophe and for days after the patient could think of nothing else. Subsequently, she lost all capacity to think clearly as her mind was filled with a great variety of obsessional thoughts and anxieties, most of them centred around the irretrievable loss of the spectacles.

The way that I tried to understand what had happened to this patient makes great use of the distinction between the normal or neurotic ways of functioning and psychotic functioning. My account is based upon the ideas of Bion, Rosenfeld and Segal, who used Melanie Klein's original work on the distinction between the depressive and the paranoid–schizoid positions (see Chapter 2 of this volume for a brief explanation of these concepts, and Spillius (1988) and Anderson (1992) for more extended accounts). It was Bion (1957) who first worked out in detail the distinction between the normal, or neurotic, area of the personality and the psychotic area. In doing this he was describing characteristic differences in ways of functioning rather than reified parts of the personality operating semi-autonomously, although, in certain pathological states, they may seem to function like independent organisations.

My hypothesis with Mrs C was that to some degree she was able to tolerate the mental pain connected with the prospect of parting from her children. This is characteristic of a normal or neurotic way of functioning. Mrs C could have thoughts and ideas and function symbolically. As she walked the children home she was preoccupied with parents being together with children but her preoccupation was not so much in the form of thoughts as a picture in her mind's eye, her visual fantasy of the scene in the lighted living room. Her collision with the metal post was an accident waiting to happen. It was an externalisation, an acting out, as a result of which her problem was no longer in her mind; the emotional problem of tolerating the parting from her children and all that that loss meant to her both in and for itself and in what it stirred up from her past she was no longer capable of bearing in her mind. She was unable to be mentally preoccupied and so was visually preoccupied. As a direct result she was not able to look where she was going.

It was mental sight that she could not tolerate and its problems were evacuated from the personal psychological sphere, an experience with meaning, to a visual and therefore sensual experience and subsequently an irreversible preoccupation with physical objects – her glasses, which had been broken and endowed with an awful significance which by rights they should not possess. This last is one characteristic of psychotic functioning where the material world is inappropriately imbued with emotional objects. Bion described this as the schizophrenic living in a world of objects that are more usually the furniture of dreams. Such patients can be neither fully awake nor fully asleep. The gramophones that 'listen' to the schizophrenic person and the walls that 'have ears' indicate that the 'sense organs' of the mind have been projected into material objects in the external world to produce what Bion described as 'bizarre objects'.

Mrs C's children were a great reassurance to her against her feelings of dreadful loss and guilt, which were in part connected with her incapacity to put right her mind and her internal world; this includes her unconscious memories and internalisation of her personal relationships both now and when she was an infant. The imminence of the loss of the children threatened to expose her to that pain and also to a much more harsh confrontation with her internal situation.

Perhaps I should make it clear that these conjectures of mine were not just ideas aimed at reconstructing what had happened when some weeks before Mrs C had bumped into the metal post. Several times in the consultation itself Mrs C was able to approach the experience of loss, pain and frustration. I regarded this as evidence of her capacity for normal or neurotic functioning but she would be unable to sustain this and instead would become whimsical or completely preoccupied with her spectacles and their damage. In this way something of the interaction between psychotic and neurotic ways of functioning was observable in the present.

More detailed psychoanalytic investigation of a patient like this might reveal a number of features that are characteristic of those liable to develop psychotic problems. Often, there may have been severe environmental failures resulting in an infant or child experiencing very difficult emotional states without the presence of a caretaking object able to help in processing these states. There may be certain, possibly inherited, qualities of the personality that predispose. Whatever the precise pattern of complex causation, there results a personality with a hatred and fear of emotionally very painful experience and a determination to drive that experience out of the mental sphere. In addition, there may be powerful unconscious feelings of envy that exert an enormously destructive effect on the individual's capacities.

There are many types of interaction between neurotic and psychotic ways of functioning. For instance, psychotic areas of the personality of this sort can sometimes invade the more normal ego functions. In part, this feature follows necessarily from the problem the whole personality has with tolerating meaning and symbolic thought, for any experience of meaning carries with it the awareness of separateness of other objects and awareness of other difficulties and losses, not least the individual's awareness of his/her own disorder. In any seriously adverse upbringing, of course, there will be many painful experiences to be dealt with, for even in the very best of circumstances there are problems and losses to be faced as an intrinsic part of development.

Anything that stirs up awareness stirs up the prospect of pain from these various sources and there will be a pressure to turn to psychotic ways of operating to dismantle the more normal experience. So, Mrs C's ability to experience mental pain was replaced by a dominating preoccupation with spectacles and vision, which in a fundamental sense was meaningless to her. Sometimes these negative reactions against movements towards greater normality can be of quite terrifying violence and intensity – dangerous to the patient and to others. In these situations the forces operating within the patient seem to be profoundly hostile to meaning and development. The exercise of this hostility seems to be inherently and addictively gratifying to the omnipotent area of the personality which, in these situations, does not seem to be operating solely as a defence against pain.

Some implications for assessment and treatment

In these circumstances, how do we respond to the many psychotic patients (the majority?) who express a strong desire for psychotherapy and for being understood? It is far from uncommon for patients to feel that if only there were someone who understood them and to whom they could talk they would feel alright. One reason for this is that the experience of being psychotic – or in some post-psychotic state – is profoundly disabling and awful. As well as the wrecking of many of their life's hopes, so many of their enjoyable or satisfying mental capacities have been lost or damaged. The normal part of the personality mourns the loss of the experience of having a life and mind capable of meaning and significance either to the world as a whole or in personal relationships or in their own life. The loss of the meaning of life is a profound and terrible one.

The destructive mental mechanisms brought into play originally to dismantle meaning and bypass mental pain end up producing more torture than is ever resolved. These patients' idealised views of someone curative to understand them comes about partly as a result of their great actual dependence upon another person's understanding, the original antagonism to understanding having dismantled their own capacities and being able to do so again should the need arise. It is this conflict that patients will repeatedly encounter in their lives. Our awareness of it may help in working out ways of using psychotherapeutic understanding in the treatment of the seriously ill.

In the patient described in the clinical example below, the wish to be understood was very strong. In addition, when the process of understanding began, psychotic ways of functioning were also stimulated, resulting in a number of familiar difficulties for both patient and therapist. Not least among these was a shift from a feeling of relief at understanding, to one of anxiety that the situation was getting out of hand. When treatment is undertaken with a naïve, idealised view of psychotherapy this sequence can lead to the breakdown of therapy, either because the therapist unconsciously avoids real understanding so as not to stir up trouble, or because one or other party brings treatment to an end.

> The patient, Mrs G, who was seen for a single consultation, was a 25-year-old woman living at her mother's home. She had been referred, slightly reluctantly, by her consultant. She had been hospitalised for some months with a diagnosis of schizophrenia and was taking antipsychotic medication. The breakdown occurred during her second year of working at Cambridge University, when she gradually became unable to cope. She felt alone and was granted a year out from her work. During that time she moved into a religious community, where gradually her thinking became muddled. She began to believe that there was a higher link between people and she searched for this. During her admission she was angry, labile and frustrated with herself, and although it was affirmed that there were no depressive features

she kept bursting into tears. At other times she would laugh inconsequentially. She was placed on medication, was described as making a good recovery and on discharge as no longer frustrated, upset or thought disordered. She was followed up as an out-patient for over a year, when it was noted that she expressed occasional feelings of guilt at being immoral sexually and that she was sometimes perplexed.

Mrs G described herself as suffering from anxiety and depression. She said her confidence was low and she felt worried and nervous. She had been working as a lecturer part time but she found work very stressful and stopped because she was unhappy about it and because she felt so anxious. She often felt lethargic and had no energy and felt very depressed at certain times. She hoped the treatment would involve her having someone to share and discuss her thoughts and feelings.

Both her parents were now in their late fifties. Her father was an engineer and her mother a lawyer. In addition to two older sisters, there was a half-sister nine years younger from her father's second marriage. When she was three or four years old her parents divorced and although she saw her father occasionally she was brought up by her mother. She seemed to have had problems as a child and went to a child guidance clinic. She found her father difficult and would have liked to talk to him but he had high expectations and could be very critical. Her relationship with her husband, with whom she had been for two and a half years, was largely platonic – she was not very interested in sex. She was close to her mother, perhaps overclose she thought, but she found her very supportive and could not manage without her.

In the consultation the patient presented as an anxious, stiff-faced young woman who, although she talked very quietly in a rather mouselike fashion, also spoke under some pressure. She described how she was worried and how she could not teach and was at pains to get across to me that people tried to reassure her and tell her that she was competent whereas she knew that really she was not. People assumed she was competent because she had a 2:1 degree. This was supposed to be a reassurance to her but it was not. She knew that she only just scraped through parts of her course and there were parts of that she avoided because she felt too anxious. She told me again that she had been working on a voluntary basis but found she could not cope with it. Eventually she had stopped working and was terribly apologetic about letting people down. She had taken a present to one of her former colleagues. The senior lecturer there had said that the patient was a good teacher.

The patient went on saying that she found she could not cope with little things, she felt depressed and she lay in bed and got up late. She felt very guilty about herself and felt that she should be able to do more. She recollected that she was angry with her father when she was ill but now that feeling did not seem to be accessible to her.

I thought that she was very concerned to get across to me how troubled and insecure she felt. In some ways she was in quite a desperate state, feeling very depressed and disabled. I thought too that she was worried about her future and felt that no one had understood this. I pointed out how she was concerned that other people formed a too favourable opinion of her, but on the other hand I thought that she felt that if people took seriously how troubled she felt then that also was very worrying for she was deeply pessimistic about herself at root. I felt that the patient listened to this and she responded by rather wanly asking me if I thought that religion was a help. Her psychiatrist thought that religion was crap. I was surprised by the directness of this language, which I had not expected. She said that in some ways she also thought it was crap, but also she did not. She went to religious meetings and this helped her in some way. At this point I felt very unsure about the nature of her religious involvement and although there had been some understanding in the interview thus far, little of real dynamic significance had taken place.

After a while I asked her for an early memory and she told me with some difficulty how she could remember when she was about three or four years old sitting on the stairs eating a banana. The patient apologised for what she thought of as the poverty of her thought and memory. Clearly she felt she should be offering something much more substantial to help me. In contrast, I was struck by something odd about the way she spoke of eating a banana and wondered to myself if it represented some kind of suggestive imagery. However, what I pointed out was the patient's feeling that she should be providing more, that what she did was unsatisfactory. I linked the fact that the age of her early memory – three or four years – coincided with the age she had said that her parents divorced. More spontaneously then the patient told me a dream that came from the time when she was unable to continue at college and when she was worried about not keeping up with people and her state of mind. In the dream she was in bed but she was just falling out. I pointed out to her that she had had the dream when she had fallen out of something, when she was leaving college. That had been very difficult for her and had had serious consequences. Gradually, as a result of these exchanges, I felt there was some deepening of emotional contact with her and I thought that the patient began to feel that I might have understood something about her. At this point it was interesting how this previously immobile patient crossed her legs in a way that seemed self-conscious. I wondered whether it represented some way of tightening herself up against some imagined opening. It had brought to my mind some kind of closure against sexuality.

However, I was keenly aware that other than the 'suggestive' move-ments and language, I had very little upon which to base these thoughts of mine. I found myself thinking that my thoughts were rather strange and sexualised. These ideas began to seem less autochthonous and more provoked by something in Mrs G when she began to tell me how just before her breakdown she had felt that God had entered her. She had been sitting in a church. Speaking quickly, she talked of feeling guilty about sexuality and of how she had become ill after first having sexual intercourse.

At this point in the consultation the general atmosphere was much changed. The patient was now involved, more overtly anxious and troubled by what she was speaking of. I suggested to her that before she became ill she might have had the thought that in some way or other having intercourse would in some very magical way put something right inside her that she had felt was very wrong. Maybe, I continued, she had found that having intercourse had not put things right in the way she had expected and perhaps instead she had felt something very strange and disturbing had taken place which might have made much worse her pre-existing feelings of unease and guilt. The patient was quite surprised that I should say this but, for what it is worth, I did think that my 'imaginative' reconstruction meant something to her.

At this point two things happened. Firstly, she began to tell me that she had been troubled earlier – she had had many difficulties as a child, she said, and she had found it very difficult to think and work. Secondly, she became more disturbed and her stiff, immobile, mouse-like quality changed and became much more excitedly interested in what I was saying and preoccupied with religion. I thought that she was getting very excited, feeling that I was interested, like her, in religion and also that I 'understood' her. I felt that the signs of some kind of delusional union were evident. I drew Mrs G's attention to her growing excitement with these religious ideas and suggested that some part of her might feel that, by becoming totally immersed and preoccupied, talking here with me, there would then be none of her painful feelings, some from the four-year-old with the separating parents, some from less formulated feelings inside her, and that also there would not be an end to this appointment and as a result no return of depression with having to struggle for knowledge. My impression of her response to this comment was that she only very partially understood it. Perhaps she mostly took it as some kind of cooling-down comment which, I suppose, it partly was. At this point certainly the heat seemed to have gone from the situation and the final part of the consultation was taken up with discussing what could be offered to Mrs G.

At the beginning of the consultation Mrs G presented the familiar picture of a post-psychotic state with some post-psychotic depression. If this is examined more closely I think that it can be seen that there is a neurotic area of the personality and also how much more this comes alive when there are more or less accurate attempts to make contact and understand. Mrs G was relieved when her quite profound worries about herself could be faced without false reassurance or flinching. She felt that everyone was expecting her to be normal and strong while she knew she was anything but this. This understanding seemed to enable her to make meaningful contact with an evocative 'memory' of herself as a child at around the time of the break-up of her parents' marriage. I found myself wondering if the patient's profound anxieties of this time, her awareness of what was going on between the parents and the various fantasies that this would necessarily stir up in a child, was causing a state of paralysis in her thinking and, probably, great sadness and suffering. I think too that the banana might have represented some rather desperate mastur-batory response to her difficulties at that time.

If these considerations have any validity or usefulness – and for a number of reasons I think that they do – it would also seem that this area of her feeling and personality continued to exist at some level within her and became more intense as she moved through adolescence to early adulthood. Intercourse for this patient meant very directly to have contact with her very damaged internal world.

However, this example has been given to illustrate a number of other issues as well. In particular, as we have seen, one of the dilemmas for psychotic patients and their therapists is that the patient longs for someone to listen to and to take in their state. When this happens it can have beneficial effects but it can also result in an intensification of depressive pain and meaning. This stimulates more psychotic areas of functioning, which attack the knowledge and experience gained by the neurotic capacities of the patient. As Mrs G felt more understood, so the emergence of more omnipotent functioning, with her delusional ideas emerging into the transference, could be seen. In this, the psychotic area of the personality, there is no waiting for knowledge and no depression but the need for all that is denied as everything is put right immediately, in fantasy. In some psychotic personalities the hostility to significance is very intense and a part of the patient's personality operates to deny any meaningful experience.

Referrals of patients like Mrs G are frequent. Typically, the patient exerted some pressure to be referred for psychotherapy while the consultant felt uncomfortable, thinking that she was not really suitable and that she might get ill again in the course of treatment. At the same time the referrer felt for Mrs G, whom he sensed was very unhappy, and she made him wish that more could be done for her. It is one of the more difficult burdens of psychiatric work to be looking after people who are suffering and unhappy and who would like to be helped while one also has the feeling, sometimes despairing, that little can be done. But these patients present difficulties too for the psychoanalytic psychotherapist. Only a limited number can be offered individual psychotherapy, which quite often needs to be long term, and the outcome of these treatments is, as we know, quite complicated, with some gains and benefits but also with difficulties and failures.

One of the most valuable benefits of treatment is a lessening of the patient's isolation from meaningful relationships and experience. The hypertrophic use of schizoid mechanisms leads to patients being cut off from important parts of their own personalities. When the fundamental preoccupations and desires of life cannot be risked for fear of the emotional and psychological consequences, the result can be a disabling impoverishment.

Hopefully, in a therapeutic encounter patients can begin to 'process' more of their experience in a more neurotic way, subtly lessening the pressure to resort to more damaging defences. For a sizeable group of borderline and psychotic patients this can make all the difference, enabling them to keep working or to maintain meaningful areas of their life.

However, these benefits are not achieved without hazard. The stimulation of psychotic ways of functioning can present major emotional problems for both the patient and the therapist. Malignant regressions are not uncommon and therapeutic impasse not always avoidable. As a result patients can deteriorate and treatment breakdown is frequent, although often something in the way of learning is usually gained from even the most fraught of therapies. Achieving a reliably constructive balance between benefits and risks is difficult, and no easy formula, routinely applied, will serve.

Towards the end of Mrs G's consultation we discussed the issue of her future treatment. In reporting this I felt uncomfortably aware of the possible inadequacy of what she received from me. For Mrs G I did not consider that there was a realistic possibility of finding her a vacancy for individual treatment with a therapist with sufficient experience to be able to deal with the problems that would arise in the course of any meaningful treatment. I therefore told her that I did not feel I could find the right vacancy for her. I said I would discuss the consultation with her psychiatrist and we would see if some further therapeutic intervention could be found. What I had in mind was some more supportive relationship with someone who had an idea and understanding of what kind of person Mrs G was. I thought in that context she could be helped to have a better contact with some of her feelings about her father, for instance, and with understanding better her relationship with her mother.

In this kind of generally sentient setting I thought she might be able to make some progress. Outcomes of this sort are not uncommon, and sometimes these consultations produce a tantalised, angry and disappointed patient and a referrer who feels that yet again he/she has to carry the patient and there has been a pointless referral. With Mrs G this was not the case, although I recognise that it could well have been. In fact, the referrer felt helped by the discussions we had and the ideas produced about the emotional origins and nature of the patient's problems. He felt freed from the burden of just seeming to say no to this patient and more able emotionally to take her in as a person – although clearly he had in a way already done this by making the referral – for his ability to use his own capacities freely had been compromised by the feelings of guilt, inadequacy and despair which so much attended Mrs G.

The contribution of applied psychoanalytic psychotherapy to psychiatric services

The consultation with Mrs G raises some important issues about how the National Health Service can best respond to the needs of patients like her, as well as those with more severe psychotic illnesses. People who are potential patients for individual psychoanalytic psychotherapy, as she was, vastly outnumber vacancies or therapists, but at the same time it must be acknowledged that the 'ecosystem' is not so simple as this numerical shortage might imply. We must ask why are there so few vacancies or so few therapists capable of doing this work? Part of the answer to this question does lie simply in resources and training but also this is very difficult work that is personally disturbing; not everyone can do it and very few people can do a lot of it. So there is a strong and, to some extent, a natural tendency to avoid it among all of us, and this needs to be taken seriously. However, I do think it is still realistic to suppose that with a better resourced and supported mental health service it would be possible and useful for a larger group of seriously disturbed patients to have formal long-term psychoanalytic psychotherapy. More mental health workers could be trained in the requirements and exigencies of psychotherapeutic work with the seriously disturbed. It is necessary for the training to include personal therapy, which should enable an increased tolerance and understanding of more disturbed areas within the therapist's own personality. Within certain limits, the more that understanding at an emotional level can be combined with a rigorous intellectual appreciation of the nature of these problems, the better it is. This means that training should include seminars and lectures about the nature of these types of psychopathology. As this is difficult work, the more supportive the environmental structure can be made for both the patient and the person doing the therapy, the better the outcome.

I would also like to mention some other ways by which favourable treatment outcomes for the very seriously ill may be obtained. The psychoanalytic psychotherapist may make a limited but still significant contribution. Through its knowledge of the meaning and nature of psychotic states, interpretive psychotherapy can contribute indirectly to the general clinical management of the patient through the impact of teaching, case discussion, and personal supervision. Not all such work should be second-hand or indirect, however. Sometimes the psychoanalytic psychotherapist should actually be engaged in the clinical management of these patients.

An important aspect of these contributions lies in resisting, and helping others to resist, the movement against understanding that has been identified with psychotic functioning earlier in this chapter. While psychotic thinking may have arisen in the first place from the dismantling of the capacity for symbolism, it is still helpful to be able to recognise psychotic states as communicative and meaningful. For instance, Lucas (1993) describes how a schizophrenic patient asked for admission by saying she was going to explode. The patient was admitted and within a day needed to be contained in a locked ward. In a previous admission she had drawn a picture of a volcano exploding. Lucas advises that when psychotic patients say they are frightened or anxious, even when this is apparently without content, this should to be taken seriously. It may be that the patient is sensing the activity of some very violent part of the personality that may be about to find expression in destructiveness towards the self or others.

Psychotic functioning can be externalised in groups and institutions, where it can have a negative effect on the capacity to work. Examples of this can be found in Chapters 5 and 14. Psychoanalytic understanding of the processes involved can, however, be used to create and maintain a therapeutic function. This is described within a specialised day hospital by Bateman (1995), while Chapter 15 in the present volume describes a different attempt to apply understanding of this kind to the rehabilitation unit of a large mental hospital.

The transition to community-based mental health care, while creating enormous problems for staff and patients with the dismantling of traditional methods of containing anxiety, at the same time may offer an opportunity to redesign our psychiatric services in new and better ways (see Alanen, 1993, and Pylkkanen, Chapter 16 of this volume, for a description of the Finnish approach to the treatment of schizophrenia in the community). In this context it may not be appropriate to perpetuate the unproductive split between biological and psychotherapeutic approaches to psychiatry that has characterised British psychiatry for so long.

Considered singly, each of these various suggestions can make only a small contribution. However, if combined and applied with an appreciation of the ubiquity of psychotic mechanisms there is the possibility of a different approach to mental health in our society. Necessarily, this involves quite fundamental questions about which values matter and a realisation of how damaging can be the persuasiveness of a whole range of quick-fix mechanisms.

References

ALANEN, Y. O. (1993) Psychotherapy of schizophrenia in community psychiatry. *Bulletin of the British Psycho-Analytical Society,* **29**, 15–27.

ANDERSON, R. (ed.) (1992) *Clinical Lectures on Klein and Bion.* No. 14 of the New Library of Psycho-Analysis. London: Tavistock/Routledge.

BATEMAN, A. (1995) The treatment of borderline patients in a day hospital setting. *Psychoanalytical Psychotherapy,* **9**, 3–16.

BION, W. R. (1957) Differentiation of the psychotic from the non-psychotic personalities. *International Journal of Psycho-Analysis,* 38. Also in W. R. Bion, *Second Thought,* Maresfield Reprints (1967).

BLEULER, M. (1970) Some results of research in schizophrenia. *Behavioral Science,* **15**, 211–218.

LUCAS, R. (1993) The psychotic wavelength. *Psycho-Analytical Psychotherapy,* **7**, 15–24.

SPILLIUS, E. B. (ed.) (1988) *Melanie Klein Today, Vol. 1, Mainly Theory,* and *Volume 2, Mainly Practice.* London: Routledge.

5 Psychosis and groups

JOHN WALSHE

"We are all of us born mad: some of us remain so." (Samuel Beckett, 1956)

I intend in this chapter to discuss briefly what is meant by psychosis and psychotic phenomena and come to an operational definition. The definition essentially will centre around the idea that the unreal, the unconscious, the fantasy world is the base from which psychosis emerges. In the Samuel Beckett sense we all have the potential to be 'mad' or psychotic; humans have an unconscious and their perception of the world is coloured by fantasies. I will then use this definition to discuss the occurrence of psychosis in different types of groups and situations. I will also consider what ideas and models are most helpful in understanding the psychotic phenomena and to some extent suggest how they might be used.

There is a problem in the mental health caring professions about the meaning of the word psychosis. It was first used in the mid-19th century (Gregory, 1987), when it tended to mean any kind of mental disturbance. It gradually, however, began to have a more specific meaning and today it is generally accepted as a term that signifies a serious mental illness. Problems with the term arise when there is an assumption about the origin and cause of the psychosis. The argument is usually linked in some way to the nature–nurture duality. For example, is it genetic or early experience? Is it predisposition or early trauma? There are many theories around these themes, including the organic model based on the observation of phenomena and a supposed objectivity about the behaviour, feelings and ideas reported by the patient – an objectivity that is linked to empirical and dualistic philosophies developed by Descartes, Kant and others. This empirical philosophical drive informs the phenomenology of Karl Jaspers (1963), which underpins psychiatric nosology and its diagnostic categories. Directly opposing this view, and intrinsic to the psychodynamic model, is the idea that the unconscious, both repressed and preconscious, has a large effect on our consciousness and objectivity. Freud particularly emphasised this effect of the unconscious on our conscious and supposedly objective lives in *Psychopathology of Everyday Life* (1901) and *Jokes and their Relation to the Unconscious* (1905). Between these polarities are many other ideas and models that take from both sides of the debate, such as the development model recognising the importance of early experience but also pointing to innate imprinting mechanisms (Bowlby, 1978).

These differences can make it extremely difficult to reach an agreement about what we are discussing and in what way we might treat the problem. Professionals tend to use all these perspectives within a discussion, which generates irritation or incomprehension because of the confusion that this creates in their audience or even themselves. Constant linguistic difficulties arise across these polarities as to the meaning of words and phrases. The same words and ideas have different connotations within each theoretical structure. For example, one individual professional may use the word psychotic in several different ways – developmentally, phenomen-ologically or diagnositically – within one conversation. There are also sociolinguistic difficulties that professionals are often caught in when words enter common usage. Again, the word psychosis is linked to severity of illness both in society and by professionals. One cannot be psychotic unless one is very ill: this becomes a tautology. Patients are often entangled in this sort of knot, which diminishes the usefulness of the word as a clinical description.

Broadly, there are three distinctive arenas from which various subtexts are attached to psychosis. These are the psychiatric medical model, the psychoanalytic developmental model, and a sociological, countercultural post-Laingian view. The medical model supports its arguments by observation of specific phenomena and empirical research. It assumes that, when certain phenomena are observed, the patient has psychosis and is suffering from a physical brain disease which today is usually described in terms of some biochemical deficiency or lack of brain substance.

The psychoanalyst, on the other hand, theorises and uses heuristic and hermeneutic methods of research. These methods suggest that someone who presents with psychotic phenomena has regressed or has not been able to develop normally from an early stage in their lives. They also suggest that their unconscious and their fantasies are dominating their existence with no control or need to check their ideas and feelings with external reality. The main forms this has taken are reviewed in Chapter 2.

There are many sociological views, the core of which is that society in some way is the dominant force that is causing the mental health problem. This contextual view overlaps with the systemic approach to psychosis reviewed in Chapter 10. Laing, Bateson and others thought that complex and skewed reactions within the family have driven a particular member into psychosis and into bizarre beliefs and reactions that are then labelled by society (Laing, 1968).

These are the polarised views used by some professionals likely to invoke names such as Freud, Klein, Laing, Mead and so on as if these theorists and clinicians had maintained a constant view without having any doubts of their own. Their original works show that this is not so. These professionals, whose views concerning psychosis often seem opposed, are likely still to agree that the person who is psychotic is acting or reacting in an unreal way, that they are out of touch with a reality external to them. This respects the historical evolution of the term, as reviewed in Chapter 1.

According to the psychodynamic view of psychosis, this apparent loss of touch with reality happens because the unconscious has broken through into consciousness and patients are operating in the external real world as if it were the unconscious world. They therefore believe that their fantasies are true. It is as if the comedian and the audience believed that the jokes that are told are absolutely true. At the most psychotic level, there is an inability or failure to hold the symbolic at a thinking intellectual plane and to be able to play with it. This is reflected in the importance placed in psychiatric diagnosis of a schizophrenic psychosis on how patients understand proverbs.

In talking about psychosis in groups, I am referring to a wide range of phenomena that suggest that the person or group is not in touch with the reality of the world around them or the situation external to themselves. They are signs that the unconscious or fantasy world is no longer balanced by the reality of what is outside the person or the group. There will always be a disagreement about what reality is, and what is outside a person and what is inside. (This philosophical conundrum will not be considered here: some pointers will be found in Gregory, 1981.) I do hope that the descriptions I shall give will make the unreality, that which makes the phenomena psychotic, sufficiently clear. I believe that both the individual and the group can operate at the reality level in one particular area, but be totally unreal in their reactions in another. Moreover, all people seem to move in and out of psychosis or back and forth from the real to the unreal. The diagnoses of the medical model therefore may have picked out a particular population of patients who are different because their sense of the world outside themselves has broken down over a broad area, or who seem unable to move out of psychosis, or who get stuck in it at times.

Psychotic phenomena can also be viewed as similar to unconscious dream-like material. They have links to childhood fantasy and primary process thinking. It is important to recognise that the person or group is operating at a psychotic level. The therapist's understanding and response to the situation may then be more enlightened. Therapists tend to be frightened of psychotic phenomena and either feel that they cannot do anything with them or try to deny their existence. They may try to suppress psychosis in the individual or group – "We don't want to open that can of worms".

When individuals meet in groups, this movement from reality to unreality becomes more obvious, particularly in groups run in an analytical way. There also seems to be an increase in psychotic phenomena the larger the size of the group. Surprisingly, the situation and locality of the group also have an effect. Taking these observations into consideration I now wish to remark upon some actual psychotic phenomena in groups, how they arise and the theoretical ideas that illuminate them. This includes specific examples of different types of groups with regard to their locality, their size and the reactions of the members.

Psychotic phenomena in groups

The propensity of individuals to produce psychotic phenomena seems to heighten once they are in a group. What are the processes and factors in a group that produce this effect? A large element of this may be the increase in tension and anxiety that prevails in groups. Linked to this is the social proximity of others, and the feelings of insecurity that arise when others are present who are not necessarily known and with the increase in complexity of inter-relationships within a group. The theory that the growth in the cerebral hemispheres in the individual is also linked to an increasing complexity in relationships shows how important this is to the human species (Humphrey, 1986). Certainly there is a heightened anxiety and a more general increase of feeling in any group. Le Bon, at the end of the 19th century, thought that there was a 'contagion' in groups (cf. Freud, 1921). He thought that emotional feelings dominate in groups at the expense of the intellect, resulting in less civilised responses ('the mob rules, OK'). Freud suggested that the anxiety and libidinal energy in groups were directed towards the leader by processes of identification and idealisation. He believed that the main way the group psychosis or disturbance could be controlled was through these processes being linked to the leader with libidinal energy (Freud, 1921).

McDougall (1920) suggested ways of reducing the chaos and emotion in groups and organisations by developing a structure and culture in the group. Bion (1961) also differentiates the work of a group, the agreed conscious task for which they have come together, from basic assumption material, which is without logic and full of emotional colouring. In our own reactions in large crowds, as spectators when our local team or hero figure is playing, it is not unusual to find ourselves shouting and jumping up and down, although in 'normal' circumstances we would not dream of doing such a thing. These experiences (and perhaps the reaction of society to them in the way the police try to contain the emotion and the football clubs try to direct it) elucidate the theories of Bion and McDougall. It is interesting to note how the common expression that I have used above – we would not *dream* of doing such a thing – shows the connection between madness or psychosis, dreams and groups. It is notable how groups, in order to deal with emotional contagion, develop rules, rituals and agendas to prevent the dominance of psychotic elements and feelings. They may even appoint an authoritarian figure to rule them, or bring in the forces of law and order.

At the conference on which this book is based, I took two workshop groups, which exhibited some of these phenomena. In the first group, at a morning session, I made a statement about how an introductory process tends to reduce anxiety and lessen the chance of a psychotic reaction and then said nothing more. I did not offer any agenda or process of introduction. As the group progressed, emotion was heightened and there was a very strong demand throughout the group for me to produce an agenda, or 'overheads', despite my various statements about how psychotic phenomena could become more manifest if we did not do so. It is interesting to note that, in reality, few people actually remember other people's names when introduced in groups of five or more, although we often behave as if this were a possibility by proceeding to introduce everyone.

In the second group, held in the afternoon, there was less anxiety and less expression of primary process thinking. We began by introducing ourselves and I produced an agenda and a set of overheads. What I was trying to achieve in the first group was to demonstrate, through having no agenda or ritual of introduction, how psychosis arises in groups and, by comparison in the afternoon, how having a ritual and lecture makes the space safe enough to contain our own internal fantasies in the external world. I think it is useful for people to have both experiences to understand these phenomena – something that was not possible at the conference, as those who chose the workshop either had one or the other.

It has been noted already that individuals, when they get into groups, can behave differently. Patients who, when seen individually, seem to have strong ego boundaries and are assessed as having neurotic defence mechanisms can, once they are in a group, be seen as narcissistic, full of primary anxiety and determined to view the world and the group as a dangerous place. Their emotions overwhelm them and they easily regress to a more primitive state. The core problem in their psyche becomes more obvious. For example, a patient who complained of being phobic and of finding it difficult to go to work once in the group became severely regressed, refused to talk to anyone and became enraged with the world, her workmates and her parents, for their refusal to operate in the way she thought they should. It was almost impossible to move her from this position, which she held to with delusional intensity.

Group-specific phenomena may also be released. Perhaps the most prevalent and astonishing psychotic phenomenon in groups is how they persist in not doing the work that is expected of them. In the terms of Bion (1961), the work function is rejected and a basic assumption predominates. This is particularly true of analytical groups. In this type of group the work, the real task to be done by the members is to consider their relationships within the group and in their own lives, to free associate and bring the unconscious meaning of what they do to the surface in the group. But members will persist in talking about the weather, the government, the state of the economy – anything but the work of the group. It is not unusual for an analytical group, particularly early in its life, to continue on in this way through an hour-and-a-half session until the last one-third or so of the session, when they may then turn to the task and begin to speak about their relationships both within and outside the group. A similar phenomenon linked to this is the group's reaction to therapist's interventions. Quite often these are ignored as if the therapist did not exist, or anything that the therapist might have to say is somehow not relevant to the group or the members. There is a resistance to the work here which is psychotic in nature. Through the mechanism of projective identification, this can leave therapists feeling paranoid (that whatever they say is wrong) or feeling psychotically depressed (that as therapists they are no good or what they do is a waste of time). By way of comparison, the resistance in individual work seems to involve processes of thinking more. Individual patients in analytical psychotherapy resist in a more neurotic defensive way. They may associate to and talk about unconscious feelings and emotions, but they are usually neurotically defending a core area against the analytical process.

Transferential material – transference to the therapist, between members and to the group – is also a group phenomenon that commonly occurs and is out of touch with the reality of the object chosen, that is, the therapist, the other group members or the situation. These transferences are sometimes held for a long time with psychotic intensity. There is then a clear gap between the real and the fantasy world, for example in the transference to the therapist shown by a patient I met in a supermarket who insistently protested that it was impossible that I should ever go shopping. Psychosis in transference to the group is illustrated by the woman who felt that it was all right for her to go at any time on a holiday but there was no need for the other members of the group to have a holiday at any time.

As for transference between members, consider a not uncommon situation in mature groups. It has become clear to everyone in the group that member A is relating to another member, B, at the transferential level and that A is unable to realise what is happening despite the attempts of several members of the group to point this out. In one instance of this kind, a woman whose father totally denigrated her felt that another man in the group was acting in the same way towards her, although it was obvious to the rest of the group that he was far too mild a man to denigrate anyone and that he had communicated with her in a helpful way.

Another common group phenomenon that is unreal is the tendency to insist that the members are all the same: 'We are all equal here'. The idea is obviously incorrect using external reality criteria, in that in the group there will be men and women, and the members will have different ages, different skills, different emotions, responses and so on. However, this insistence of equality is a primal emotional idea that is driven by primary process thinking. It may dominate a group for a long time. Multidisciplinary teams are prone to fall into this predicament in order to deal with the anxiety of their differences and the problem of competition. I watched one particular team who, after two years, were still trying to prove to each other and to their managers that they all had the same skills. This was in spite of some horrendous difficulties and anxieties for the individuals within the team in trying to make everyone equal when they were obviously not equal in skill, experience and qualifications. It felt like they were trying to square the circle. Some patients clearly saw that there was a difference and this insistence upon being equal was confusing for patients who were referred and attended for treatment. At times they seemed more sane than the team. Something similar to this occurs with feelings of omnipotence in a group: this group is all-powerful, it is the best group ever and, particularly, no other group is as capable as they are, no one knows as well as they do. Any suggestion outside of this way of thinking is taken up in a paranoid way. The reverse may also be seen as a kind of negative omnipotence, when the members can think and feel that they are the worst group ever.

Psychosis and the group context

It is helpful for the therapist to be aware of phenomena like these because the situation, and of course the membership, of a group can increase or decrease the amount of psychotic phenomena present. In some groups they are seen more often and more obviously. These phenomena should influence the choices made in groups about where they are held and the type of members who would be suitable. The position that the therapist holds in the group, and his/her emotional insight and knowledge, is crucial in these situations.

Out-patient groups

Out-patient groups tend to be less psychotic because the members are still functioning in the outside world. Some of them will have jobs, or will otherwise have to deal with the complexities of day-to-day living. They bring the reality of the environment, social life and immediate family or friends' reactions into the group. They are more in touch with their ambivalence and social reality. Therapists are also aware that it is difficult to hold a largely psychotic individual in an out-patient group and therefore they usually invite less psychotic members to join. This applies even more if, immediately outside the group room, the situation is not very holding (e.g. an empty clinic or one with only non-mental health personnel). However, if the place where the group is held is a day centre where there are experienced mental health staff outside the group room, then it is possible to have more psychotic patients in the group and the therapist will probably take this into consideration when selecting members for the group.

In out-patient long-term groups, it is useful to have one or two psychotic patients. As outlined above, the members of these groups generally have stronger egos, and are more able to differentiate between the world of fantasy and the world outside in which some of them will be working. Their boundaries are clearer to them. The psychotic episodes in these groups tend to be momentary or to be confined to one particular operation. Two psychotic members at the most is as much as this type of group can take. What may happen depends to some extent upon the intensity of the psychotic phenomena. If both psychotic members are too out of touch with reality then they tend to form a subgroup of their own, which is not helpful to them or the group. They may be depressed, and feel the world is a totally disappointing place (including themselves) and they cannot bear it, or they may have paranoid ideas and feelings, and the world seems to be to blame for everything. They remind the group members of their own feelings of disappointment with the world – a whole body of feeling usefully described by Craib (1994). They may realise the madness of blaming others entirely for their problems.

For the psychotic individuals, if they are able to stay in the group, there is power in several other people telling them the opposite to what they assume is reality. They begin to realise the unreality of their belief systems and behaviour. The strength of the assumption that their fantasy life is the correct perception of the world is reduced. As an example, take the patient who is determined to view the world and the relationships within it as always manipulative, untrustworthy, and 'crass': to quote her, "all relationships are like this". She very soon learns that it is only her that feels that way, and that not all relationships are like that (i.e. not those of the other members and therapist in the group). Instead, it is "all *my* …", that is, her own feelings about her relationships that are like this. She learns that people do not automatically dislike her for thinking in this way, and that the members are able to empathise with what she is saying to some degree without agreeing with her that it is true all the time.

In-patient groups

In in-patient groups there will be more psychotic phenomena (Yalom, 1983). This reflects the type of patients who get admitted to hospital. They are usually more profoundly disturbed. Some patients are admitted under the Mental Health Act; their number is increasing at present. The number of trained staff who are available to deal with psychotic behaviour will also have an effect. There is, moreover, the possibility that patients regress more easily in this secure environment. It is sometimes difficult to assess whether they are regressed to their psychotic state because of the situation or because of their intrinsic illness. There is an increased intimacy for both staff and patients with each other physically and psychologically, as they are with each other for much longer periods. This tends to increase the anxiety level and opportunities for disagreements and arguments, which leads to feelings of insecurity and lack of holding. Uncontrollable emotions – rage, envy – and their accompanying fantasies are more likely to emerge.

In in-patient open groups it is possible to have more disturbed individual patients and a greater number in the group. The amount of disturbance psychically and physically can be higher because of the holding environment outside. Paranoid and depressive anxieties may sometimes operate outside the group, both about the group and in the feelings of the staff generally. Acute in-patient units tend to be the 'bins' for all kinds of early and primitive anxiety and this sometimes infects the staff. They then wish to get rid of these feelings and a target outlet for this can be the therapist who comes to the unit only to run a small in-patient group. Feelings develop about the therapist who does not have to deal with these patients all the time and the consequences of what might be happening in the group. In-patient group members tend to act out a lot more and the staff have to deal with it. For example, the patient who suddenly leaves a group and begins to break up the furniture in another room causes the staff to feel, with some justification, in an objective sense, that the group is to blame. The problem is that staff are not able on occasion to separate their internal feelings of paranoid and depressive anxiety from the external objectivity which then hooks on to these situations. In these circumstances it is essential for the therapist to ensure there is good communication with the staff of the unit.

In large groups, there are also more psychotic phenomena present. Unconscious elements can break through the structures that are set up to control them, such as agendas, social formulated interchanges and rituals. In large analytical groups where these structures are at a minimum this is more likely to happen. Besides, it is part of the purpose of the group to meet to consider the unconscious motivations, thoughts and patterns of response to internal and external stimuli of its members. And again, as might be expected, the larger the group the more psychotic elements are present. The individual tends to lose his/her sense of self, the large number seems to make it more emotionally powerful, and there is increased anxiety. I remember a large group of psychotherapists agreeing that 'we are all English here' (a variant of 'we are all equal here') despite the clear fact that there were people from all over the world in that group. It is much more difficult to get agreement about the rules, rituals and what is acceptable behaviour in a large group. It may therefore become much more psychotic. Politicians seem to be instinctively aware of the unreality of large groups: this may be the reason why they talk a lot but say nothing. They try to avoid a commitment in public, an external reality situation. Perhaps, like the bard described by Tacitus (cf. Bion, 1961), they realise it is the noise they make that matters.

It is important to avoid having members in a large group who are overtly psychotic or who are liable to become psychotic because of these psychotic phenomena breaking through. The higher anxiety level present also adds to the problem. It can be devastating both for the group and the individual. This becomes quite clear in encounter groups and some religious groups where there are very strong pressures to act or think in a particular way. It is not uncommon to see patients who have become psychotic after an encounter group experience. Mass suicides in religious sects – the temple of Jones' people, the Waco experience – show how psychotic people can become under pressure in large groups. They are not in touch with the reality of what is happening in the external world.

Psychosis and useful theories in group practice

To understand and make use of psychosis in a group I have found the following theorists and models the most helpful.

Freud described how libidinal energy operates in groups through the leader by the process of identification and idealisation (Freud, 1921). The insistence by the patient on the reality of the transference to the leader absorbs tremendous energy and can absorb other group members in its unreal dimensions. A group once for a whole year kept up the idea that I definitely did not have any children, which had arisen from the transferential statements and belief of one of the female members. This idea was ultimately challenged by the arrival of a new member. Unfortunately this resulted in an admission episode to hospital for the female patient, who found the shattering of her fantasy too much. However, it produced a reassessment of the reality of the situation for the rest of the group; that is, they did not in fact know whether I had children or not, and the patient was able to return to the group after her admission. The fantasy and power of the libidinal attachment to the leader can lead to an unreal world where the ideal of the superego, projected into the leader, is the only one allowed to operate, keeping control over an individual's own ego and the world around it. Freud's (1923) structural description of the mind is very helpful in providing a model to help understand these processes.

Klein's ideas about the paranoid and depressive positions and the mechanisms of projection, introjection and splitting are summarised in Chapter 2 and illustrated in a one-to-one setting in Chapter 4

(Klein, 1935, 1946). They are immensely useful in understanding groups. They may be seen in the whole group or in a particular member retreating to one of the positions or using the different defensive mechanisms. For example, one particular psychotically depressed and paranoid member believed that she was hopeless and there was no point in life. She had made several serious suicide attempts. She described how she would often look out of her window and believe that people she could see in the street were talking about her, and "saying nothing good". In a Kleinian sense she was projecting her bad feelings about herself on to the people in the street, thus remaining in the paranoid position. The group then took up the theme of how they also have fantasies about how other people see them, both outside and in the group – how they put on to others their own feelings, which have nothing to do with how the other is thinking or being. The depressed member was surprised by other people having the same feelings and began to talk about her own internal world, where there was something that made her feel very bad, and connected this, through an interpretation, to early life experiences.

The group itself can also become paranoid or depressed. The paranoia becomes dominant when the group project their problems on to the outside world, "the system is wrong", "the government is the cause of the problem''. At that moment, or for some time, the members all agree with this mode of being and of feeling, despite the evidence to the contrary, which they themselves have itemised in previous group sessions. A more subtle and perhaps more anti-depressive mode is the feeling that the group is the best place in the world and the external world is "the mad place" or where "other people consistently attack you".

Bion's basic assumptions extend Kleinian ideas in that his description of what operates at the basic feeling and fantasy levels, the unconscious world of the group, is more detailed and specific to groups (Bion, 1961). His ideas help to clarify the internal life of the group as much as its relationship with the world outside. The basic assumption of fight/flight is about how the group can take flight or begin a fight either within the group or carry the same operations into another group. A group takes up a row about race so they do not have to look at the fact that they are actually in direct conflict with each other. They discuss at length an idea that is far away from the reality of the situation or they focus on the unreal hope that a particular member or members will have the solution to everything, a basic assumption pairing. As with the Freudian leadership mechanism, the group will try to place all their dependence on the leader or some external institution, bible or agenda.

Bowlby's (1978) ideas about the secure base and attachment and loss in connection with that secure base also help therapists to pick up some specific psychotic moments on the boundary of the group and its administration. For example, a patient who consistently arrives late for the group and, despite this being pointed out to him by the group many times, gives a consistent reply about "not knowing why I do it". However, it is clear from his history and his reactions within the group that he has enormous unconscious fears about being attached to and/or losing anyone whom he needs or becomes close to. The ghosts of difficult past separations and deaths are still powerful emotive forces in his unconscious that affect his arrival at the group. He had lost both his parents through conflict and a much-needed partner through separation.

Conclusion

The points that I would like to emphasise are that in groups the unconscious world becomes available for analytic understanding. The psychotic dimensions of this can be understood and linked to observed phenomena, linguistic meaning and various analytical models. Therapists can use this understanding in a helpful way for patients. And it is unfortunate that they sometimes wish to ignore it or do not consciously pick it up and make use of it. The can of worms, Medusa's head, or Pandora's box becomes too fearful and anxiety-provoking for them and for the patient, and thus a useful therapeutic intervention is missed.

References

BECKETT, S. (1956) *Waiting for Godot.* London: Faber & Faber.
BION, W. R. (1961) *Experiences in Groups and Other Papers.* London: Tavistock.
BOWLBY, J. (1978) *Attachment and Loss.* Harmondsworth: Penguin Books.
CRAIB, I. (1994) *The Importance of Disappointment.* London: Routledge.
FREUD, S. (1901) Psychopathology of everyday life. *Standard Edition, Volume 6.* London: Hogarth Press.
—— (1905) Jokes and their relation to the unconscious. *Standard Edition, Volume 8.* London: Hogarth Press.
—— (1921) Group psychology and the analysis of the ego. *Standard Edition, Volume 18.* London: Hogarth Press.
—— (1923) The ego and the id. *Standard Edition, Volume 19.* London: Hogarth Press.
GREGORY, R. L. (1981) *Mind in Science: A History of Explanations in Psychology and Physics.* London: Weidenfeld & Nicolson.
—— (ed.) (1987) *The Oxford Companion to the Mind.* Oxford: Oxford University Press.
HUMPHREY, N. (1986) *The Inner Eye.* London: Faber & Faber.

JASPERS, K. (1963) *General Psychopathology* (translators J. Hoenig & M. W. Hamilton). Chicago: Regenery.

KLEIN, M. (1935) A contribution to the psychogenesis of manic depressive states. In *Love, Guilt and Reparation*. London: Hogarth (1975).

—— (1946) Notes on some schoid mechanisms. In *Envy Gratitude and Some Other Works*. London: Hogarth (1975).

LAING, R. D. (1968) *The Politics of the Family*. Toronto: Hunter Rose Company.

McDOUGALL, W. (1920) *The Group Mind*. Cambridge: Cambridge University Press.

YALOM, I. D. (1983) *Inpatient Group Psychotherapy*. New York: Basic Books.

6 Borderline phenomena in analytic groups

MALCOLM PINES

The group analytic situation as devised by S. H. Foulkes combines strength with sensitivity. The model has been adequately outlined elsewhere (Foulkes & Anthony, 1984; Pines & Hearst, 1993) and I have described experiences with difficult and borderline patients in other publications (Roberts & Pines, 1992), as have other group analysts. In this chapter my aim is to describe and to discuss situations that strain and test the capacity of the group analytic setting to and sometimes beyond its limits. Particular to the group analytic approach is the clarification and emphasis that the group analyst has a dual function as a group leader. First, this is to be the 'dynamic administrator', who has the responsibility for establishing and maintaining the group analytic setting. After this the analyst can become the 'group conductor'.

As dynamic administrator his/her responsibilities are to select patients:

(a) for membership of the group;
(b) on the basis of the desired composition of the group, so that there is an adequate balance of resources to enable the group to function therapeutically.

The conductor must take into account the psychological strengths and weaknesses of the various members; for instance, if the group includes quite ill patients then there must also be a potential for health in the other members of the group, to fulfil what Foulkes called his "basic law of group dynamics". By this he meant that although each member of the group may represent some form of deviance from the social and cultural norm, together the group members will have a built-in developmental thrust towards regaining that norm. This can be expressed in terms of regression and progression: the individuals may in different ways show different forms of regression, but the group itself will have an inherent tendency to higher levels of organisation, that is, of progression. The exception to this is when there is a heterogeneous population who, however, all come from some form of deviant subculture, for instance of psychopaths or other severely deviant characters. Such a group will not have an inherent developmental thrust towards the social norm.

The dynamic administrator has responsibility for control of the group boundaries, for determining who enters and exits the group, for the boundaries of time and place. Any analytic group is, at an interface with its surrounding and encompassing environment, a larger group. This can be a clinic, an in- or out-patient service, and so on. The dynamic responses of this wider setting to the dynamics of the analytic group will be especially important when 'boundary' incidents occur, that is, when issues provoked and arising in the group itself impinge on the human and physical surround. In the clinic this can involve the interactions with and responses of other staff, other therapists, administrators, secretaries, domestics, and other patients. In private practice this may affect the therapist's own domestic arrangements – his/her family space and privacy.

The group analytic situation has much in common with the dyadic situation. Common to both is the creation and opening up of a dynamic force field. In that force field there are different levels of organisation, different levels of progression and regression, although there are many more so in the group than in the dyad. The organising effect of responses, verbal and non-verbal, are common to both. In group analysis the verbal responses of the patients to each other are both organising and disorganising. In their relationships and in their conversations the group members relate and provoke responses that are disorganising, releasing transferential levels of object relationships. These experiences, which are essential to the therapeutic process, are shared and witnessed by the other group members, who, through their own resonances, can help to reorganise through acceptance and understanding the experiences that have disturbed its members.

Intrinsic to the notion of the therapeutic function of regression is that contact is made with earlier forms of experience and that these have been blocked from integration with the central self (Fairbairn, 1952). These integrations can take place in therapy and thereby the patient is ultimately enriched and strengthened. The setting must be able to allow such regression to take place, to protect the patient from too powerful and primitive a regression and to provide resources of understanding and responding that the patient is not for him/herself alone.

What can affect the range of responses? At one extreme is a strongly defensive group who will not allow such re-experiences to occur. Group relationships and discussions remain on a mainly conscious and safe level. This can come about for a variety of reasons, such as faulty selection and balance of the group, putting together a group of persons all of whom are strongly defensive and none of whom have the resources or willingness to go beyond such defended areas. It can also occur when there is an obviously disturbed or fragile patient or patients and the other members are afraid to open up lest a dangerous situation erupts.

At the other end of the scale is the group that quickly reaches to regressed levels and will not relinquish them. The group becomes a forum for acting out an avoidance of the painful work of understanding and reintegration. Here again selection is important. Has the therapist as dynamic administrator failed to balance the group: are there insufficient 'healthy' aspects of personality function to integrate and work with the regressed levels of the other members?

Foulkes shows that by sharing a common 'foundation matrix' members of a group are able to understand each other on quite deep levels as the group analytic situation develops, aided by the therapist. But when we reach to the levels of borderline functioning and psychotic functioning the situation becomes much more threatening. For understanding and containment at this level, either the group analyst has to be the provider or fortuitously there may be other group members who can do so because they can be in touch with such levels of experience, but are more able to verbalise and to organise themselves than are the more disorganised and disturbed patients. When, however, this is not possible, one patient can become isolated and vulnerable for scapegoating and for premature drop-out.

It is with the more disturbed borderline patients that the profoundest levels of primitive rage and destructiveness are encountered. Once the defences against exposing this rage are weakened or removed the patient becomes terrified by the intensity of the savagery, becomes frightened of the fantasised destructiveness and often appalled by the overwhelming sense of evil and destructiveness that he/she now experiences as originating within the self. Desperate attempts to remove this inner threat by projection then ensue, leading to paranoid attitudes, a constant search for the weaknesses or flaws in the environment that will enable this projection to hold and, in line with the mechanism of projective identification, an attempt unconsciously and also partly consciously to manipulate the recipient of the projection into fitting the internal schema of persecution. The greatest intensity of this type of desperate rage is,

in my experience, encountered more in individual therapy and
becomes an extremely painful situation both for the patient and for
the therapist. Therapists have to be able to contain the negative
projections in which such patients attempt to envelop them. They
have to experience, without retaliation and with a sensitive acceptance and understanding, the patient's overwhelming need to see
them as evil and as the origin of all the pain. It is a great demand
upon the tact and sensitivity of therapists, and one that they cannot
always be expected to demonstrate.

Transference and countertransference considerations at the borderline

Perhaps unusually, I will begin with countertransference, because
with the borderline patient the countertransference is often acute
and difficult to manage. The patient uses primitive defence mechanisms, projective identification, splitting into ideal and persecutory
part object relations. Because the narcissistic defences of devaluation,
arrogance and contempt are used, the therapist and the other
patients in the group, if the group is one of neurotic and borderline
patients, are often in a situation of acute stress. As therapists, we try
to maintain the capacity for relatively neutral yet empathic responses
to our patients. We try to monitor our internal reactions, to think
about them, try to use them in understanding the experience of the
patient to form a basis either for interpretation or for some other
appropriate form of action. One of the pleasures of effective
psychotherapy is this capacity to understand another person and to
see how well one's understanding of them is often received. Anxiety
is reduced, the patient becomes more relaxed and more open when
a well-timed empathic interpretation is given. One person has
understood another person and they can become closer and less
defensive. One of the diagnostic signs with the borderline patient is
that this desirable and pleasant position for the therapist is rarely
attained; the therapist and the other patients in the group, who
might otherwise be able to function as co-therapists, feel themselves to be distanced and often bewildered. The patient maintains
a prickly distance, remains isolated and yet will often subject the
other members of the group to very powerful and intrusive
comments. Rage, anger and contempt may suddenly erupt, leaving
the recipient of the attack shaken and alarmed and, of course,
these attacks can be followed by counterattacks and thus a vicious

cycle of escalating conflict arises. When these phenomena occur, we know that we are in the presence of primitive projection and introjection processes.

Early on in his work, Foulkes saw that destructive forces in the group are consumed in attacking each other's resistances and that this allows the loving, constructive forces in the group to predominate over the destructive ones. With borderline members, the destructive forces are not used to attack the other person's resistances because these members do not see or understand the need that other persons have for such defences. That another person needs sensitive handling, that we protect ourselves from conflict and psychic pain by defence mechanisms, is not understood by them. They wish to be gratified instantly by the other person's complete attention and to derive narcissistic nourishment from them. They are excessively gratified by hurting other people and seek to be able to project unwanted aspects of the self into other persons and, in order to do so, need to manipulate others into a position to receive them. Thus, if I want to get rid of bits of myself that seem very bad, very destructive, very contemptible or frightening, because they represent needs and greeds that are too primitive to know about, then I will seek not only to find someone who will take in these characteristics but to try to induce them to behave in such a way that the projection and their behaviour will fit. For instance, a patient who is very frightened of her own sadism focuses on the physical characteristics of a man in the group (this case, of Sara, is presented in detail below). This man is a rather quiet, inhibited man, very much the passive, weak partner in a marriage, whose voice is quiet and gentle and his sensitive understandings of other people is quite marked. All this is meaningless to her. All that she relates to in him is the fact that he has large hands. For her, these are the hands of a murderer or a butcher. The fact that the man is in a profession where sensitive and accurate use of his hands is called for makes no difference to her. For her, he is simply the brutal male to be kept at a distance by her attacks and who can also be the recipient of her sadism. Thus she has a part-object relationship to the man and can easily incite him to respond to her aggressively. Much of the work of therapy with these patients is making sure that the response to the primitive attacks is not simply a reciprocal mirroring. It is only by the constant exposure to a more benign and a higher level of psychological responsiveness that a more benign cycle of projection and introjection can occur. This is what I have called 'trading' part-object for whole-object relationships. This leads me on to the transference of these patients to other members of the group, to the group as a whole and to the therapist.

The experience of a patient in one of my groups, Sara, illustrates this.

Sara was a single woman in her early thirties, tall, quite good-looking but thin, as if she had severe anorexia earlier on in life. She was often very poorly dressed but always appeared to be clean. She spoke very rapidly and explosively with a sharp tongue, a mordant wit and a rather rich yet oblique form of symbolic language that was difficult to comprehend. Her language was idiosyncratic, but she was very impatient if it was not immediately understood. It was allusive in drawing upon a rich knowledge of the English language and literature, in which she was a graduate. She lived a chaotic life and had an obsessive attachment to a married man, who was also in therapy, and she was constantly tormented by her feelings of jealousy and rage.

Most members of the group experienced her as disruptive and almost intolerable. She would attack almost anyone mercilessly and impatiently interrupt anything that she felt did not interest or involve her or would otherwise withdraw into stony silence. Only after about a year in the group did she sometimes show an interest in other people's problems or respond constructively to some issue that she had not herself initiated. She always sat next to the therapist and at times spoke quietly, almost under her breath, in a way that he alone could hear. What she said at these times was often much more sensitive and constructive than the words that the rest of the group could hear.

She provoked a split of the group into factions – those who could tolerate her and those who disliked her. She provoked great hostility in those whom she disliked, and she was expert at derisive remarks and comments, particularly to people with whom she felt herself to be in competition. It was clear that she experienced her family situation as an unfair one in which her father was a very absent figure. She was sensitive to her fear of, and capacity for, fusion with others and she needed distancing in order to preserve her own sense of self. She needed to keep herself clearly defined and sharp, and used hostility as her main capacity to do this; she was either hostile or withdrawn. She was threatened by contact with other persons whose boundaries and outlines seemed to her to be blurred. This was shown in her response to an older member of the group whom she saw as always being vague and weak, and as usual there was a core of reality in her perceptions and responses.

She had a fear of being taken over and being rendered passive and becoming only a ventriloquist's dummy. However, she defended herself against a recognition that much of her behaviour was motivated through anxiety and fear. She was impulsive and used her rapidity of thought and speech evasively to avoid finding out what was behind her actions and responses. The group gradually helped her to slow down and to be a little bit more reflective.

She evoked positive transference feelings in the therapist, who felt quite protective towards her, aware that she was the most disturbed member of the group, bordering on a psychotic breakdown. However, his protectiveness of her aroused jealousy, particularly in other women.

They also resented his enjoyment of her impulsiveness and verbal wit. What he approved of in her seemed to be those aspects of herself of which approval was denied in the family.

She avoided allowing herself to get into any triangular situations and maintained one-to-one relationships in the group.

She demanded that her egocentricity be accepted and therefore had little capacity for empathy with members whom she attacked. However, she could be empathic with persons with whom she felt an identification through similarity of life situations or emotional problems.

Sara could manipulate other persons in the group into becoming receptacles for her contempt and for devaluation. She tried to devalue all the achievements of one man with whom she felt rivalrous. Another man she used as a receptacle for the disturbance of her body image distortions. She was confused about whether she was male or female in body and outline, and she seized upon this man's body as something that she could try to distort. The vulnerability of her own boundaries was consciously recognised by her because she could say such things as "anyone can get inside me and I cannot protect myself from invasion".

She had a very difficult relationship with a violent boyfriend, which seemed constantly to lead her sadistically to revenge herself upon the men in the group, thereby turning passive into active. She actually succeeded in getting one man to feel that she was a threat to his own positive self-evaluation, and that she seemed to get right inside him as a destructive bad object. In this way, she forced him to experience what she herself experienced in relationship to her boyfriend, who did not seem to value anything that she felt was good about herself.

Sara had very clear and definite ideas about each member of the group and had a different type of relationship within each of them. Let us first take the women; the oldest member of the group, who had great problems with a teenage daughter with whom she had very destructive and aggressive attacks and whom she could not value, she saw as being shallow, manipulative and essentially worthless. She had no compunction in attacking her ruthlessly and enjoyed the counter-attacks this produced. She and the other patient, in fact, reproduced the relationship between the older woman and her daughter. In contrast to this, she idealised another older woman in the group and saw her as a person who had been able to deal successfully with her own rage and bad feelings. One of the reasons for her to continue to come to the group, she said, was because she could enjoy seeing how this older woman would unthaw from her frozen personality. She often failed to understand the depth of this person's unhappiness and how she aroused painful feelings in her; she was unaware of her sadism towards the woman whom she was idealising. Towards a third woman in the group she had nothing but contempt, seeing her as dull and uninteresting, again accurately pinpointing an area of considerable concern in the other person. This is another characteristic of the borderline patient, a particular form of 'borderline empathy'. This is that the borderline patient is extremely empathic to particular and restricted sectors of the other person's personality, those that are necessary for these particular forms of externalisation and protection to occur. The rest of the person is of no significance to them and can be thrown away like the pulp of an orange from which the juice has been extracted. Thus the relationship remains on a primitive part-object level and they are not in touch with the higher-level structures and functions of the other personalities.

Towards the men in the group she displayed equally selective perceptions. I have already mentioned the man with the large hands; another man, who was a successful entrepreneur, again aroused nothing but contempt. In fact he seemed to be a more successful version of herself: he, too, had a very ready wit, a very good command of language and could himself be very destructive. Towards a third man in the group, an older man who on the surface appeared rather weak, she was full of rage and contempt and accused him of being impotent and half dead. The fourth man in the group, a younger one, whom she could identify with in a more benign way, she was encouraging to. In fact, at one time she tried very hard to get this particular man to see that he ought to strive to improve his relationship with the therapist. To the therapist himself she also preserved a benign relationship. It was very important to her that he was accepting and tolerant of her behaviour, and that he did not insist on analysing everything that she did and that he supported her right to behave in her own way until such time as she could begin to modify it.

Over the course of several months the intensity of her reactions began to diminish and she became more comfortable to be with. She became a very regular attendant at the group, apologised at times for her rude behaviour, began to give up a very destructive sado-masochistic relationship with a very disturbed man and began to show some sadness and depression. The other members learnt more about her as a person, of her childhood and there was the beginning of a capacity for mutual empathy between her and the other group members. She began to be supportive and caring and even minimally to allow herself to be cared for. For this to happen she had first of all to experience the therapist and the group entity as relatively benign, not overwhelming and invasive.

During the first months, when her behaviour was so provocative and difficult, the therapist was often accused by the group of being overprotective to her, of making her a favourite and of enjoying her behaviour rather than being critical of it. I often had the feeling that I was the only person who cared for and could see anything positive about her and had hopes for her future, that she might benefit from the group and use it as a place for constructive change. I often had to act as a *negotiator* between her and the other group members when quarrels took place, usually when she succeeded in provoking another member into a vicious counterattack.

Regrettably, in the end I had to ask Sara to leave the group. This was after an episode in which another patient felt so abused by some racially coloured comments that physical violence broke out. Sara, although somewhat apologetic, was not able to understand sufficiently and therefore to repair the injury that she had caused and seemed relieved that she would not have to continue in the group, which would have meant altering her position in it. I heard a few months later that she had moved to another part of the country and was working, and I have not heard from her since.

Negotiation, mediation and other techniques

I believe that it is characteristic of borderline patients that therapists are often drawn into these intense and bitter strifes, where they have to act as a *negotiator* or *mediator* (Pines, 1984). They have in a way to reconcile the two persons to each other and help them to see that the outcome of such quarrels can be constructive. The criterion for the constructive resolution of these quarrels is that both people must recognise that they are partly right and partly wrong, that what the other person says about them has some validity, that this validity can be acknowledged but that it is accepted that this is not the complete truth. Each is a whole person and whatever is at issue represents only one aspect of that person. Furthermore, whatever each is accusing the other of is something that is an aspect of themselves. Thus, in the destructiveness and in the attack upon the other, there is a hidden mutuality. It is the job of the therapist to bring out this hidden mutuality. In so doing the therapist, I believe, raises the level of the interaction from a destructive diadic one to a constructive triadic one. In this, therapists, with their capacity for reflection and distancing from the destructive struggle, their capacity to remain relatively uninvolved, to reflect and to think about what is happening, and their position as the relatively uninvolved third person in the situation, bring about triangulation. The level of triangulation is a higher level of psychological development than the level of diadic confrontations. I am reminded here of the myth of Perseus and the Gorgon. Perseus could be in the presence of the Gorgon and not be petrified by her only by using a mirror that was derived from the armour of the Goddess Pallas Athene. This goddess represents wisdom, the highest reflective level of psychic function and organisation, symbolised by the mirror which enabled Perseus to catch the image of the Gorgon. Catching the image on the mirror represents the act of symbolisation that is possible through the capacity for reflection.

I have already mentioned splitting and the intensity of the projections and the need to contain and not to retaliate with counter-projections. Patience, caring and above all fairness are needed for patients to be able to realise that they do not take into account others as separate and autonomous persons. To do so and to behave differently, they need to interact in non-interpretive modes with the therapist or other patients. The therapist must often try to show the other members of the group the meaning of the patient's behaviour before that patient can begin to grasp its meaning. Stone & Gustafson (1982) make the point that the idealisation by the patient of the group or of the therapist is a necessary state in accepting group membership. At this stage, idealisation is not defensive and to interpret it as such is faulty technique and often leads to the patient leaving the group. Later on, the idealisation may need to be interpreted as defence against the underlying negative feelings, but this can only be done when the patient is securely embedded in the group and held by the experience of support and understanding.

A summary of basic points

My recommendations are that we treat borderline patients in mixed groups, that we make sure that these patients do not predominate either qualitatively or quantitatively, and that the group to which they belong has sufficient resources to withstand the regressive pulls of their primitive mechanisms. An understanding of the nature of their defences and an appreciation of their inner anguish and the great need that they have for help will sustain the therapist through the many difficult episodes that are bound to come.

The characteristics of group analytic therapy with the more disturbed patient can be summarised in eight points.

(a) Borderline patients will not behave as relatively separate independent and autonomous persons. Because of developmental arrests and faults, they will inevitably in varying degrees seek to merge or to fuse with the therapists, or in a group with other members or with the group as a whole. Very intense feelings of need, and inevitably of deprivation, will be evoked and anger and rage are to be expected.

(b) In a similar manner other persons involved with the patient are not treated as separate autonomous persons, centres of their own motivation and activity. They are mainly related to as 'need-unsatisfying objects'. The subjective response of the other persons range between hurt, bewilderment, anger and rejection, to fascination and submission.

(c) Great fluctuations and swings in mood, attitudes and relationships are to be expected. Typical cycles are those between closeness, leading to threat of merger, and consequent great distancing and aloofness.

(d) The varying ego states are not integrated or acknowledged as belonging to a unitary personality. There is often a poorly established observing ego, little capacity to see that "I feel this and that, I have more than one self and I know the difference between them and can see that at one time I feel this way and at other times I feel and behave that way, which is totally different". The ego states are vigorously kept apart and the therapist's efforts to bring these contradictions to the patient's attention are strongly resisted. Often the warded-off contradictory part is experienced as being in some other person. That person will then be feared or attacked and have to be controlled.

(e) There is a tenuous hold on psychic reality. What feels real is treated as if it were real. The patient will often treat fantasy as reality and act upon this. This will occur when affect has been raised or when some other aspects of psychic reality have to be warded off. Therapists or other patients will often find themselves caught up in the patient's fantasy world without knowing what is happening. The patient may be living a waking dream and other persons are often a part of it. It is often very difficult to understand what is happening between oneself and the patient. One feels lost and under pressure. The patient reacts to this loss of understanding catastrophically, and the management of these catastrophes is the essence of the treatment. Treatment has to fail, to be annihilated and then to recover from this. The therapist or the group has to be reliable and caring when the patient is despairing and annihilating. They must respond to the patient as a whole person when the patient is feeling and behaving primitively and relating to other people not as whole persons.

(f) Relationships must be maintained when interpretation fails.

(g) The treatment is full of traumas. It will be long and the most primitive stages of human development will be reactivated.

(h) Do not expect the patients to care for you. By the time they are able to do so they are well on the way to recovery.

References

FAIRBAIRN, W. R. D. (1952) *Psychoanalytic Studies of the Personality.* London: Tavistock.

FOULKES, S. H. & ANTHONY, E. J. (1984) *Group Psychotherapy. The Psychoanalytic Approach.* London: Karnac.

PINES, M. (1984) Reflections on mirroring. *International Review of Psychoanalysis*, **11**, 27.
—— & HEARST, L. E. (1993) Group analysis. In *Comprehensive Group Psychotherapy* (3rd edn) (eds H. I. Kaplan & B. J. Sadock), pp. 146–155. Baltimore: Williams & Wilkins.
ROBERTS, J. & PINES, M. (1992) Group analytic psychotherapy. *International Journal of Group Psychotherapy*, **42**, 469–494.
STONE, W. N. & GUSTAFSON, J. P. (1982) Technique in the group psychotherapy of narcissistic and borderline patients. *International Journal of Group Psychotherapy*, **32**, 29–47.

Part II. Behavioural and cognitive approaches to psychosis

This section is in marked contrast to those on psychodynamic and systemic approaches. Its language belongs to the empirical tradition, and the overview and individual chapters all rely heavily on research evidence to support their contentions.

Behavioural and cognitive treatment strategies combine the removal of unwanted symptoms with an increase in the individual's personal resilience in the face of illness. These approaches are exemplified in the detailed discussions of the cognitive therapy of delusions by Kingdon and Turkington (Chapter 8) and the impact of enhancement of coping skills by Tarrier and colleagues (Chapter 9). These were the foci of key presentations at the York conference, and current research has tried to differentiate which of these approaches is the more effective.

Many other strategies have been used with psychotic patients, Drummond and Duggal (Chapter 7) grouping these into: treatment of positive symptoms; treatment of antisocial behaviours; dealing with negative and deficit symptoms; and relapse prevention. Some of the approaches described in the historical section of the review by Drummond and Duggal have not stood the test of time, and the non-specialist is struck by the pace of change in this field. For example, the use of token economies, at one point providing seemingly irrefutable evidence for the success of an approach based on conditioning and learning theory, was revised in the light of a 'dismantling' research strategy. That is, the elements of the package were disaggregated and tested separately, and the specific use of the tokens was found to be subsumed under a more general effect probably relying on a combination of enhanced ward morale and social learning opportunities.

Inevitably, there is overlap with work described elsewhere in the book as some of the treatments involve integrative elements, and may use behavioural strategies in a family setting. The review does cover family approaches briefly, although some of the themes are expanded in greater detail in Chapter 12, and discussed in the review of systemic and family treatments in Chapter 10.

Developments in this area continue at a rapid pace. Since the York conference a major prospective multicentre trial of cognitive therapy for schizophrenia has been funded which will deal with some of the uncertainties remaining about the optimal way of targeting specific symptoms while also minimising relapse rates. The project will be led by the authors of Chapters 8 and 9 (David Kingdon and Nick Tarrier) in collaboration with Richard Bentall from Liverpool and Shôn Lewis from Manchester.

The dissemination of the findings of behavioural and cognitive therapy into everyday practice has been slow, and educational initiatives to train practitioners in appropriately focused techniques have been developed to address this problem, with preliminary results from the Manchester group on the effectiveness of training community psychiatric nurses already available (Brooker *et al*, 1992). Despite these initiatives the empirical work on symptom reduction, reduction of challenging behaviours, amelioration of functional deficits, and relapse prevention (at family and individual level) has been remarkably slow in becoming established in mainstream practice. All innovatory treatments have an inevitable time-lag, but the contrast with the rapid introduction of novel antipsychotic drugs is salutary.

A principal aim of this book is to introduce knowledge already available to improve practice to a wide readership. A great deal of truly useful knowledge is bound to be of a procedural kind, learned by example rather than declarative. However, the cognitive–behavioural tradition has always been distinguished by the faith it has placed in precise description and replication of its methods. Notes on some guiding practical principles are offered as a preface to the remainder of this section.

Principles of designing a cognitive–behavioural management plan

Most clinicians favour a combined approach to deal with multiple problems concurrently. Planning a behavioural package requires close attention to the consistency of the team's response. Other staff, patients and relatives can easily disrupt a management plan, but this is part of the problem of generalising the results to a less controlled environment. The use of punishment as a behavioural technique has fallen out of favour in place of a 'constructionist approach' that builds on existing desired behaviours and differentially reinforces these, rather than applying aversive stimuli to reduce behaviours directly.

The principles of reinforcement are widely known, but are frequently misunderstood. An important link with the other sections of this book lies in the understanding that important interpersonal principles underlie successful treatment plans. (This is one explanation of why 'tokens' appeared to be less important than social reinforcement in ward-based contingency programmes.) While reinforcement from anyone is likely to have some effect, most regimes rely on the establishment of a good working alliance through which the social reinforcement can be applied.

Modelling desired aspects of behaviour is common in behavioural programmes. Therapists need to be quite explicit about the aspects of behaviour that are to be modelled. If this is not done, the patient is much less likely to be able to use this type of social learning. Therapists in training often need to be reassured that it is desirable to make these 'process commentaries', whether in psychodynamic or behavioural mode. The 'here and now' quality of a good therapeutic style is enhanced by making comments as close to the event as possible.

Part of the skill in developing an effective programme is to set the goals just beyond the patient's current repertoire so that there are frequent experiences of success and mastery.

The systemic aspects of behavioural therapies are described in the overview chapter and elsewhere; the management of the family system, the ward milieu, and the therapeutic team all require a practical understanding of social systems.

One vital aspect of social systems concerns ethical practice and the maintenance of high standards of care. The report of the Ashworth Inquiry has a separate volume on case studies that should be read in conjunction with the relevant section of the Mental Health Act Code of Practice (Chapter 19) to give an overview of the ethical and practice principles to be aware of in establishing behavioural regimes in in-patient settings.

Recommended additional reading

BROOKER, C., TARRIER, N., BARROWCLOUGH, C., *et al* (1992) Training community psychiatric nurses for psychosocial intervention: report of a pilot study. *British Journal of Psychiatry*, **160**, 836–844.

Code of Practice: Mental Health Act 1983. Section 19. Psychological Treatments. London: HMSO.

EKDAWI, M. Y. & CONNING, A. M. (1994) *Psychiatric Rehabilitation: A Practical Guide.* London: Chapman & Hall.

KAVANAGH, D. J. (ed.) (1992) *Schizophrenia: An Overview and Practical Handbook.* London: Chapman & Hall.

Report of the Committee of Inquiry about Ashworth Hospital, Volume II: The Case Studies, Cmnd 2028-II. London: HMSO.

SHEPHERD, G. (1983) Planning the rehabilitation of the individual. In *Theory and Practice of Psychiatric Rehabilitation* (eds F. N. Watts & D. H. Bennett). London: Wiley.

WATTS, F. & BENNETT, D. (1983) Management of the staff team. In *Theory and Practice of Psychiatric Rehabilitation* (eds F. N. Watts & D. H. Bennett). London: Wiley.

7 Cognitive–behavioural approaches to psychosis: an overview

LYNNE M. DRUMMOND and ANITA DUGGAL

Cognitive–behavioural psychotherapy has traditionally been applied in response to a functional analysis of the patient's problem rather than after a psychiatric diagnosis. As is common in psychotherapy research, however, much of the literature is based on discrete diagnostic groups. For the purposes of this review, we will concentrate on the treatment of schizophrenia. Nevertheless, many of the treatments described will also be applicable to other psychotic conditions. The first section briefly reviews the research on the other psychotic disorders before concentrating on the substantial literature on the treatment of schizophrenia. Throughout, we have concentrated on properly conducted controlled trials or review papers wherever these are available.

Cognitive–behavioural psychotherapy and non-schizophrenic psychoses

Although cognitive intervention has been shown to be at least as effective as antidepressant medication for patients with mild to moderate depressive disorder (Williams, 1984; Dobson, 1989; Andrews, 1991), in more severe depression, with or without psychotic features, the position is less clear. Many studies have failed to find differences between drugs or cognitive and behavioural treatments, but some of these excluded patients with psychotic symptoms (e.g. Hollon *et al*, 1992). There is a fuller discussion of this in the description of the Collaborative Treatment of Depression Research Programme (Elkin *et al*, 1992), but, overall, there is currently little work that indicates whether behavioural and cognitive psychotherapy has much to offer patients with psychotic types of depression. There is some evidence from in-patient settings for patients with more severe disorders to support the use of cognitive therapy, but the studies did not specifically target patients with psychotic symptoms as part of their major depressive disorder. There were also methodological difficulties in all three of the main studies.

Thase *et al* (1991) assessed 26 patients, of whom 16 completed psychological treatment (the other 10 having medication, electroconvulsive therapy, or too severe symptoms, or they did not comply). Bowers (1990) conducted a comparison trial of nortriptyline, relaxation, cognitive–behavioural therapy (CBT), or treatment milieu as usual. There were some advantages to CBT, but small numbers and high drop-out rates make firm conclusions difficult, and in any case there were no controls for amount of attention. Miller *et al* (1989) assigned 47 patients to standard treatment (drugs plus in-patient treatment), standard treatment plus CBT or standard treatment plus social skills training. There was a trend to better recovery in the 'enhanced treatments' that reached significance at follow-up, but there were high drop-out rates, particularly from the standard treatment, somewhat less from CBT and only 14% from the social skills training group. *All* patients from the standard treatment group had dropped out at the end of follow-up, so that interpretation is difficult.

Behavioural and cognitive techniques have been used successfully to treat some patients with monosymptomatic psychoses. Most of the research evidence, however, is based on single case studies and case series. For example, Marks has demonstrated that exposure can be successfully used in the treatment of dysmorphophobia (Marks, 1987). A case series by Salkovskis & Warwick (1985) also demonstrated that cognitive therapy could alter overvalued ideation, some of which appeared to have been held with delusional intensity. (The treatment of personality disorder has recently become an area of research in the cognitive literature, with promising early results. For example, a controlled trial found that patients who had a diagnosis of borderline personality disorder and were treated with a model known as dialectical behaviour therapy showed a marked reduction in suicidal and other self-injurious behaviour and required fewer psychiatric admissions than patients treated in a standard psychiatric community clinic (Linehan *et al*, 1991).) However, it is unclear whether such patients, while clearly disturbed, would fit into the category of psychosis. The group of conditions most similar to schizophrenia within the 'borderline disorders' are schizotypal disorders, but these have not been studied as a separate subgroup.

Overall, the literature on the psychoses other than schizophrenia is remarkably lacking. While it may be expected that some disorders will respond similarly to schizophrenia, there is still an under-developed research base for adequate treatment decisions. Clinically, the role of psychological treatments in improving compliance rates has been stressed, and research is currently under way to develop training packages for patients to improve their ability to detect early signs of relapse in manic–depressive illness, in order to reduce the severity and duration of subsequent episodes.

Schizophrenia

Schizophrenia is the most widely researched psychotic illness. The management and treatment of patients suffering from schizophrenic psychosis are a key challenge to mental health services today and the treatment of such enduring mental illness is crucial to the reduction in severe psychiatric morbidity suggested by the *Health of the Nation* targets produced by the Department of Health in England and Wales. Schizophrenia is a huge cause of severe disability, with approximately 1% of the population suffering from the disorder. There is growing public pressure for effective treatment or at least containment of sufferers, particularly following well publicised, although rare, violent incidents. Old psychiatric institutions have been closed and large numbers of patients with schizophrenia now live in the community, sometimes with greatly increased autonomy, but sometimes with inadequate treatment and social support. The role of psychological treatments has grown against this backdrop of altered social policy. This section reviews both the historical background to the psychological treatment of schizophrenia and the development of modern techniques, which have a crucial role in minimising the disruptive effects of the illness so as to allow successful rehabilitation into community settings.

Cognitive–behavioural psychotherapy has been used in a variety of ways to try to tackle the symptoms, sequelae and social effects of schizophrenia. These will be described under the headings 'Positive symptoms', 'Antisocial behaviours', 'Negative symptoms and deficit states' and 'Relapse prevention'.

The terminology is not entirely consistent in the literature, and sometimes the terms positive and negative are replaced by acute and chronic. The term 'positive', while in itself somewhat ambiguous, is preferred because it implies that an experience has been added; typically the aim of treatment is to reduce its frequency.

The term 'negative' implies that previously gained skills have atrophied and need to be reintroduced to improve social function. The time course of one symptom group can be independent of the other and it cannot be automatically assumed that by removing intrusive, positive symptoms that the person's social function will spontaneously improve.

'Antisocial behaviours' are again heterogeneous. The features may be directly associated with positive symptoms but may include features consequent upon frontal lobe disinhibition; attempts by the patient to deal with distressing experiences; and behaviours that would normally be controlled by social pressure but that have been allowed to continue in understaffed and understimulating in-patient environments.

The term 'relapse prevention' subsumes several strategies, but at this point it is worth reflecting that the implied model is of a recurrent and at times episodic state. This is crucially different from the chronic deficit model implied in the old 'asylum' model and terms like 'burned out schizophrenia'. Relapse prevention incorporates several of the above themes: relapse is measured by the frequency and intensity of positive symptoms, by the need for readmission, by the breakdown of community placements, and by the successful resolution of long-term reduction in volition.

For ease of reference, Table 7.1 summarises the treatments discussed.

Positive symptoms

The positive symptoms described are primarily delusions and hallucinations. Although in recent years there has been considerable work on treating these directly using behavioural and cognitive methods, treatment aimed at negative symptoms alters the frequency of positive symptoms. For example, in their controlled trial of the use of a token economy in a chronic schizophrenic population, Baker *et al* (1977) found that a stimulating and motivating regime caused some increase in acute symptoms. This finding, however, was opposed to that of Paul & Lentz (1977), who found that increasing self-care skills in patients using token economy methods resulted in a reduction in acute symptoms. The relationship between the successful resolution of deficit symptoms and the concurrent reduction or increase of positive symptoms requires more empirical study.

Delusions

One of the first studies to be performed in this area was a single-case experiment. Verbal reinforcement was found to reduce dramatically the delusional talk of a chronic institutionalised patient

TABLE 7.1
Summary of possible goals of cognitive–behavioural interventions in psychosis

Type of symptom	Intervention
Positive	
Delusions	
Early approaches	Verbal reinforcement
	Feedback
	Reinforcement programmes
Later approaches	Cognitive therapy
	Self-instruction
	Challenging beliefs
Hallucinations	
Early approaches	Reinforcement
	Self-monitoring and feedback
	Self-administered aversion
	Identifying antecedent anxiety and exposure
	Modifying subvocal speech
Later approaches	Distraction
	Thought-stopping
	Attention-switching
	Challenging beliefs
	Practising controlling the experience
	Enhanced reality testing
	Coping strategy enhancement
	Modelling
	Contingency management
	Stimulus control
	Biofeedback
Antisocial behaviours	Milieu or staff team approach
	Group behavioural regimes
	Individual behavioural approaches
	Individual cognitive–behavioural approaches
	Differential reinforcement of desired behaviour
Negative symptoms and deficit states	Token economy
	Social skills training
Relapse	Decreasing environmental stress
	Reducing vulnerability to stress
	Illness self-management
	Compliance enhancement
	Early detection of relapse
	Family-based interventions
	Psychoeducational approaches to reduce critical high expressed emotion
	Problem-solving enhancement
	Structuring family interaction
	Brief, intense focused approaches
	Communication enhancement
	Anxiety reduction
	Behavioural family management (BFM) combining: optimal drug management; stress management for patient and carers; skills training package

with schizophrenia (Rickard *et al*, 1960; Rickard & Dinoff, 1962). Several other workers also reported success with reinforcement approaches. Wincze *et al* (1972) compared reinforcement and feedback procedures in their efficacy in reducing delusional talk in ten patients with paranoid schizophrenia. They found that the reinforcement was more potent in symptom reduction in most patients.

There are, however, obvious shortfalls and criticisms of this approach. Firstly, although delusional talk may be reduced by reinforcement regimes, it does not necessarily mean that the patient has any fewer delusional ideas or is less distressed by the condition. Secondly, there are difficulties in generalising the improvements. A patient may learn to reduce delusional speech in a ward setting but not in the community. For example, Liberman *et al* (1973) found that delusional speech was reduced in four patients when talking to their therapists but did not generalise to the ward setting until reinforcement programmes were also introduced by other staff.

Cognitive techniques have also been used over the last 25 years with some success in reducing delusions. In an early study of schizophrenic patients, Meichenbaum (1969) noted that following contingency reinforcement methods aimed at reducing delusional speech, those patients who were able to generalise their improvements outside the treatment sessions often gave themselves verbal instructions. These verbal instructions often consisted of commands such as "Be logical" and "Be coherent". He therefore decided to try to teach these commands in a procedure he called 'self-instructional training' (Meichenbaum & Cameron, 1973). Initially, patients were taught to verbalise these self-instructions, but using modelling and social approval they were taught to internalise their thinking. This study showed that this self-instructional training significantly improved patients' problem-solving abilities and decreased inappropriate and delusional speech (Meichenbaum & Cameron, 1973).

More recent cognitive therapy based on Beck's model has been used with schizophrenic patients. The usual approach of collaborative empiricism is adopted by the therapist and the patient. Abnormal beliefs are then identified and challenged by testing their validity (Alford & Beck, 1994). This approach is contrary to much traditional psychiatric thinking, in which delusions have been thought to be unamenable to reasoning. The level of belief in delusional ideas does fluctuate and it is this variability that can be used in cognitive therapy (Rudden *et al*, 1982). Traditional behavioural approaches aimed to reduce delusional speech, whereas in cognitive therapy the aim is to modify the strength of the beliefs.

While it is possible to reduce delusional speech without altering the patient's belief systems (Alford & Beck, 1994), success in achieving a change at the belief level should lead to wider and more sustained benefit. There have been multiple-case series of this method, which have been reviewed in a number of excellent papers (e.g. Kingdon *et al*, 1994; see also Chapter 8 of this volume). Although many studies suggest that delusional beliefs can be modified using cognitive therapy, there are some difficulties in patient selection, target-symptom selection and generalisation of treatment (Watts *et al*, 1973; Rudden *et al*, 1982; Chadwick & Lowe, 1994).

Hallucinations

Reinforcement regimes have also been used to reduce hallucinations and hallucinatory behaviour. In an early study, Rutner & Bugle (1969) asked a woman with severe hallucinations to self-monitor the frequency of her symptoms over three days. This self-monitoring in itself led to a marked reduction in hallucinations. Thereafter, her chart was placed on the wall of the ward and she was given praise and social reinforcement whenever the frequency of her hallucinations reduced. The patient reported that her hallucinations disappeared within two weeks and she remained symptom-free at six-month follow-up.

Aversion techniques whereby the patient administers an electric shock to him/herself whenever hallucinations occur have also been reported to be successful in many patients (Bucher & Fabricatore, 1970; Weingaertner, 1971). However, few patients can be persuaded to use this technique (Anderson & Alpert, 1974).

Another approach followed Davison's (1969) theory that antecedents to the hallucinatory behaviour should be examined and that the hallucinations are related to anxiety. Treatment programmes based on exposure principles were designed by several workers. The results of these experiments were controversial, with several papers reporting early success which was not maintained at follow-up (e.g. Slade, 1973).

The link with subvocal muscular activity has been tested (Corrigan & Storzbach, 1993). Bick & Kinsbourne (1987) found that schizophrenic subjects in their study, prescribed specific subvocal exercises involving the mouth, reported fewer hallucinations than the control group whose prescribed exercises involved the eyes or hands. Similarly, Green & Kinsbourne (1990) found that prescribing humming to their schizophrenic subjects resulted in increased subvocal muscular activity as measured by the electromyograph (EMG) and fewer reports of hallucination. There was little relation between EMG measurements and auditory hallucinations and so they also examined distraction and interference with cognitive processes, although neither was found to be a wholly satisfactory explanation.

Behavioural techniques have been employed to help patients cope with hallucinations, including thought-stopping, distraction techniques, switching attention to external stimuli, and engaging in alternative, incompatible, activities (Hemsley, 1986).

The main problem has been one of generalisation of improvements to outside the sessions, which may be due to beliefs concerning the reality of the hallucinations (Fowler & Morley, 1989). A preliminary study by Fowler & Morley (1989) aimed to tackle beliefs about hallucinations and increase control over symptoms. They treated five patients with chronic psychotic symptoms with a cognitive–behavioural approach that included coping strategies and attempts to restructure beliefs about their hallucinations through the identification of moods and situations associated with the symptoms, and through the presentation of possible alternative explanations in terms of abnormal perceptions. Fisher & Winkler's (1975) method was employed to bring on and dismiss hallucinations and so gain some control over them. Coping strategies involved focusing attention on external stimuli. Four of the five patients believed that they had gained some control over their hallucinations, but this was associated with a decrease in frequency of hallucinations and belief in them in only one case. This preliminary study supported the hypothesis that control over hallucinations was influenced by the degree of conviction in the hallucinations and degree of motivation.

Beck's model of cognitive therapy has also been used to reduce the frequency, distress, intrusiveness and intensity of belief in hallucinatory experiences. Kingdon *et al* (1994) described how a high proportion of the general population reported that they have experienced hallucinatory phenomena. Cognitive therapy was used to help patients with hallucinations to distinguish between real and hallucinatory experience. The patient is taught to question the reality of the experience in a similar way to those members of the 'normal' population who have hallucinations.

As with delusions, there are grounds for optimism that cognitive therapy can complement medication in schizophrenic hallucinations. Indeed, modern cognitive approaches developed in University College, London, and in Manchester have focused on reasons for non-compliance (such as incompatible beliefs and associated mood disturbance) in an attempt to reduce relapse rates.

Recent cognitive–behavioural therapy for hallucinations (see Chapter 8) has involved reality testing, which is used to demonstrate to patients that their experiences are not shared by others and that were the hallucinations originating from external sources, they would be accessible to others (Kingdon & Turkington, 1991; Kingdon *et al*, 1994). The hypothesis that hallucinations originate from within the mind is tested with arguments for and against them, and alternative explanations relate the hallucinations to stressful circumstances, for example sleep deprivation.

Coping-strategy enhancement (CSE) is a treatment devised by Tarrier *et al* (1990, 1993; and Chapter 9 of this volume) that aims to decrease symptoms by training the patient to cope with and control the cues and reactions to positive symptoms. As far as hallucinations are concerned, patients are taught to recognise and monitor them. Interventions used include: cognitive strategies such as attention switching and attention narrowing; behavioural strategies such as social interactions, increased solitary activities and reality testing; and other measures such as relaxation and breathing exercises. A controlled trial of two cognitive–behavioural methods, CSE and problem-solving (PS) on residual positive symptoms, demonstrated that those receiving either treatment experienced a reduction in psychotic symptoms compared with those in the waiting period, but the evidence in favour of CSE was not as conclusive. The study also found that delusions rather than hallucinations appeared more responsive to these approaches (Tarrier *et al*, 1993).

In tackling positive symptoms, Birchwood *et al* (1992) have concentrated on a different strategy, that of early detection and intervention, which involves training the patient and family to detect and act upon early prodromal symptoms suggestive of relapse (discussed below). Their model draws on earlier descriptive studies suggesting that there are four stages to relapse:

(a) a loss of control over cognitive and perceptual processes, perhaps with initial euphoria;
(b) depressive symptoms;
(c) impulsivity and exaggeration of emotions with reduced capacity to control the expression of personal thoughts and disinhibited sexuality and anger;
(d) a 'prepsychotic' stage with delusional mood, ideas of reference, loss of trust in others and early perceptual misinterpretations.

Most studies agreed on the presence of a prodromal period with dysphoria, interpersonal sensitivity and low-level psychotic experiences. Birchwood *et al* have developed intervention strategies that rely on identifying the characteristic prodromal features, a 'time window' for action, and an early intervention package – usually involving counselling, advice and medication.

Antisocial behaviours

The role of treatment aimed at reducing undesirable behaviour and increasing socially acceptable behaviour has increased in the past few years with the closure of psychiatric institutions and a move towards community care. Discharge to the community or even admission to a psychiatric unit of a district general hospital often means that bizarre or socially unacceptable behaviour is not tolerated. The generic term 'challenging behaviour' is sometimes used to refer to a range of actions that vary from being socially criticised or bizarre (eating habits, urinating in public places) through to violent and potentially dangerous acts. Hogg & Hall (1992) provide a clear overview of the management of such challenging behaviours and their distinction from behavioural deficits, as described in the next section of this chapter. The challenging behaviours most commonly reported include:

(a) aggression to people and things;
(b) antisocial actions (e.g. shouting, screaming, spitting, vomiting and stealing);
(c) sexually inappropriate behaviour (e.g. nakedness in public, exposure of genitals and/or masturbation in public, sexual harassment and even assault);
(d) bizarre behaviour (rocking, odd speech, unusual gait and hand movements, altered routines such as day–night reversal, and unrestrained eating, drinking or drug-taking).

The behavioural strategies developed to deal with these behaviours clearly require an understanding of their context and, often, a full behavioural analysis. The measures used should ideally be unambiguous, easy to assess and sensitive to change. Contextual and antecedent factors such as environmental state (isolation/crowding, heat/cold, for example), social pressures, the concurrence of intrusive positive phenomena, mood state, arousal, and physiological state (for example pain, hunger, intoxication) need to be assessed systemically. The behaviours themselves need to be expressed as neutrally and descriptively as possible to increase precision and also to avoid 'halo effects': it may be difficult to delineate early, small positive changes without clear descriptors. As always in a behavioural analysis, the immediate results of the behaviour (consequences) need to be recorded in case they have a maintaining role.

Interventions will depend to some extent on the agreed goals, but can usefully be divided into four groups (after Hogg & Hall, 1992):

(a) milieu and staff team approaches;
(b) group behavioural regimes;
(c) individual behavioural approaches;
(d) cognitive–behavioural approaches.

Individual rehabilitation programmes based on reinforcement principles are often used to increase the social acceptability of patients' behaviours. These simple procedures can often be useful, but it is important to remember that finding an effective reinforcer can be difficult in these patients, who often lack motivation and have few enthusiasms. Premack's principle (1959) addresses this finding by observing that high-frequency preferred activity can be used to reinforce lower-frequency, non-preferred activity. By far the most commonly applied form of reinforcement to be used is positive reinforcement (Table 7.2). Negative reinforcement or even punishment is hardly ever used and usually only in dangerous or

TABLE 7.2
Summary of reinforcement strategies to increase or decrease specified activities

	Strategy
Increase activity	
Positive reinforcement	Social approval
	Feedback reinforcement, e.g. social skills group
	Food reinforcers
	Higher frequency preferred activities (Premack principle)
	Tokens – given for certain activities and exchanged for reinforcers
Negative reinforcement (removal of negative reinforcer)	Removal of an aversive event after a specific response is obtained (also known as aversive relief)
Decrease activity	
Punishment (the application of negative reinforcer)	Overcorrection Positive punishment
Response cost (removal of positive reinforcer)	Time out, i.e. brief removal from reinforcing environment Penalty involving some time and effort Removal of other positive reinforcer

life-threatening situations. The ethical problems with negative reinforcement and punishment are obvious, but clear ethical dilemmas may also arise with positive reinforcers, particularly if necessary items such as food are used.

There have been many case reports over the years describing successful reinforcement programmes in chronic schizophrenic patients. Controlled trials, however, have usually been performed on groups of patients with similar problems. Outcome of this kind of treatment has been described in the management of delusions and hallucinations. Group reinforcement treatments are described below with token economy and social skills research.

Negative symptoms and deficit states

The patient may have great difficulty with daily tasks because of underactivity and apathy, anhedonia, poor attention and concentration, impaired or slowed speech and thought, and a reduced range of emotional expression. Some of these may overlap with the concept of antisocial or challenging behaviours, but it is worth keeping the conceptual distinction between challenging behaviour in the sense of an excess of socially unacceptable behaviour and the concept discussed here, of a deficit in certain expected behaviours (which may be challenging or distressing to family and neighbours but that require the patient to fill a 'behavioural gap' rather than lose unacceptable or threatening behaviours).

Two forms of treatment were developed to provide opportunities for increasing the patient's behavioural range. Unfortunately the first of these, the 'token economy', suffered from excessive claims of success, but, in fact, many of the principles of managing a therapeutic environment and maintaining the morale of the staff team are still relevant in modern treatment settings, whether in hospital or in community settings such as hostels, or settings that provide structured employment.

Token economy systems

Ayllon & Azrin (1968) pioneered token economy systems in the US. Following the publication of their work, token economy was hailed as a major breakthrough in the management of chronic schizophrenia. In the token economy environment, individual target behaviours and problem areas are identified for each patient as well as an individualised reward system. Instead of the usual reinforcers, tokens were rewarded (or even sacrificed) in response to target behaviours. These tokens could then be exchanged by the patient for a number of rewards, each of which had a certain token 'price'. The rewards used included a single room, food, cigarettes, outings and even, on occasion, meals (if a meal was not earned, a liquid meal substitute was given). Early research on token economy systems was extremely encouraging. Soon it was applied to all chronically hospitalised psychiatric and learning disabled patients, with apparently excellent results. A controlled evaluation performed in the UK, however, threw some doubt on the efficacy of tokens themselves. Hall *et al* (1977) performed a controlled trial in a hospital in Wakefield. Taking chronic schizophrenic patients who had been in hospital continuously for at least two years, they matched them and randomly allocated them to one of three wards.

The 'experimental' group were admitted to the token economy ward, where there was a highly motivating environment with new staff and many activities in addition to the token economy. Another group moved to a control ward where the same highly motivating and stimulating environment with new enthusiastic staff existed. A third group remained in a traditional chronic ward. It was found that whereas the introduction of tokens had an initial effect on target behaviours, this was not sustained. Both active rehabilitation wards resulted in greater improvement in negative symptoms and more discharges to the community, although this was at the expense of a slight increase in positive symptoms of schizophrenia in the stimulating environments. Although this study failed to demonstrate the efficacy of tokens themselves, the nursing staff involved in the study requested that the system be continued at the end of the research as they found the structure and their ability to reward certain behaviours useful.

The above research has been described in some detail as it raises a number of vital clinical issues. Firstly, it demonstrates the importance of an enthusiastic and fulfilled ward-based staff and emphasises the need for maintaining staff morale. Secondly, a moderately stimulating and interesting environment was beneficial to the patients. Thirdly, the structure and ability to reward patients was seen as valuable and important by the ward-based staff. The apparent success of good token economy systems may thus be due to the effect on morale they have on ward staff. The disadvantages of tokens are that they are sometimes a difficult concept for patients to grasp and many people working in this field prefer to use more tangible reinforcers such as money. There has been widespread discussion about the ethics of providing cigarettes as tokens, given the risk to health.

Social skills training

Social skills training packages are used to modify maladaptive behaviours and improve social functioning. The package generally consists of instructions, modelling, behavioural rehearsal, reinforcement and homework assignments. A number of studies, of both single-case and group design, have demonstrated significant improvements of targeted behaviours and specific behavioural components of social skills, but evidence of generalisation and maintenance of these skills has been inconsistent (Curran *et al*, 1982). One explanation is that treatment was not empirically based on observation of the individual patient but provided a package leading to socially sanctioned behaviour. This hypothesis was supported by Goldsmith & McFall's study (1975), which was empirically based and did appear to generalise. Following the success of skills training in improving social and independent living skills in schizophrenic patients, Eckman *et al* (1992) developed a new module of skills training designed to overcome the specific problems of cognitive deficits and symptom interference. They were particularly alert to the disruptive role of negative symptoms, which impede the learning of complex skills. By reducing the interference of negative symptoms, patients could learn skills relevant to managing their illness better. As in the work on relapse prevention (see below), the package included skills relevant to symptom management, such as identifying early warning signs and seeking assistance appropriately, coping with persistent symptoms through specific techniques, and avoiding alcohol and illicit drugs. It also consisted of developing skills in relation to medication management – obtaining information on antipsychotic drugs, learning to self-administer correctly, identify side-effects and seek assistance when problems with medication arose. The methods employed included: cognitive restructuring and considerable positive social reinforcement aimed at overcoming lack of motivation; video modelling; behavioural rehearsal and role-play to overcome poor attention; and focused instructions with prompting and coaching to compensate for cognitive deficits and interference from psychopathology. The package also included problem-solving and resource management training.

In a controlled trial, Eckman *et al* (1992) compared this model of skills training with supportive and insight-oriented group psychotherapy, and found that the patients receiving the skills training gained significantly greater skills in the areas outlined than those receiving group therapy, and that this improvement was independent of initial level of psychopathology. Furthermore, there was little loss of skills at 12-month follow-up. This module demonstrates clearly that cognitive impairments and symptomatic interference associated with schizophrenia can be compensated for using specific cognitive and behavioural techniques and that these patients are able to acquire important illness-management skills.

Relapse prevention

Although antipsychotic drugs are effective in preventing relapse, 30–40% of patients will relapse on maintenance treatment (Leff & Wing, 1971; Johnson, 1976). The reasons for an acute relapse may include irregular compliance with treatment, found to be commoner than good compliance (Kane, 1983), or high levels of environmental stress (Falloon, 1988). A high level of expressed emotion (EE), particularly of a critical kind, is a specific form of environmental stress that has been demonstrated to be associated with acute relapse and is a strong predictor of course of illness in schizophrenia (Brown *et al*, 1972; Leff & Vaughn, 1985; Tarrier & Barrowclough, 1990). Current levels of knowledge support a vulnerability/stress model of schizophrenia that suggests an interaction between inherent biological vulnerability and environmental psychosocial stressors, which act as precipitants of acute psychotic episodes (Falloon & Shanahan, 1990). It is postulated that antipsychotic drugs act at the level of biological vulnerability to prevent relapse, whereas behavioural and cognitive interventions attempt to reduce psychosocial stressors, such as EE, or increase coping strategies and skills (Falloon, 1992) to enhance personal strengths and reduce weaknesses, thereby reducing morbidity and preventing relapse. These new forms of behavioural treatment provide a means of influencing both the person and the environment (Liberman, 1988).

Cognitive–behavioural approaches including family interventions, reviewed by Lam (1991), training in illness self-management (Eckman *et al*, 1992) and training in coping strategies (Tarrier *et al*, 1993), discussed earlier in this chapter, have been successful in reducing relapse rates and morbidity. Studies focusing on the family have examined the effect of simple educational packages and more intensive family interventions (see also Chapter 10, this volume). The rationale behind family education is that high-EE relatives, unlike low-EE relatives, have unrealistic expectations, tending to believe that patients have control over their symptoms. This leads to increased critical comments in response to negative symptoms (Leff & Vaughn, 1985). In educating these relatives it is postulated that their expectations and critical behaviour can be modified. The educational programmes aim to enlighten families as to the nature of schizophrenia, sessions covering areas such as symptoms, diagnosis, aetiology, management and outcome (McGill *et al*, 1983; Berkowitz *et al*, 1984; Barrowclough *et al*, 1987; Smith & Birchwood, 1987; Cozolino *et al*, 1988). Evidence from these studies tends to suggest that although education may improve levels of knowledge and reduce family distress and burden, alone it is insufficient to change family beliefs and attitudes. Education alone would appear to have little effect in preventing relapse (Tarrier *et al*, 1988) in either high- or low-EE groups. A combination of family education, problem-solving and a short-term family intervention studied by Abramowitz & Coursey (1989) was associated with a more promising outcome than the education-only programmes.

It is clear from the evidence available that simple education packages are insufficient to shift family attitudes and prevent relapse, and that more comprehensive interventions are required. A number of carefully controlled studies have clearly shown the effectiveness of family interventions in reducing relapse rates in schizophrenia (Falloon *et al*, 1982, 1985; Leff *et al*, 1982, 1985, 1988, 1990; Hogarty *et al*, 1986, 1987; Tarrier *et al*, 1988, 1989; Randolph *et al*, 1994). The aim of family interventions has been to modify EE, which at high levels is associated with a re-emergence of positive symptoms, and to enhance the family's coping capacity. It has been postulated that these interventions work by modifying an environment that produces a situation of information overload in individuals who have information processing deficits that make them vulnerable to relapse (Tarrier *et al*, 1989). Family interventions, illustrated in Chapter 12 of this volume, have included attempts to focus on strengths and weaknesses of the family, education of the family (with the use of cognitive restructuring techniques enabling relatives to understand the nature of the patient's illness as well as their own reactions), prescribing regular structured contact with the patient within clear limits, the setting of behavioural tasks and goals, training to improve communication, and training in problem-solving strategies.

Family interventions have also included training in cognitive–behavioural techniques to reduce anxiety (Tarrier *et al*, 1988, 1989; Brooker *et al*, 1992) and the enhancement of coping skills through adopting a problem-centred approach. Outcome of these studies has revealed a significant impact on relapse rate. In Falloon *et al*'s study (1982, 1985), 6% of the family treatment group relapsed as opposed to 44% of the control group at nine months, with 17% of the experimental group relapsing at two years and 83% of the control group. Leff *et al* (1982, 1985) also demonstrated a significant difference in relapse rate between a group receiving a package of family intervention and a control group receiving only routine clinical management (9% and 50% respectively at nine months and 40% and 78% at two years). Randolph *et al*'s (1994) results of a clinic-based study comparing behavioural family management (BFM) with customary care revealed a positive outcome for those receiving BFM on rates of symptom exacerbation (14% as opposed to 55%), and the effect appeared to have been beneficial for both high- and low-EE families.

Hogarty *et al* (1986, 1987) compared family treatment, social skills training, combined family treatment and social skills training, and simple out-patient management in a sample of patients suffering from schizophrenia or schizoaffective psychosis. Their results confirmed the significant impact of family intervention on relapse rates, but also demonstrated the cumulative beneficial effect of combining social skills training with family intervention; 23% of the family treatment group relapsed in the first year, compared with 49% of the control group, 30% of the social skills training group and only 9% of the group receiving combined social skills training and family treatment. Family treatment was found to be effective independently of the degree of drug compliance.

Tarrier *et al* (1988, 1989), comparing specific behavioural family interventions with education alone and routine clinical treatment in high-EE groups, found reduced relapse rates in those receiving enactive and symbolic behavioural treatment compared with those on education alone or routine treatment, at both nine-month and two-year follow-up. Expressed emotion was clearly shown to have been modified in the behavioural treatment groups.

Leff *et al* (1988, 1990) attempted to compare the effectiveness of family treatment with a relatives' group in high-EE households of schizophrenic patients, and obtained results demonstrating the superiority of family treatment over the relatives' group in reducing relapse rate. They also reported improvement in negative symptoms in both groups at two years.

As well as making the re-emergence of symptoms less likely in schizophrenia or schizoaffective psychosis, behavioural family intervention has been shown to give improved social adjustment. Falloon *et al* (1985, 1987) found that patients who received family interventions had had longer periods of activity in terms of employment or rehabilitation than patients in the control group at nine-month follow-up, and that they demonstrated greater social and family adjustment measured by the Family Adjustment Scale and the self-reported Social Adjustment Scale. These findings are supported by the results of a study by Barrowclough & Tarrier (1990), who reported significant improvements in social functioning in the high-EE group over the nine months after family intervention, as measured by the overall score on the Social Adjustment Scale and its subscales (measuring withdrawal, interpersonal functioning and prosocial activities), compared with the high-EE control group. It has been suggested that the improvement in social functioning reported in the high-EE treatment group may not reflect an actual improvement but a shift in the attitudes of relatives rating the social performance of the patient as their status changes from high to low EE (Lam, 1991).

Evidence to date supports the role of behavioural family management, in conjunction with optimal antipsychotic treatment, in reducing significantly the risk of acute relapse in schizophrenia and schizoaffective psychosis through reducing the stress in the household and in improving stress management. Falloon (1992) argues that all patients with schizophrenia should receive carer-based stress management. The integrative programmes recommended by Falloon (1992) include optimal drug treatment and stress management that involves patient and carers, and skills training. This combination has been shown to be effective in reducing morbidity, reducing relapse rates and improving social functioning (Falloon, 1985; Falloon *et al*, 1987; Hogarty *et al*, 1986, 1991).

Conclusion

Overall it appears that a combination of behavioural and cognitive approaches can often be applied, usually in combination with standard pharmacotherapy, to reduce symptoms and improve general functioning and prognosis for psychotic patients. Further research in this area will define more clearly the most useful components of the therapeutic regime and help to identify the patient characteristics that predict successful outcome with the various approaches.

References

ABRAMOWITZ, I. A. & COURSEY, R. D. (1989) Impact of an educational support group of family participants who take care of their schizophrenic relatives. *Journal of Consulting and Clinical Psychology*, **57**, 232–236.

ALFORD, B. A. & BECK, A. T. (1994) Cognitive therapy of delusional beliefs. *Behaviour Research and Therapy*, **12**, 369–380.

ANDERSON, L. R. & ALPERT, M. (1974) Operant analysis of hallucinations frequency in a hospitalised schizophrenic. *Journal of Behaviour Therapy and Experimental Psychiatry*, **5**, 13–18.

ANDREWS, G. (1991) The evaluation of psychotherapy. *Current Opinion in Psychiatry*, **4**, 379–383.

AYLLON, T. & AZRIN, N. (1968) *The Token Economy*. New York: Appleton Century Crofts.

BAKER, E., HALL, J. N., HUTCHINSON, K., *et al* (1977) Symptom changes in chronic schizophrenic patients on a token economy: a controlled experiment. *British Journal of Psychiatry*, **131**, 381–393.

BARROWCLOUGH, C., TARRIER, N., WATTS, S., *et al* (1987) Assessing the functional issue of relatives' knowledge about schizophrenia: a preliminary report. *British Journal of Psychiatry*, **151**, 1–8.

—— & —— (1990) Social functioning in schizophrenic patients. 1. The effects of expressed emotion and family intervention. *Social Psychiatry and Psychiatric Epidemiology*, **25**, 125–130.

BERKOWITZ, R., EBERLEIN-FRIESS, R., KUIPERS, L., *et al* (1984) Educating relatives about schizophrenia. *Schizophrenia Bulletin*, **10**, 418–429.

BICK, P. A. & KINSBOURNE, M. (1987) Auditory hallucinations and subvocal speech in schizophrenic patients. *American Journal of Psychiatry*, **144**, 222–225.

BIRCHWOOD, M., MACMILLAN, F. & SMITH, J. (1992) Early intervention. In *Innovations in the Psychological Management of Schizophrenia: Assessment, Treatment and Services* (eds M. Birchwood & N. Tarrier). London: Wiley.

BOWERS, W. A. (1990) Treatment of depressed inpatients: cognitive therapy plus medication, relaxation plus medication, and medication alone. *British Journal of Psychiatry*, **156**, 73–78.

BROOKER, C., TARRIER, N., BARROWCLOUGH, C., *et al* (1992) Training community psychiatric nurses for psychosocial intervention: report of a pilot study. *British Journal of Psychiatry*, **160**, 836–844.

BROWN, G. W., BIRLEY, J. L. T. & WING, J. K. (1972) Influence of family life on the course of schizophrenia disorders: replication. *British Journal of Psychiatry*, **121**, 241–258.

BUCHER, B. & FABRICATORE, J. (1970) Use of patient-administered shock to suppress hallucinations. *Behavior Therapy*, **1**, 382–385.

CHADWICK, P. D. J. & LOWE, C. F. (1994) A cognitive approach to measuring and modifying delusions. *Behaviour Research and Therapy*, **32**, 355–367.

CORRIGAN, P. W. & STORZBACH, D. M. (1993) Behavioural interventions for psychotic symptoms. *Hospital and Community Psychiatry*, **44**, 341–347.

COZOLINO, L. J., GOLDSTEIN, M. J., NUECHTERLEIN, K. H., *et al* (1988) The impact of education about schizophrenia on relatives varying in expressed emotion. *Schizophrenia Bulletin*, **14**, 675–687.

CURRAN, J. P., MONTI, P. M. & CORRIVEAU, D. P. (1982) Treatment of schizophrenia. In *International Handbook of Behaviour Modification and Therapy* (eds A. S. Bellack, M. Hersell & A. E. Kazdin), pp. 209–242. New York: Plenum Press.

DAVISON, G. C. (1969) Appraisal of behavior modification techniques with adults in institutional settings. In *Behavior Therapy: Appraisal and Status* (ed. C. M. Franks). New York: McGraw-Hill.

DOBSON, K. (1989) A meta-analysis of the efficacy of cognitive therapy for depression. *Journal of Consulting and Clinical Psychology*, **57**, 414–419.

ECKMAN, T. A., WIRSHING, W. C., MARDER, S. R., *et al* (1992) Technique for training schizophrenic patients in illness self-management: a controlled trial. *American Journal of Psychiatry*, **149**, 1549–1555.

ELKIN, I., SHEA, M., WATKINS, J., *et al* (1992) National Institute of Mental Health treatment of depression collaborative treatment programme. *Archives of General Psychiatry*, **46**, 971–982.

FALLOON, I. R. H. (ed.) (1985) *Family Management of Schizophrenia: Clinical, Social, Family and Economic Benefit*. Baltimore: Johns Hopkins University Press.

—— (1988) Expressed emotion: the current status. *Psychological Medicine*, **18**, 269–274.

—— (1992) Psychotherapy of schizophrenia. *British Journal of Hospital Medicine*, **48**, 164–170.

——, BOYD, J. L., McGILL, C. W., *et al* (1982) Family management in the prevention of exacerbation of schizophrenia. A controlled study. *New England Journal of Medicine*, **306**, 1437–1440.

——, ——, ——, *et al* (1985) Family management in the prevention of morbidity of schizophrenia. Clinical outcome of a two-year longitudinal study. *Archives of General Psychiatry*, **42**, 887–896.

——, McGILL, C. W., BOYD, J. L., *et al* (1987) Family management in the prevention of morbidity of schizophrenia: social outcome of a two-year longitudinal study. *Psychological Medicine*, **17**, 59–66.

—— & SHANAHAN, W. J. (1990) Community management of schizophrenia. *British Journal of Hospital Medicine*, **43**, 62–66.

FISHER, E. & WINKLER, R. (1975) Self-control over intrusive experiences. *Journal of Consulting and Clinical Psychology*, **43**, 911–916.

FOWLER, D. & MORLEY, S. (1989) The cognitive–behavioural treatment of hallucinations and delusions: a preliminary study. *Behavioural Psychotherapy*, **17**, 267–282.

GOLDSMITH, J. B. & McFALL, R. M. (1975) Development and evaluation of an interpersonal skills training program for psychiatric inpatients. *Journal of Abnormal Psychology*, **84**, 51–58.

GREEN, M. F. & KINSBOURNE, M. (1990) Subvocal activity and auditory hallucinations: clues for behavioural treatments? *Schizophrenia Bulletin*, **16**, 617–625.

HALL, J. N., BAKER, R. D. & HUTCHINSON, K. (1977) A controlled evaluation of token economy procedures with chronic schizophrenic patients. *Behaviour Research and Therapy*, **15**, 261–283.

HEMSLEY, D. R. (1986) Psychological treatment of schizophrenia. In *A Handbook of Clinical Psychology* (eds S. Lindsay & G. Powell). London: Gower.

HOGARTY, G. E., ANDERSON, C. M., REISS, D. J., *et al* (1986) Family psycho-education, social skills training and maintenance chemotherapy in the aftercare treatment of schizophrenia. 1. One-year effects of a controlled study on relapse and expressed emotion. *Archives of General Psychiatry*, **43**, 633–642.

——, —— & —— (1987) Family psychoeducation, social skill training and medication in schizophrenia: the long and short of it. *Psychopharmacology Bulletin*, **23**, 12–13.

——, ——, ——, *et al* (1991) Family psychoeducation, social skills training and maintenance chemotherapy in the aftercare treatment of schizophrenia. II. Two-year effects of a controlled study on relapse and adjustment. *Archives of General Psychiatry*, **48**, 340–347.

HOGG, L. & HALL, J. (1992) Management of long-term impairments and challenging behaviour. In *Innovations in the Psychological Management of Schizophrenia: Assessment, Treatment and Services* (eds J. Birchwood & N. Tarrier), pp. 171–203. Chichester: John Wiley.

HOLLON, S., DeRUBEIS, R., EVANS, M., *et al* (1992) Cognitive therapy and pharmacotherapy for depression: singly and in combination. *Archives of General Psychiatry*, **49**, 774–781.

JOHNSON, J. A. W. (1976) The duration of maintenance therapy in chronic schizophrenia. *Acta Psychiatrica Scandinavica*, **53**, 298.

KANE, J. M. (1983) Problems of compliance in the outpatient treatment of schizophrenia. *Journal of Clinical Psychiatry*, **44**, 3–6.

KINGDON, D. G. & TURKINGTON, D. (1991) The use of cognitive behaviour therapy with a normalising rationale in schizophrenia; preliminary report. *Journal of Nervous and Mental Disease*, **179**, 207–211.

——, —— & JOHN, C. (1994) Cognitive behaviour therapy of schizophrenia: the amenability of delusions and hallucinations to reasoning. *British Journal of Psychiatry*, **164**, 581–587.

LAM, D. H. (1991) Psychosocial family intervention in schizophrenia: a review of empirical studies. *Psychological Medicine*, **21**, 423–441.

LEFF, J. P. & WING, J. K. (1971) Trial of maintenance therapy in schizophrenia. *British Medical Journal*, **iii**, 599–604.

——, KUIPERS, L., BERKOWITZ, R., *et al* (1982) A controlled trial of social intervention in schizophrenic families. *British Journal of Psychiatry*, **141**, 121–134.

—— & VAUGHN, C. (1985) *Expressed Emotion in Families*. New York: Guilford Press.

——, KUIPERS, L., BERKOWITZ, R., *et al* (1985) A controlled trial of social intervention in the families of schizophrenia patients: two-year follow-up. *British Journal of Psychiatry*, **146**, 594–600.

——, BERKOWITZ, R., SHAVIT, N., *et al* (1988) A trial of family therapy versus a relatives' group for schizophrenia. *British Journal of Psychiatry*, **153**, 58–66.

——, ——, ——, *et al* (1990) A trial of family therapy versus a relatives' group for schizophrenia. Two-year follow-up. *British Journal of Psychiatry*, **157**, 571–577.

LIBERMAN, R. (1988) *Psychiatric Rehabilitation of Chronic Mental Patients*. Washington, DC: American Psychiatric Press.

——, TEIGEN, J., PATTERSON, R., *et al* (1973) Reducing delusional speech in chronic paranoid schizophrenics. *Journal of Applied Behavior Analysis*, **6**, 57–64.

LINEHAN, M. M., ARMSTRONG, H. E., SUAREZ, A., *et al* (1991) Cognitive–behavioral treatment of chronically parasuicidal borderline patients. *Archives of General Psychiatry*, **48**, 1060–1064.

MARKS, I. M. (1987) *Fears, Phobias and Rituals.* New York: Oxford University Press.

McGILL, C. W., FALLOON, I. R. H., BOYD, J. L., *et al* (1983) Family educational intervention in the treatment of schizophrenia. *Hospital and Community Psychiatry*, **34**, 934–938.

MEICHENBAUM, D. (1969) The effects of instructions and reinforcement on thinking and language behavior of schizophrenics. *Behaviour Research and Therapy*, **7**, 101–114.

—— & CAMERON, R. (1973) Training schizophrenics to talk to themselves: a means of developing attentional controls. *Behavior Therapy*, **4**, 515–534.

MILLER, I. W., NORMAN, W. H., KEITNER, G. I., *et al* (1989) Cognitive behavioral treatment of depressed inpatients. *Behaviour Therapy*, **20**, 25–47.

PAUL, G. I. & LENTZ, R. (1977) *Psychosocial Treatment of the Chronic Mental Patient.* Cambridge, MA: Harvard University Press.

PREMACK, D. (1959) Toward empirical behavior laws: 1. Positive reinforcement. *Psychological Review*, **66**, 219–233.

RANDOLPH, E. T., ETH, S., GLYNN, S. M., *et al* (1994) Behavioural family management in schizophrenia: outcome of a clinic-based intervention. *British Journal of Psychiatry*, **164**, 501–506.

RICKARD, H. C., DIGMAN, P. J. & HORNER, R. F. (1960) Verbal manipulation in a psycho-therapeutic relationship. *Journal of Clinical Psychology*, **16**, 364–367.

—— & DINOFF, M. A. (1962) A follow-up note on "Verbal manipulation in a psycho-therapeutic relationship". *Psychological Reports*, **11**, 506.

RUDDEN, M., GILMORE, M. & ALLEN, F. (1982) Delusions: when to confront the facts of life. *American Journal of Psychiatry*, **197**, 929–932.

RUTNER, I. T. & BUGLE, C. (1969) An experimental procedure for the modification of psychotic behavior. *Journal of Consulting and Clinical Psychology*, **33**, 651–653.

SALKOVSKIS, P. M. & WARWICK, H. M. C. (1985) Cognitive therapy of obsessive–compulsive disorder: treating treatment failures. *Behavioural Psychotherapy*, **13**, 243–255.

SHEA, M. T., ELKIN, I., IMBER, S., *et al* (1992) Course of depressive symptoms over follow-up. *Archives of General Psychiatry*, **49**, 782–787.

SLADE, P. D. (1973) The psychological investigation and treatment of auditory hallucinations: a second case report. *British Journal of Medical Psychology*, **46**, 293–296.

SMITH, J. & BIRCHWOOD, M. J. (1987) Specific and non-specific effects of educational intervention with families living with schizophrenic relatives. *British Journal of Psychiatry*, **150**, 645–652.

TARRIER, N., BARROWCLOUGH, C., VAUGHN, C., *et al* (1988) The community management of schizophrenia: a controlled trial of a behavioural intervention with families to reduce relapse. *British Journal of Psychiatry*, **153**, 532–542.

——, ——, ——, *et al* (1989) Community management of schizophrenia: a two-year follow-up of a behavioural intervention with families. *British Journal of Psychiatry*, **154**, 625–628.

—— & —— (1990) Family interventions for schizophrenia. *Behavior Modification*, **14**, 408–440.

——, HARWOOD, S., YUSOPOFF, L., *et al* (1990) Coping Strategy Enhancement (CSE): a method of treating residual schizophrenic symptoms. *Behavioral Psychotherapy*, **18**, 283–293.

——, BECKETT, R., HARWOOD, S., *et al* (1993) A trial of two cognitive–behavioural methods of treating drug-resistant residual psychotic symptoms in schizophrenic patients: 1. Outcome. *British Journal of Psychiatry*, **162**, 524–532.

THASE, M., BOWLER, K. & HARDEN, T. (1991) Cognitive therapy of endogenous depression: part 2: preliminary findings in 16 unmedicated inpatients. *Behaviour Therapy*, **22**, 469–477.

WATTS, F. N., POWELL, G. E. & AUSTIN, S. V. (1973) The modification of abnormal beliefs. *British Journal of Medical Psychology*, **46**, 359–363.

WEINGAERTNER, A. H. (1971) Self-administered aversive stimulation with hallucinating hospitalized schizophrenics. *Journal of Consulting and Clinical Psychology*, **36**, 422–429.

WILLIAMS, J. M. G. (1984) Cognitive behavior therapy for depression: problems and perspectives. *British Journal of Psychiatry*, **22**, 254–266.

WINCZE, J. P., LEITENBERG, H. & AGRAS, W. S. (1972) The effects of token reinforcement and feedback on the delusional verbal behaviour of chronic paranoid schizophrenics. *Journal of Applied Behavior Analysis*, **5**, 247–262.

8 Cognitive therapy of schizophrenia: collaborative and integrated approaches

DAVID KINGDON and DOUGLAS TURKINGTON

Cognitive–behavioural therapy of schizophrenia has developed from a long, although variably successful, tradition of psychosocial management of schizophrenia and other disorders. It uses a vulnerability–stress model (Zubin & Spring, 1977) that brings together diverse beliefs about the nature of the group of schizophrenias by integrating biological, psychological and social theories. It also utilises cognitive therapies of depression and anxiety in the management of these disorders, as both conditions coexist with the positive and negative symptoms of schizophrenia in most patients. Organising 'schemata' that may underpin cognitive distortions have been identified in these disorders, and schema-focused therapy developed to elucidate and, where appropriate, question and alter them. This work has become particularly relevant to pervasive disorders of personality (Beck *et al*, 1990).

Over the past 30 years, general psychiatry has emphasised the importance of accurate diagnosis but provided limited guidance about further dialogue once that diagnosis has been made. The use of supportive counselling is generally advocated, with Slater & Roth (1969, p. 236), for example, stressing that "it is a waste of time to argue with a paranoid patient about his delusions". Hamilton (1984, p. 145), in *Fish's Schizophrenia*, advised psychiatrists "not to go along with the patient's delusions and hallucinations; on the contrary, the patient should be encouraged to ignore them". These views have proved influential in psychiatric training, although they lack empirical verification and have been unsatisfactory to many. Biological theories of the aetiology of schizophrenia have held out hope, at least implicitly, that medication or other physical interventions may eventually cure schizophrenia. In the meantime, while medication is very valuable, many patients with schizophrenia remain disabled and distressed by their symptoms through lack of compliance or efficacy.

Psychotherapy has taken many forms in schizophrenia, as described elsewhere in this book. Briefly, Rudden *et al* (1982) summarised the views of psychotherapists as opposing "confronting the reality of the delusion", in contrast to cognitive therapists (e.g. Lowe & Chadwick, 1990). Techniques used instead have included: ignoring delusional content while focusing on conflict-free areas; exploring delusional beliefs and experiences to assist in forming a rapport; and even participating in the delusion. Of relevance to the development of cognitive therapy in schizophrenia, Sullivan (1962) described *Schizophrenia as a Human Process* promoting 'normalisation' and the importance of interpersonal relationships in therapy. With his more 'direct analysis', Rosen (1953) based his therapy on the dream psychology of Freud because of the similarity between psychotic and dream material:

> "What is psychosis but an interminable nightmare in which the wishes are so well disguised that the psychotic does not awaken? Why not then awaken the psychotic by unmasking the real content of his psychosis?"

The governing principle of direct analysis was that the therapist must be an omnipotent protector and provider for the patient:

> "When the patient is mute, he is generally rigid. In that case, it must be understood that what the patient is saying is 'I am frightened stiff'. You have to tell him what you see or hear him to be saying so that somewhere inside of him, he will gain the sense that he is no longer alone; he is understood. Somebody is trying to help."

He also describes the use of 'recovered' patients as aides in the treatment of others using an intensive model – treating one patient at a time. This demonstration that he valued patients' contributions and the self-help element incorporated may have contributed to the process of treatment. However, controlled trials of the use of psychotherapy in schizophrenia (e.g. Stanton *et al*, 1984) did not provide evidence of efficacy.

The use of cognitive therapy in schizophrenia was first described by Beck (1952). He encouraged a person with chronic schizophrenia to scrutinise the appearance and behaviour of alleged FBI agents who were visiting his shop, in order to reality-test his belief that these persons had him under surveillance. The patient succeeded in narrowing down his original group of 50 'suspects' to two or three possibilities and reported that he felt he would soon be able to "eliminate them completely". Despite the existence of the delusion for seven years it proved modifiable:

> "The combination of tracing the antecedents of the delusion, and helping the patient to test his conclusions systematically, helped him to recognise and to gradually do away with the irrational and rigid belief-system."

There are now many other case studies in the literature (e.g. Turkington & Kingdon, 1991; Bentall *et al*, 1994; John & Turkington, 1997), uncontrolled follow-ups (e.g. Kingdon & Turkington, 1991; Perris & Skagerlind, 1994) and a small number of pilot controlled studies. Garety *et al* (1994) describe reductions in delusional conviction, general symptoms and depression using cognitive–behavioural therapy for drug-resistant psychosis in 13 patients treated over six months, compared with a non-randomised waiting-list control group. Kingdon *et al* (1997) found a significant reduction in global symptom assessment between patients treated over two months with cognitive therapy compared with a randomised 'befriending' control group. Both groups are now involved in more extensive studies to explore these preliminary findings.

Continuities between 'normality' and schizophrenia

Perhaps the most distressing and disabling aspect of schizophrenia is the belief held by most people, including some mental health workers and patients themselves, that people experiencing the illness are qualitatively distinct – not just different in degree but in type. At one extreme, they are defined as 'schizophrenics' rather than people with schizophrenia, but even from the latter, more holistic, viewpoint, they are still regarded as being categorically different. Yet there is evidence that delusions have much in common with 'normal' beliefs and that other phenomena encountered in schizophrenia can occur under certain types of stressful circumstances, such as organic confusional states, sensory deprivation, hostage situations and sleep deprivation.

Strauss (1969) has also demonstrated that:

> "phenomena like delusions and hallucinations represent points on continua. All intermediate gradations of experience exist, from

normal perceptions to hallucinations and from normal ideation to delusions."

It is reasonable to conclude that schizophrenia lies on a continuum with normality. People experience episodes or continuing signs and symptoms of it when their individual degree of vulnerability has combined with specific or excess stress; their difference from others is only a question of degree, with all the implications for self-concept and stigmatisation. However, such a reconceptualisation should not lead to a devaluation of the degree of distress and disability caused.

In the formation of normal beliefs and delusions, two factors appear to be significant: expectation shapes belief formation, that is, "what you expect affects what you believe"; and disproportionate importance is given to current information provided by the environment, that is, the "events occurring at the time and circumstances you find yourself in" (Hemsley & Garety, 1986). Strongly held 'normal' beliefs can be highly resistant to change even where strong counterargument is employed. Logical reasoning frequently is not utilised (Dulit, 1972). The differences between 'normal' thinking and that in schizophrenia were examined by Tissot & Bernand (1980), who, after concluding that differences were in degree rather than type, stated that "when rational explanations and the certainty they produce are lacking, magical causality and subjective certainty take their place".

The description of delusions as irrational beliefs, out of keeping with a person's cultural (or socio-economic) background, that are not amenable to reason, needs re-evaluating (Roberts, 1992; see also Chapter 9 of this volume). It incorporated a series of subjective judgements about irrationality, a person's cultural background and amenability to reason, which could be expected to vary along a series of dimensions. We have suggested that these include: the strength of the belief; the consequences of its relinquishment; how well the assessor understands the beliefs presented and their antecedents; the cogency of explanations used; and the relationship between the patient and the assessor (Kingdon & Turkington, 1994; Kingdon *et al*, 1994). There is substantial evidence that verbal material produced by patients has meaning to them (e.g. Harrow & Prosen, 1978), but that this may not be appreciated by others at the time it is uttered.

Techniques used

Basic techniques used when therapy commences include assembling available information from case notes and referrers. While initial interview of the patient without potentially prejudicing information might be attractive, the nature of delusions and thought disorder is such that initial contacts can be incomprehensible without it, and opportunities for engagement are lost. The personal history is particularly important as it can assist greatly in understanding the context and thus meaning and significance of statements made.

An outline agenda needs to be developed for the initial session and then used flexibly; this could comprise introductory statements, discussion of cognitive model, inquiry into major concerns, tracing of antecedents to symptoms, and personal history. Introduction might be a clear explanation of who the interviewer is and why the patient is seeing him/her (e.g. "to talk about the problems you've been having" or "concerns that your family or doctor have about you"). Inquiry into major current concerns might start with "Maybe you could tell me about what's been happening". Generally, initial conversation will be non-directive and involve gentle exploration. If the patient is unresponsive, prompts from known history can open up discourse; if thought-disordered, initially this can be allowed to flow, but for a short period only before focusing on one problem or theme at a time.

Tracing the antecedents of onset is of prime importance. This means identifying the circumstances that formed the basis for misinterpretations and delusional beliefs, and using them to develop a rationale for symptoms that is acceptable to the patient. Determining exactly when symptoms began by gentle questioning (e.g. "When did this all start?", "When did you last feel well?") enables the therapist to build up a picture of the preceding period and explore cognitions using a Socratic approach. Misinterpretations of life events and circumstances can be identified along with the associated 'faulty cognitions' – personalisation (taking things personally), selective abstraction (getting things out of context) and arbitrary inference (jumping to conclusions).

The next step is to attempt to correct them by reattribution, analysis of evidence, and the generation of alternative explanations. Such explanations commonly include the use of vulnerability–stress interactions. Vulnerabilities are identified, such as family history, birth difficulties, personality characteristics, or brain injury. Stressors are isolated, for example work, school, university, family, sexuality, isolation, and drug or alcohol misuse. A 'normalising' rationale for individual symptoms may be developed: sleep deprivation – "Were you sleeping properly at the time?"; sensory deprivation – perhaps through isolation because of work circumstances or a house move – "What can happen is that when things are getting you down or confusing you, there is nobody around to help you work it out and stop it getting out of proportion". Symptoms may be reframed as cultural beliefs. Thought broadcasting and insertion can be explored: "Do you think people read your thoughts or that you can read theirs?", "How can they do that?", "Do you mean something like telepathy?", "Do you know much about telepathy?" An understanding of non-verbal communication may assist, that is, discussion of how a sensitive appreciation of non-verbal cues can lead to others understanding mood which may be interpreted as thought broadcasting. Passivity can be explored: "Do you think people are making you do/think/feel things against your will?", "How do you think they can do that?", "Do you mean some sort of hypnotism?", "Hypnotism is a well demonstrated phenomenon, but you do need to agree to it for it to work and it couldn't make you ...". Alternatively the therapist could suggest, "Do you mean some sort of magnetism or waves is occurring?" and then discuss this; for example, "I don't know of any way they could affect people like that ... perhaps we should find out more about these phenomena". Reattribution of somatic symptoms of anxiety is frequently necessary in response to bizarre beliefs. Questioning establishes "What did you actually feel?". Frequently the sensations involved are paraesthesia or a startle reflex misinterpreted as, for example, 'electric shocks', or hyperventilation as pressure on the person's chest. Explanations of the physiology of anxiety can provide credible alternative explanations.

Formulation

The formulation of an individual's experience of schizophrenia is one of the cornerstones on which techniques build. The formulation is worked out collaboratively with the patient once a full assessment has been completed in the early sessions of therapy, frequently around session 2–5. Trust-building and teaching the cognitive model, along with a non-confrontational, non-colluding therapist style, generally lead to the development of a viable therapeutic alliance, although with especially paranoid and grandiose patients this can take longer. The formulation should be clearly written down for the patient and therapist to consider the development of the symptoms in relation to the personal history and key life events and circumstances.

Schema-based techniques

The development of schema-based approaches in depression, anxiety and personality disorder has provided ways of tackling entrenched beliefs that have been resistant to standard techniques of cognitive therapy. These approaches have common ground with insight-oriented psychodynamic techniques, although they are based on collaborative questioning and 'guided discovery' rather than interpretation. The organising frameworks that exist to shape the interpretation of information received by individuals, for the most part, act in a way that benefits the person by helping him/her to understand and interact with the environment and those within it. However, sometimes they can perpetuate false beliefs about the self that depress mood or exacerbate anxiety, such as a global belief that "I am a failure". Evidence disconfirming such a belief would tend to be discounted, while that which could be taken to support it will be focused upon.

Where discussion of the specifics of delusional ideas or thought disorder is failing to make inroads and rapport is being impaired or necessitating agreement to differ, it may be that attempting to understand the theme of the thought disorder (Bannister, in Dryden, 1985) or identifying schema underpinning delusional ideas can allow the impasse to be overcome. In developing a formulation, the therapist may elucidate particularly traumatic early pressures, events and relationships. These events may need to be managed through the use of brief focal psychotherapeutic or cognitive–behavioural techniques alongside cognitive therapy for psychotic symptoms. However, engagement to work on them necessitates agreement between the patient and therapist that these events are significant and are continuing to affect the patient. Where there appear to be no specific early life events of significance, it may be useful to review how the developing child interacted with parents and peers. In particular, persistent criticism (with the implication that "I am flawed/worthless") or overprotection ("I am special") need to be considered.

Critical events are often discovered from an examination of the antecedents (using inductive questioning/imagery or role play) or from an inductive formulation. The technique of inductive formulation involves going through each phase of a patient's life systematically, over the space of two or three sessions, to detect predominating mood states and particularly critical events, which are often not clearly elaborated in straightforward history-taking. The immediate antecedents, personality traits and sociocultural milieu of the development of psychotic symptoms should all be clearly outlined.

Next, current symptoms with maintaining variables and the rationale that has been developed to explain the symptom emergence are delineated. This should be an integrative experience for the patient to understand the development of the illness from childhood to the present date. It should also inspire hope that if the therapist can understand such a bewildering set of symptoms, then perhaps there might be a way forward with cognitive therapy to help symptoms, stress or disability to improve. The appetite of patients with schizophrenia is often whetted for further exploration and understanding of the condition, while the therapist is floundering without a clear understanding of the case formulation. One of the biggest reasons for the failure of isolated techniques is a lack of this crucial individual patient knowledge. The process of developing a formulation, therefore, should assist in understanding why a particular patient in his/her own unique situation should have developed particular symptom patterns. Content may also become less incomprehensible than it appears at the outset.

The key schema related to the psychotic symptoms should start to emerge from the formulation, and the appropriate techniques and the sequence of their application become clearer. The main schema can be detected by looking for themes in negative automatic thoughts or by ascertaining the meaning of critical schema-forming life events or childhood situations. Schema related to drug-resistant psychotic symptoms need to be elucidated, but often they will also be resistant to the use of peripheral and Socratic questioning and graded homework assignments based on reality testing.

The 'downward arrow' technique is used in depression to identify schema (Blackburn & Davidson, 1990); it involves following through the implications or inferences of delusional ideas. For example, for a patient who describes being followed, the therapist response could be "So let's for the moment assume that is actually happening, why does that worry you?" And the answers would be followed through to identify the underlying concerns and possible schema.

The key schema related to delusions can often be understood using inference chaining (downward arrow technique), as used in this example of a patient with a grandiose belief:

Patient: I am the second coming of Christ.
Therapist: What does this mean for you, if indeed it was the case that you are the second coming of Christ?
Patient: It means I have to save the world from Satan.
Therapist: And, what does that mean for you – if you are as you believe placed in such a vital role?
Patient: It means I have to do this on my own and that I will have no friends or wife to help me.
Therapist: What is the worst thing about that particular situation?
Patient: I am very, very alone.

This final statement is the 'hot' cognition existing beneath this grandiose material – delineating the key core maladaptive schema, that is, "I am separate/different/alone".

Schema-focused cognitive therapy uses a sequence of techniques to help patients gradually to work on and shift such very painful beliefs about the self. Working at the schema level may involve patients experiencing depression briefly when they reach an understanding of the core belief; however, it is essential that any persisting feelings of depression are dealt with immediately, by psychological or pharmacological means. It is important that the relationship between the therapist and patient is well established before any attempt is made at such schema identification. Potentially, this could be damaging to a developing relationship between therapist and patient, who might view such discussion as implying either that the therapist is not taking the beliefs, or the patient him/herself, seriously or even that the therapist is actually part of the conspiracy against the patient.

Core maladaptive schema are usually unconditional: "I am ..." "out of control", "bad/evil", "worthless/a failure", "unlovable". They need to be tackled cautiously and almost always later in therapy. Occasionally, a patient describes a core schema very early on in therapy and may be extremely disturbed by it. For example, a suicidal person with schizophrenia reported in the first session that he was evil and should be continually punished, if necessary by self-inflicted wounds or overdosing. In such a situation, the core maladaptive schema is tackled at the initiation of therapy as it is difficult to ignore without appearing to disregard the patient's concerns. This in turn can mean that engagement cannot take place until exploration of the beliefs occurs. Following such exploration, it may be appropriate to work with these beliefs, but if they are too distressing it is often possible to agree to return to them later, after exploring other areas. In general terms, high levels of anxiety or depression seem to be poorly tolerated by patients and can be damaging to the therapeutic relationship and the patients themselves, and so unless there are very good reasons for proceeding, the safest and probably most effective course is to withdraw and then return later.

A number of other schema issues emerge. Often a compensatory schema is related to particular psychotic symptoms. For example, in relation to paranoid delusions there are often thoughts of "they are out to get me, there is a conspiracy, they are talking about me on radios, the television was referring to me" and so on. Tracing the antecedents of symptom onset often locates the critical events, for example the loss of a job that traumatised a key personal schema (e.g. "I must be successful" and consequently "I am a failure").

Invalidation of key personal schema at critical points in a person's life by external life events may lead to the emergence of psychotic symptoms, especially delusional beliefs, which serve to protect against low self-esteem.

A number of other schemas occur in schizophrenia. The response to the development of schizophrenia itself, and the feelings of loss of control that emerge, may well impinge upon control-related schema ("I must be completely in control of myself and my environ-ment"), or on schema relating to fairness ("Life must always be fair"). In relation to treatment, including hospitalisation and neuroleptic drugs, pertinent schema may also relate to issues of control and independence.

In tackling the schema in psychosis, it is important to use 'guided discovery' to help patients to articulate the schema, rather than didactic interpretation, and so to be clear about what they actually believe about themselves or their world. Once the schema is articulated and clearly described, there are a number of techniques used to try gradually to change this. Collection of evidence is particularly useful and this can be linked into homework assignments to see just how consistent, or not, the schema appears to be with the patient's experiences and general life situation. This can be tackled using positive and negative recording of events and thoughts of relevance to the schema and reporting this from session to session, along with a percentage belief allocation in relation to the particular schema and the monitoring of this as homework proceeds. Weighing the pros and cons of holding a particular schema can be useful, although in general tackling directly how the schema functions in schizophrenia (e.g. as a protection against low self-esteem) has not been found to be a particularly useful technique. Tackling the 'demandingness' and the 'extreme evaluation' inherent within these schema, for example with "I must be successful or life is unbearable", tends to be extremely useful and can be done in relation to the nature of demandingness itself or by placing the outcome of the feared situation in context, for example in relation to situations that are much less bearable, like serious road traffic accidents and earth-quakes. Schema that are particularly difficult to shift may be tackled directly or using imagery, through asking the patient to act directly against the schema where possible. However, again caution is essential to retain rapport and avoid undue distress.

An example of how experiences in psychodynamic psychotherapy might be able to assist in identifying and understanding schema occurred at the conference on which this book is based. A patient with schizophrenia was described who had developed a fear that the moon was going to fall to the earth and, as far as the patient was concerned, upon him (described in Kingdon & Turkington, 1994). This was viewed as being an example of a specific lack of social knowledge (Cutting & Murphy, 1988) and an educational approach was used. This involved discussion of basic physics to establish the reasons why the moon remains in its orbit and was successful in overcoming the distress that the patient felt. A member of the workshop, however, postulated that the moon might have represented the maternal breast and that the fear may have been related to engulfment by the mother. While this seemed initially to be speculative and even irrelevant, consideration of the patient's history established that his mother was indeed a dominant figure in his life, had frequently interfered with his psychiatric management, and his difficulty in separating from her was a key factor in his current situation. Whether this interpretation could be useful in his management was less clear, but nonetheless a possible reason for such a bizarre belief became apparent.

Depression and suicide

Delusions have been considered to form defensive mechanisms against depression. In our series of patients, there have been circumstances in which as delusional ideas recede or, as discussed earlier, maladaptive schema are identified, depressive symptoms emerge. These have been dealt with directly as they become apparent; cognitive therapy of depression and antidepressants have been used along with the range of community interventions available (e.g. day care, befriending, and means of improving socialisation). The use of an illness model has also proved valuable in protecting self-esteem; this has involved reattribution of delusional ideas to the illness, schizophrenia, rather than personal failure. Suicide occurs in about 10% of people with schizophrenia, and methods to minimise its likelihood have been considered during the development of cognitive–behavioural therapy with this group. Patients and carers have been encouraged to make direct contact with the mental health team, usually through the consultant or his secretary when the patient has deteriorated, especially where suicidal thoughts developed. Therapy itself has aimed at sustaining hope, decatastrophising symptoms, and explaining and normalising them. Treatment of depression and anxiety with cognitive therapy, interpersonal therapy or medication at an early stage has been emphasised with the close involvement of relatives and other carers. 'Command' hallucinations of an abusive or self-destructive nature have received particular attention. The principle of 'safety first' has predominated and appears to have been successful; none of the 64 patients followed up over 10 years has committed suicide.

Hallucinations

Visions, voices, and feelings of being touched that are not produced by any external stimulus commonly occur in schizophrenia and can cause great distress. A few patients view their voices in a positive manner (Romme & Escher, 1994), sometimes enjoying their 'company' when they are lonely and isolated, or being excited by them. However, most patients simply want to get rid of their hallucinations. Such a direct target is difficult, if not impossible, to achieve and needs to be mediated by other steps. Usually the most distressing aspect of hallucinations is their feeling of omnipotence (Chadwick & Birchwood, 1994) and the belief that they are being created by another, malevolent, agency, person or being.

The collaborative development of an acceptable alternative explanation of them is therefore usually the first step to take. For auditory hallucinations, establish with the patient that, if a voice sounds as if it comes from outside the patient, other people ought to be able to hear it and if not, why not? Any alternative suggestions by the patient are explored until it is possible to move on to discuss three theoretically possible alternative explanations: first, the therapist and others are lying – they can hear it; second, the voice is directed specifically at the patient so that others cannot hear it (if the patient thinks this is a possibility, ask about possible mechanisms); finally, it is suggested that the voice might be coming from within the patient's own mind, caused by a combination of stress and vulnerability, perhaps the illness called schizophrenia. Such gentle inductive questioning frequently sows doubt in the patient's mind about the origins of the hallucinations and assists in the development of insight, reducing the fear attached to them. In turn, the reduction in distress often seems to reduce the frequency and intensity of the hallucinations.

Command hallucinations cause particular concern and can prove resistant because of the intense distress associated with them, which in turn appears to increase their intensity. Reality testing nevertheless can assist in producing insight, such that the content can be discussed. Frequently what is said is sexual, violent, especially self-harming, or extremely abusive, and the patient feels unable to disclose its nature. Such disclosure within a therapeutic relationship and the unconditional acceptance of it and continued acceptance of the patient by the therapist can have a marked effect on reducing distress. However, therapeutic inquiry can easily be construed as 'probing' and needs to be very cautious. Gentle examination with the patient about the onset of the voices may identify a precipitant – or sometimes simply a precipitating thought. Discussion of "Do you think you have done anything to deserve this?" may assist in identifying relevant material to work through. Establishing with patients that voices – that is, their own thoughts – cannot directly make them act in a specific way can undermine the sense of impotence they have. All-or-nothing thinking tends to predominate (e.g. "They always make me do things"), but it is often possible to elicit inconsistencies and to discuss methods of resisting the voices and development of coping strategies.

Somatic hallucinations are also quite common but frequently not elicited. Discussion of their nature, which is frequently sexual or anxiety-related, and possible mechanisms can establish the precise nature of the sensations. There may then be specific actions that can help; for example, one of our patients believed that she was being repeatedly touched and assaulted. When asked who did this, she named other patients and staff members, but on further discussion it was established that, if they did this, she should be able to see them do so. She was encouraged to look at where she felt she was being touched – which surprisingly she had not done previously or at least consistently. Nursing staff reinforced this message, leading to a marked reduction in the symptom's occurrence. At times other mechanisms may be cited, such as rays, electricity or magnetism. Sensitive exploration of these and the development of alternative explanations – like sexual feelings which are disowned, somatic symptoms of anxiety – has the potential to modify them.

Conclusions

The specific techniques described here may assist patients to feel less stigmatised, to develop and sustain a strong rapport with the therapist, and to reduce the frequency and intensity of their psychotic symptoms, especially delusions and hallucinations. This in turn can contribute to the overall goal of cognitive–behavioural therapy of schizophrenia, which is to reduce the distress and disability that this disorder causes.

References

ALFORD, B. A. & BECK, A. T. (1994) Cognitive therapy of delusional beliefs. *Behavior Research and Therapy*, **32**, 369–380.

BECK, A. T. (1952) Successful outpatient psychotherapy of a chronic schizophrenic with a delusion based on borrowed guilt. *Psychiatry*, **15**, 305–312.

——, FREEMAN, A., *et al.* (1990) *Cognitive Therapy of Personality Disorders*. New York: Guilford.

BENTALL, R. P., HADDOCK, G. & SLADE, P. D. (1994) Cognitive behavior therapy for persistent auditory hallucinations: from theory to therapy. *Behavior Therapy*, **25**, 51–66.

BLACKBURN, I. & DAVIDSON, K., (1990) *Cognitive Therapy for Depression and Anxiety*. Oxford: Blackwell.

CHADWICK, D. & BIRCHWOOD, M. (1994) The omnipotence of voices. A cognitive approach to auditory hallucinations. *British Journal of Psychiatry*, **164**, 190–201.

CUTTING, J. & MURPHY, D. (1988) Schizophrenic thought disorder. *British Journal of Psychiatry*, **152**, 310–319.

DRYDEN, W. (1985) *Therapist's Dilemmas* (Chapter 15). London: Harper & Row.

DULIT, E. (1972) Adolescent thinking a la Piaget: the formal stage. *Journal of Youth and Adolescence*, **1**, 282–301.

GARETY, P. A., KUIPERS, L., FOWLER, D., *et al* (1994) Cognitive behavioural therapy for drug-resistant psychosis. *British Journal of Medical Psychology*, **67**, 259–271.

HAMILTON, M. (1984) *Fish's Schizophrenia* (3rd edn), p. 145. Bristol: Wright.

HARROW, M. & PROSEN, M. (1978) Intermingling and disordered logic as influences on schizophrenic 'thought disorders'. *Archives of General Psychiatry*, **35**, 1213–1218.

HEMSLEY, D. R. & GARETY, P. A. (1986) The formation and maintenance of delusions: a Bayesian analysis. *British Journal of Psychiatry*, **149**, 51–56.

JOHN, C. H. & TURKINGTON, D. (1997) A model-building approach in cognitive therapy with a woman with chronic 'schizophrenic' hallucinations: why did it work? *Clinical Psychology and Psychotherapy* (in press).

KINGDON, D. G. & TURKINGTON, D. (1991) Preliminary report. The use of cognitive behaviour therapy and a normalising rationale in schizophrenia. *Journal of Nervous and Mental Disease*, **179**, 207–211.

—— & —— (1994) *Cognitive–Behavioural Therapy of Schizophrenia*. New York: Guilford Press; London: Lawrence-Ehrlbaum.

——, —— & JOHN, C. (1994) Cognitive therapy of schizophrenia. The amenability of delusions and hallucinations to reason (Editorial). *British Journal of Psychiatry*, **164**, 581–587.

——, ——, ——, *et al* (1997) Controlled study of cognitive therapy in schizophrenia. *Behavioural and Cognitive Psychotherapy* (in press).

LOWE, C. F. & CHADWICK, P. D. J. (1990) Verbal control of delusions. *Behavior Therapy*, **21**, 461–479.

PERRIS, C. & SKAGERLIND, L. (1994) Cognitive therapy with schizophrenic patients. *Acta Psychiatrica Scandinavica*, **89** (suppl. 382), 65–70.

ROBERTS, G. (1992) The origins of delusion. *British Journal of Psychiatry*, **161**, 298–308.

ROMME, M. & ESCHER, S. (1994) *Accepting Voices*. London: MIND Publications.

ROSEN, J. N. (1953) *Direct Analysis*. New York: Grune & Stratton.

RUDDEN, M., GILMORE, M. & FRANCES, A. (1982) Delusions: when to confront the facts of life. *American Journal of Psychiatry*, **139**, 929–932.

SLATER, E. & ROTH, M. (1969) *Clinical Psychiatry* (3rd edn). London: Bailliere, Tindall & Cassell.

STANTON, A. H., GUNDERSON, J. G., KNAPP, P. H., *et al* (1984) Effects of psychotherapy in schizophrenia: I. Design and implementation of a controlled study. *Schizophrenia Bulletin*, **10**, 520–562.

STRAUSS, J. S. (1969) Hallucinations and delusions as points on continua function. *Archives of General Psychiatry*, **21**, 581–586.

SULLIVAN, H. S. (1962) *Schizophrenia as a Human Process*. New York: Norton.

TISSOT, R. & BERNAND, Y. (1980) Aspects of cognitive activity in schizophrenia. *Psychological Medicine*, **10**, 657–663.

TURKINGTON, D. & KINGDON, D. G. (1991) Ordering thoughts in thought disorder. *British Journal of Psychiatry*, **159**, 160–161.

ZUBIN, J. & SPRING, B. (1977) Vulnerability – a new view on schizophrenia. *Journal of Abnormal Psychology*, **86**, 103–126.

9 The use of coping skills in the treatment of hallucinations and delusions in schizophrenia

NICHOLAS TARRIER, LAWRENCE YUSUPOFF, CAROLINE KINNEY and EILIS McCARTHY

Inadequacy of pharmacological treatment

Despite advances in the pharmacological treatment of schizophrenia, many patients continue to experience residual positive symptoms of psychosis. Although these symptoms may be less severe than those experienced during an acute episode, they are distressing to the patient and disrupt the patient's level of functioning. In a three-year follow-up study it was found that 47% of patients continued to experience some symptoms (Harrow & Silverstein, 1977; Silverstein & Harrow, 1978), and in a seven-year follow-up study 23% of the patient sample were found to be experiencing florid psychotic symptoms (Curson *et al*, 1985). Similar results to these studies demonstrating persistent symptoms in patients within a community setting have also been found in the investigation of patients in a hospital setting. Curson *et al* (1988) assessed all the patients in a large London psychiatric hospital and found that nearly half were experiencing either hallucinations or delusions. Moreover, many patients fail to comply with their medication, which can result in relapse or exacerbation of positive symptoms (Buchanan, 1992). Even in those who do comply with prophylactic medication, approximately 40–60% will suffer a relapse over the first two years after discharge (Falloon *et al*, 1978; Hogarty *et al*, 1979). It could be concluded, therefore, that neuroleptic medication as a sole intervention

strategy for the long-term care of patients suffering from schizophrenia is flawed.

Historical development of psychological treatments and interventions

Psychological treatments have a long history and have arisen from a
number of different theoretical and clinical perspectives. However,
many of these approaches were poorly evaluated and when the
appropriate studies were performed their efficacy was not confirmed.
For example, large-scale evaluative studies showed little support for
supportive or psychodynamic psychotherapy with schizophrenia (May,
1968; Mosher & Keith, 1979; Stanton *et al*, 1984; Gunderson *et al*, 1984).

Methods derived from the behavioural tradition, which had a
firmly established empirical background, had more demonstrable
benefits. Contingency management, in which rewards and punish-
ments are variously manipulated, has been used to decrease the
behavioural correlates of hallucinations and delusions (Chapter 7,
this volume). A number of methods have been used, including social
reinforcement (Ayllon & Haughton, 1964; Liberman *et al*, 1973;
Bulow *et al*, 1979), time out (Davis *et al*, 1976), social interference
(Alford & Turner, 1976; Turner *et al*, 1977; Alford *et al*, 1982),
punishment (Bucher & Fabricatore, 1970; Anderson & Albert, 1974;
Turner *et al*, 1977; Fonagy & Slade, 1982; Belcher, 1988) and negative
reinforcement (Fonagy & Slade, 1982).

Although positive results were frequently reported, there are
problems with these approaches. Improvements were rarely long-
lasting or resistant to extinction. Improvements did not generalise
to settings or situations other than those in which contingencies
were controlled. The majority of these studies were carried out with
chronic populations within institutions, and the generalisation of
contingency management to populations outside institutions is
doubtful. Furthermore, hallucinations and delusions are experiential
and largely private events, whereas the manipulation of contingencies requires overt behaviour to reinforce or punish, thus
patients may learn not to talk about their symptoms rather than their
symptoms being actually decreased because of the intervention.
Nevertheless, contingencies are an important determinant of all
human behaviour and their manipulation will be an influential aspect
of any treatment approach, even if the structured manipulation of
contingencies, as seen in the operant programmes, has not proven
that generally applicable.

Other approaches derived from the behavioural tradition have been evaluated in case studies. Stimulus control methods, in which the antecedent conditions to psychotic symptoms are identified and manipulated, have been reported with mainly positive results (Slade, 1972, 1973; Nydegger, 1972). Self-management procedures in which patients monitor their experiences, identify them as illness-related or not, and then implement a procedure to reduce symptoms when present, and reinforce themselves for their successes have also been used. However, in one well-controlled case study improvements were not maintained over time (Alford *et al*, 1982).

Meichenbaum and his colleagues produced a treatment programme for schizophrenic patients that involved training patients to use their own internal dialogue in self-instruction on on-task behaviour (Meichenbaum & Cameron, 1973). Initial reports demonstrated improvements in task performance, an increase in 'healthy talk' and a decrease in 'sick talk' (Meichenbaum & Cameron, 1973; Meyers *et al*, 1976). Other reports have failed to replicate these findings (Gresen, 1974; Margolis & Shemberg, 1976).

The first report of a cognitive approach where the patient's thoughts and beliefs were elicited and modified was by Beck (1952). Watts *et al* (1973) reported a series of controlled case studies that demonstrated that belief modification reduced the severity of the patient's abnormal belief, whereas relaxation and systematic desensitisation to social situations (a stimulus control method) did not. Following from this, a small controlled study was carried out that demonstrated the superiority of belief modification over confrontation (Milton *et al*, 1978). In some patients confrontation appeared to strengthen their conviction in the delusional belief. Other case studies have also reported positive results for this method of modifying the patient's beliefs (Hole *et al*, 1979; Hartman & Cashman, 1983).

Recent developments in the psychological treatment of psychotic symptoms

Although there has been a long history in the application of different psychological treatments to positive psychotic symptoms, it is only in recent years that there has been widespread interest in this area. This has mainly occurred in the UK, and has in part been in response to the failure of neuroleptic medication to manage positive symptoms successfully, but also because of changes in the priorities of the National Health Service towards better care for patients suffering from schizophrenia. Psychologists and psychologically minded psychiatrists have become more interested in psychosis, and effective psychological treatments have, and still are, being developed. A number of groups – such as those of Kingdon and Turkington in Bassetlaw and Newcastle (Kingdon & Turkington, 1994); Garety, Kuipers, Fowler and colleagues in London (Garety *et al*, 1994); Bentall, Slade and Haddock in Liverpool (Bentall *et al*, 1994) and Birchwood and colleagues in Birmingham (Chadwick & Birchwood, 1994; Drury, 1994) – have developed cognitive–behavioural treatments for hallucinations and delusions. These treatments have excited much interest, and although there are conceptual and practical differences between them the basic theoretical and clinical approaches are similar. A number of large-scale controlled trials are currently under way to investigate the efficacy of these therapeutic methods.

The Salford and Manchester projects

In the Salford Family Intervention Project in the mid-1980s, 29% of patients suffered persistent psychotic symptoms after discharge, despite the aggressive use of neuroleptic medication. It was an interesting question to see how the experience of these persistent symptoms affected sufferers and how they coped with them. A small study was carried out with the 25 patients who continued to experience either hallucinations, delusions or both (Tarrier, 1987). Patients were interviewed using a semi-structured interview, the Antecedent and Coping Interview (ACI; Tarrier, 1992), which elicited: the nature of each hallucination and delusion, including the frequency, duration and severity; the accompanying emotional reactions; the antecedents; the consequences; the active coping strategies used and their effectiveness. This interview was essentially a behavioural analysis of each psychotic experience, and set out to describe the topography of that experience, including the patient's reactions and attempts to cope.

Of the 25 patients, 17 (68%) experienced true auditory hallucinations, 2 (8%) pseudo-hallucinations and 19 (76%) experienced coherently expressed delusions. Thirteen patients (52%) were able to identify antecedents to their symptoms; these varied from specific stimuli (16%; e.g. traffic noise) and social situations (20%), to internal states such as feeling anxious (4%), to being alone or inactive (24%), or to a specific time of the day (16%). All patients were able to identify emotional reactions to their symptoms, although 2 (8%) said that they no longer experienced the severe anxiety that they had previously. Eighteen (72%) said that they experienced distress in response to their symptoms and 9 (36%) reported that their symptoms inhibited ongoing behaviour. Three (12%) reported recent severe social disruption, such as being arrested or attempting suicide.

Coping strategies were defined as active attempts to reduce, overcome or master the symptom or the distress resulting from its experience. The aspect to stress here is that coping is an active or wilful attempt to control or master a situation or experience. Eighteen (72%) of the patients were able to identify their use of such coping strategies. It was possible to categorise different methods of coping:

(a) cognitive strategies consisted of cognitive or mental events, such as attention-switching, attention-narrowing, the use of self-statements and rational restructuring;

(b) behavioural strategies included increased activity levels, increased social activity, decreased social activity and social disengagement, and reality testing;

(c) sensory strategies included attempts to modify sensory input;

(d) physiological strategies included attempts to modify the physiological state of the patient, such as relaxation or controlled breathing;

(e) inappropriate strategies such as the misuse of alcohol or street drugs to reduce physiological arousal were also noted.

Ten patients (40%) used cognitive strategies, nine (36%) used behavioural strategies, four (16%) used modification of sensory input, while five (20%) used strategies designed to modify physiological state (three of whom used alcohol or drugs). Eighteen patients (72%) using active coping strategies reported at least one to be moderately successful or better, and 75% of all described strategies were reported as being at least moderately successful. Eight patients (32%) reported using two or more strategies and there was a significant association between multiple strategy use and strategy effectiveness. Ineffective strategies were significantly more likely to be employed by patients using only one strategy.

Coping-strategy enhancement

This and other naturalistic studies of patients' attempts to cope with their symptoms (e.g. Falloon & Talbot, 1981; Breier & Strauss, 1983; Cohen & Berk, 1985; Carr, 1988) have suggested that psychotic symptoms such as hallucinations and delusions would be responsive to non-pharmacological interventions. Furthermore, such coping strategies may be used to form the basis of more systematic interventions to reduce psychotic symptoms. It was reasoned that such a treatment approach would have a number of advantages. Because coping strategies were something many patients did already, then they already existed within the patient's response repertoire and hence further training in their use would enhance their effectiveness. Such enhancement of coping skills might be especially effective with patients who used solitary strategies or who used their strategies inconsistently or who were unaware of antecedents to their symptoms. The fact that many of these coping strategies represented normal psychological processes would suggest that this method of treatment would be acceptable to the patient. Furthermore, treatment would be acceptable because it did not dismiss everything that patients did as pathological but communicated to them that they were coping with unusual and often frightening experiences in a normal way. (It is interesting to note the similarities of this rationale to that used by Kingdon and Turkington, which they term 'normalising rationale'.) The frequent experience of symptoms and the existence of a coping repertoire would also provide ample opportunity for *in vivo* practice of the enhanced coping skills.

So, from observations of the propensity of patients to establish their own methods of coping, a treatment method termed 'coping-strategy enhancement' (CSE) was produced and developed. This treatment approach was first reported as a number of case studies (Tarrier *et al*, 1990). Many of the coping skills that were taught to patients originated from their own established repertoires, but they were also drawn from techniques that had been reported in the literature on psychological treatments, such as self-management and self-instruction. Three characteristics tended to distinguish CSE from other approaches:

(a) there was an attempt to build upon established coping repertoires, hence using the patient's assets and strengths;
(b) *in vivo* practice of coping skills was encouraged;
(c) training in coping was not restricted to the application of a single technique but consisted of an array or combination of individual coping strategies.

The actual procedures of CSE have been summarised elsewhere (Tarrier, 1992; Barrowclough & Tarrier, 1992) and a training manual is currently being produced.

Clinical example

A clinical example will help to understand the CSE approach and how it can be applied in clinical practice.

> A 62-year-old woman, who was widowed and lived alone, with a 30-year history of schizophrenia suffered persistent hallucinations. The voices she heard were abusive, usually in the third person and the content was frequently of a blasphemous and obscene nature. This was very distressing to her as she had strongly held religious beliefs and she was a regular churchgoer. She also experienced delusions of reference and believed that other people could read her mind and that her thoughts were broadcast out loud so that others could hear. She had a fairly restricted life but she was able to attend church regularly on a Sunday and a church social group twice a week. Usually she felt relaxed and cheerful when she attended church and she rarely experienced psychotic symptoms while she was there. She was able to go shopping at the local shops and her neighbours were very caring and helpful. She coped with her voices at home by drowning them out with the vacuum cleaner. She tried to avoid going out as much as possible, other than to the church, and when she did go out she hurried as quickly as she could and avoided social contact with people.
>
> She was initially taught to improve her coping with the hallucinations that she experienced at home. These appeared to be worse in the morning and decreased in intensity and the distress they caused in the afternoon and evening. Because she used the vacuum cleaner to mask the voices she was spending an inordinate amount of time cleaning the house. She was first taught to be aware of the onset of the voices and to reattribute the cause to illness rather than reality. She found the content of the voices very distressing and appraised them as being truthful. This resulted in a cascade of negative thoughts about herself on the basis that if what the voices said was true she must be a very bad person. Thus, she was asked to generate reasons why the accusations of the voices were inaccurate and how their content was at odds with an objective evaluation of her worth as a person. She was also taught a quick method of relaxation, which she used if the distress resulting from the experience of the hallucinations became excessive. To do this she was trained to become aware of her own emotional reactions to the hallucinations and how to control them. As an alternative to using the noise of the vacuum cleaner to mask the hallucinations it was suggested that she use the radio. This also served the function of allowing her to choose radio programmes that she wished to listen to and using these to distract her thoughts from the voices and the negative cognitions that accompanied them. These strategies, systematically taught and applied, resulted in a decrease in the intensity of the hallucinations and a considerable decrease in the associated distress and preoccupation.
>
> However, she then experienced hallucinations while attending church. The voices were particularly unpleasant in their nature and she was convinced that her friends and fellow churchgoers would also

have heard them and think that it was her saying these terrible things. She became acutely upset and left the church quickly. Over the next few days she ruminated over what she thought had happened and she concluded that she could never return to church because her friends, horrified by what she had said, would be sure to reject her. This belief was confirmed when, out shopping, she saw one of her friends, who completely ignored her. This was a very important issue because the majority of her social activity and reinforcement came from her church activities and to lose these would have a very large impact on her life.

Her beliefs that her friends had heard the voices, thought it was her speaking and had been disgusted with her were then examined. By going back over the incident it appeared that there was little objective evidence that anyone had actually reacted to the voices. On further questioning about the incident when her friend ignored her it appeared that the friend was travelling in a car that quickly passed down the main street. Alternative explanations for why the friend did not acknowledge her, such as she had been unable to see her while driving, were then generated and the strength in her original belief weakened. However, she still believed that her friends at church would reject her because they had heard the voices. Two alternative explanations with their consequences were then outlined: first, that she was correct, that her friends had heard the obscene and blasphemous voices, thought it was her and were disgusted with her, and hence if she returned to church they would reject her; second, that the hallucinations were part of her disorder, they were unpleasant but private experiences and her friends could not possibly share them, and hence if she returned to church her friends would not reject her. With considerable persuasion she agreed to put these two explanations to the test. She was anxious about returning to church but with further preparation using the anxiety management methods she had been taught earlier she managed to do so. To her surprise her friends welcomed her back with concern that she had been absent for the last few weeks. The strength of her delusional belief and her distress markedly diminished. Interestingly, on being questioned some months later her original belief about what had happened had returned but it caused her no distress nor was she preoccupied by it. She rationalised that her friends had heard her voices, but as they did not seem to be bothered by the event then neither was she.

The above example demonstrates the importance of a comprehensive assessment and case formulation of a patient's psychotic experience and how this is used to direct the intervention. A range of coping methods are used, with an attempt to build these together in stages through systematic practice and training to produce a comprehensive strategy for assisting the patient to cope well with a range of difficulties. It should be noted that a range of coping techniques were used, varying in sophistication from simple distraction followed by arousal-reducing methods to more complex reality-testing tactics. Patients may differ in their ability to use the more complex methods, but it is wrong to underestimate any patient's capabilities.

Evaluation: the Salford Symptom Project

A controlled trial of CSE was carried out to evaluate its efficacy (Tarrier *et al*, 1993*a*). Outcome measures used in the evaluation included target psychotic symptoms, general psychopathology, social functioning and patient satisfaction and perceived benefit. Patients were recruited into the study if they had a diagnosis of schizophrenia, were still experiencing symptoms that were not responding further to medication over the last six months, were on stable medication, were living in the community, and were between the ages of 18 and 65. Patients were randomly allocated into either CSE or an alternative psychological treatment, problem-solving. It was hypothesised that CSE would result in a significant improvement of both psychotic symptoms and general psychopathology, and that improvements in social functioning would then follow. Therefore, CSE would have a significant effect on all outcome measures. Problem-solving was regarded as an effective general psychological treatment, but because it was not focused on psychotic symptoms it was predicted that no significant improvements in hallucinations and delusions and general psychopathology would result. However, an improvement in social functioning was predicted as general problem-solving skills would be acquired and utilised.

Both treatments were of relatively short duration, consisting of ten treatment sessions over five weeks. Treatment was carried out by four experienced clinical psychologists so that any effects of individual therapists would be controlled for. Half the patients recruited into the study were allocated to a waiting period group of five weeks, to act as a no-treatment control before entering treatment. Half the patients in each treatment group were allocated consecutively to a high-expectancy group and the other half to a low-expectancy group. This was to control for the non-specific effect of the patient expecting to benefit from treatment. In the high-expectancy group patients were told that they should expect to benefit from treatment and that that benefit would become increasingly obvious as treatment progressed. The low-expectancy group received counter-expectancy instructions, in that they were told that they should expect to benefit from treatment but that the benefits would take time to accrue and would not be apparent until after the end of treatment. Hence the expectation of the timing of change and perceived benefit was manipulated.

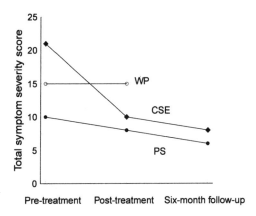

Fig. 9.1. The Salford Symptom Project: changes in positive symptoms. WP, waiting period; PS, problem-solving (n=12); CSE, coping skills enhancement (n=15).

Seventy-five patients from Salford Health Authority were screened as possibly suitable for recruitment to the trial. Of these, 49 met the entry criteria. Most of those excluded were so because of diagnostic ambiguity. A further ten patients dropped out without concluding the initial assessment. Thus 39 were recruited into the study but a further 12 dropped out before receiving treatment. Twenty-seven entered the trial and completed treatment to post-treatment assessment, and 23 were assessed at six-month follow-up. The first point of note is the high attrition rate: of the 49 who satisfied the entry criteria, only 27 (55%) completed treatment. But these figures are not dissimilar to those reported in some family intervention trials (Tarrier, 1991) and for poor medication compliance (Buchanan, 1992).

The results of the trial indicated that patients in both treatment groups showed a significant decrease in the number and severity of positive psychotic symptoms over treatment. Benefit was maintained at six-month follow-up. No change was shown in the waiting period subjects (Fig. 9.1). There was some evidence, although it was equivocal because of a pre-treatment difference, that patients who received CSE improved more over treatment than those who received problem-solving. Further analysis indicated that overall improvement was significant for delusions and anxiety, but that CSE showed a significant superiority over problem-solving for improvements of delusions, and a trend for such in anxiety. There were no significant improvements in negative symptoms or social functioning. The manipulation of expectancy did not contribute to the treatment effects and the subjects' perceived benefits of treatment were high but were not different between the two treatment groups.

Because of the importance of distinguishing between statistical significance and clinical significance, an attempt was made to compare the two treatments on the latter. Although the literature does refer to the importance of making this discrimination, there is little consensus as to what constitutes clinical significance and none as to what would constitute a clinically significant improvement in patients suffering from schizophrenia, for whom a 'return to normality' would not be a viable treatment goal. A reduction of positive psychotic symptoms of 50% or more was selected as a clinically meaningful change. A similar criterion has been suggested for agoraphobia (Jansson & Ost, 1982). Moreover, since patients in the trial had not shown symptom reduction in at least six months, this criterion seemed reasonable. After treatment, 9 out of 15 (60%) CSE patients achieved this criterion compared with 3 out of 12 (25%) patients receiving problem-solving, a difference that closely approached significance. Therefore it can be concluded that large improvements in positive symptoms were achieved in a sizeable group of patients (44%), especially those receiving CSE.

The prediction that CSE would result in a significant decrease in positive psychotic symptoms was upheld; surprisingly, a similar effect, although of lesser magnitude, was also found in the patients who received problem-solving. A significant decrease in anxiety was also found in both groups. Neither group showed significant improvements in depression or negative symptoms, although one patient who was free of positive symptoms at follow-up reported an increase in depression. When asked further about the reason for his depression he indicated that he had experienced a sense of loss now that he was symptom-free. Although this was only an anecdotal report, it was unexpected. Disappointingly, and contrary to predictions, neither group showed any improvement in social functioning; in fact, social functioning was remarkably consistent over time.

Changes in coping and problem-solving

To examine whether changes in specific skills, either coping or problem-solving, were specific to a particular treatment, the coping and problem-solving skills of the patients before and after treatment were assessed by an independent rater who was blind to the treatment group and time of assessment. Skills were rated from transcripts of the ACI and responses to hypothetical problem situations (Tarrier *et al*, 1993*b*). The CSE group showed significant increases in the use of coping skills and in their effectiveness, whereas patients who

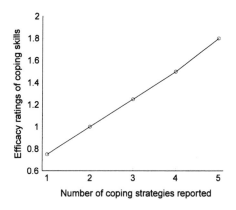

Fig. 9.2. Relationship between the number and efficacy of coping skills.

received problem-solving showed a reduction in both these measures over treatment. Both groups showed significant improvements in problem-solving skills. Changes in coping but not problem-solving were significantly related to decreases in psychotic symptoms over treatment. There were no significant correlations between any measures of coping and problem-solving before, during or after treatment. From these results it was concluded that treatment involving the teaching of coping skills had a specific treatment effect. However, the results indicated that this was not the case with problem-solving, since there was no relationship between the acquisition of problem-solving skills and improvement in psychotic symptoms. Yet the problem-solving group did show significant improvements in psychotic symptoms. How is this to be explained? It is unlikely that this is due to a decay over time, since the waiting-period patients showed no such change. Possibly these changes resulted from the non-specific supportive nature of the therapeutic interaction.

The finding reported earlier (Tarrier, 1987) that the effectiveness of coping was related to the use of multiple strategies was confirmed, as the efficacy of each coping strategy increased with an increase in the number of strategies used (Fig. 9.2).

The Manchester Symptom Project

A second project was planned to address some of the issues raised by the first project. This project, funded by the Wellcome Trust, is currently in progress. Specifically, it aimed to address the following issues.

(a) There had been an independent assessment of outcome in the first study but the evaluator had not been blind to the treatment received by the patient. Therefore to counter any possible bias it was necessary to have independent and blind rating of outcome.

(b) Since the first study indicated that both training in coping skills and problem-solving skills had a therapeutic effect, would the combination of these two interventions increase therapeutic power?

(c) Since the initial project failed to demonstrate any effect of treatment on the patients' level of social functioning, would it be possible to demonstrate improvements in social functioning if the problem-solving component was more directly focused on this aim?

(d) Would the addition of a relapse-prevention component, which taught patients to identify early signs of relapse and use coping skills to try to abort that relapse, ensure the generalisation of treatment benefits over time and decrease the rate of relapse?

(e) Since the treatment used in the first trial had been relatively short, only ten sessions over five weeks, would a longer treatment that included booster sessions increase therapeutic power?

(f) Since the supportive elements of therapy may be contributing to the treatment effect, would it be possible to demonstrate the superiority of a cognitive–behavioural intervention over an intervention of the same duration that consisted of supportive psychotherapy?

(g) The previous project had a follow-up of only six months, which is a very short period over which to demonstrate the enduring effects of a new therapy. Would it be possible to establish the benefits, if any, of this cognitive–behavioural therapy over a follow-up period of 12 and 24 months?

(h) The study also aimed to investigate predictors of treatment response, the reasons for patients dropping out of treatment, and various clinical observations such as the feelings of loss reported by some patients after the reduction of some of the symptoms.

To address these questions a treatment programme was developed that consisted of three components: coping skills, problem-solving and relapse prevention, each consisting of six hourly sessions. These 18 sessions were then followed by two summary sessions. The complete programme took place over three months. This was followed by four booster sessions, one a month, so that the complete therapeutic envelope was of 24 sessions over seven months. This cognitive–behavioural programme was compared with a 24-session programme of supportive psychotherapy, which followed a similar structure. A third comparison group, of routine care, was also included. Patients were assessed on a range of outcome measures before treatment, at the completion of treatment, and 12 and 24 months after the completion of treatment.

This treatment trial is also aimed at patients experiencing residual positive psychotic symptoms that do not respond further to medication. To be included patients must have residual symptoms and to have been on stable medication for at least six months.

There have also been changes in the therapeutic approach. The Salford study was developed directly from a behavioural tradition that merged self-management methods with naturally occurring coping skills to result in a coping-skills training programme. Theoretically this aimed at setting up new stimulus–response chains so as to decrease the probability of specific antecedents and consequences maintaining positive symptoms. We have been influenced by the development of cognitive approaches by colleagues in other centres, as mentioned earlier in the chapter, by our own clinical experience, and by the general drift to a more cognitive bias in cognitive–behavioural therapy. The coping-skills component of the treatment programme has developed to reflect this shift. This has resulted in a greater emphasis on the interpretation by patients of their experiences and how this underpins the experience itself and their emotional reactions. This still exists within the framework of behaviour analysis but represents a change of focus in practice – towards challenging interpretations and reality testing through behavioural experiments – rather than any major theoretical change.

By June 1995, 80 patients had satisfied the entry requirements of the project and 34 had completed treatment. Of those who had completed the post-treatment assessments, 15 had been allocated to routine care, 6 to supportive psychotherapy and 13 to cognitive-behavioural therapy. The results for these 34 patients are presented here to give an indication of the progress of the study. It must be emphasised that these results are only tentative and may not be representative of the final results of the trial. Because of this, these data have not been subjected to statistical analysis and are presented solely for visual inspection. Figure 9.3 shows the change in scores for the severity of positive psychotic symptoms as measured by aggregating the score of the appropriate subscale of the Brief Psychiatric Rating Scale (Lukoff *et al*, 1986) for each hallucination and delusion experienced by the patient into a single score. As can be seen, the patients who received routine care show little change

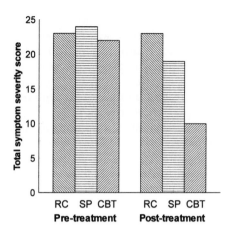

Fig. 9.3. Changes in positive symptoms (RC, routine care; SP, supportive psychotherapy; CBT, cognitive–behaviour therapy).

over seven months. This is as would have been expected, since to enter the trial the patient's symptoms had to be stable. The patients receiving supportive psychotherapy show some improvement but less than those receiving cognitive–behaviour therapy.

Figure 9.4 presents improvement in social functioning as measured by the Social Functioning Scale (Birchwood *et al*, 1990). As can be seen, the changes are in the predicted direction, with routine care resulting in a slight deterioration of social functioning, and patients

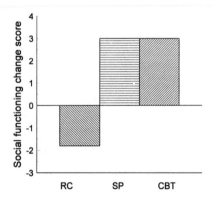

Fig. 9.4. Changes in social functioning (RC, routine care; SP, supportive psychotherapy; CBT, cognitive–behaviour therapy).

receiving cognitive–behaviour therapy and supportive psychotherapy showing improvements.

Although these results are early and incomplete, they do demonstrate an encouraging trend indicating that the extended cognitive-behavioural programme improves both symptoms and social functioning. If these results are confirmed at the end of the study and replicated by other studies currently under way, then the new cognitive–behavioural treatments will represent a major advance in the management of schizophrenia, with the very real possibility of compensating for the inadequacies of pharmacological treatments and attacking the social disabilities resulting from the disorder.

Acknowledgements

The Salford Symptom Project was funded by the NWRHA (grant no. 5107), and the Manchester Symptom Project is funded by the Wellcome Trust (grant no. 036740/1.5).

References

ALFORD G. S. & TURNER, S. M. (1976) Stimulus interference and conditioned inhibition of auditory hallucinations. *Journal of Behavior Therapy and Experimental Psychiatry*, **7**, 637–644.

——, FLEECE, L. & ROTHBLUM, E. (1982) Hallucinatory–delusional verbalisations: modification in a chronic schizophrenic by self-control and cognitive restructuring. *Behavior Modification*, **6**, 421–435.

ANDERSON, L. T. & ALPERT, M. (1974) Operant analysis of hallucinatory frequency in a hospitalised schizophrenic. *Journal of Behavior Therapy and Experimental Psychiatry*, **5**, 13–18.

AYLLON, T. & HAUGHTON, E. (1964) Modification of symptomatic verbal behavior of mental patients. *Behaviour Research and Therapy*, **2**, 87–97.

BARROWCLOUGH, C. & TARRIER, N. (1992) *Families of Schizophrenic Patients: Cognitive Behavioural Interventions*. London: Chapman & Hall.

BECK, A. T. (1952) Successful outpatient psychotherapy of a chronic schizophrenic with a delusion based on borrowed guilt. *Psychiatry*, **15**, 305–312.

BELCHER, T. L. (1988) Behavioural reduction of overt hallucinatory behaviour in chronic schizophrenics. *Journal of Behavior Therapy and Experimental Psychiatry*, **19**, 69–71.

BENTALL, R. P., HADDOCK, G. & SLADE, P. D. (1994) Cognitive behavior therapy for persistent auditory hallucinations: from theory to therapy. *Behavior Therapy*, **25**, 51–66.

BIRCHWOOD, M., SMITH, J., COCHRANE, R., *et al* (1990) The social functioning scale: the development and validation of a scale of social adjustment for use in family intervention programmes with schizophrenic patients. *British Journal of Psychiatry*, **157**, 853–859.

BREIER, A. & STRAUSS, J. S. (1983) Self-control in psychotic disorders. *Archives of General Psychiatry*, **40**, 1141–1145.

BUCHANAN, A. (1992) A two-year prospective study of treatment compliance in patients with schizophrenia. *Psychological Medicine*, **22**, 787–797.

BUCHER, B. & FABRICATORE, J. (1970) Use of patient administered shock to suppress hallucinations. *Behavior Therapy*, **1**, 382–385

146   Tarrier et al

Bulow, H., Oei, T. P. S. & Pinkey, B. (1979) Effects of contingent social reinforcement with delusional chronic schizophrenic men. *Psychological Reports*, **44**, 659–666.

Carr, V. (1988) Patients' techniques for coping with schizophrenia: an explanatory study. *British Journal of Medical Psychology*, **61**, 339–352.

Chadwick, P. & Birchwood, M. (1994) The omnipotence of voices: a cognitive approach to auditory hallucinations. *British Journal of Psychiatry*, **164**, 190–201.

Cohen, C. I. & Berk, B. S. (1985) Personal coping styles of schizophrenic out-patients. *Hospital and Community Psychiatry*, **36**, 407–410.

Curson, D. A., Barnes, T. R. E., Bamber, R. W., *et al* (1985) Long term depot maintenance of chronic schizophrenic out-patients. *British Journal of Psychiatry*, **146**, 464–480.

——, Patel, M., Liddle, P. F., *et al* (1988) Psychiatric morbidity of a long stay hospital population with chronic schizophrenia and implications for future community care. *British Medical Journal*, **297**, 819–822.

Davis, J. R., Wallace, C. J., Liberman, R. P., *et al* (1976) The use of brief isolation to suppress delusional and hallucinatory speech. *Journal of Behavior Therapy and Experimental Psychiatry*, **7**, 269–275.

Drury, V. (1994) Recovery from acute psychosis. In *Psychological Management of Schizophrenia* (eds M. Birchwood & N. Tarrier), pp. 23–52. Chichester: Wiley.

Falloon, I. R. H., Watt, D. C. & Shepherd, M. (1978) A comparative controlled trial of pimozide and fluphenazine decanoate in the continuation therapy of schizophrenia. *Psychological Medicine*, **7**, 59–70.

—— & Talbot, R. E. (1981) Persistent auditory hallucinations: coping mechanisms and implications for management. *Psychological Medicine*, **11**, 329–339.

Fonagy, P. & Slade, P. D. (1982) Punishment vs negative reinforcement in the aversive conditioning of auditory hallucinations. *Behaviour Research and Therapy*, **20**, 267–282.

Garety, P. A., Kuipers, L., Fowler, D., *et al* (1994) Cognitive behavioural therapy for drug-resistant psychosis. *British Journal of Medical Psychology*, **67**, 259–271.

Gresen, R. (1974) The effects of instruction and reinforcement on a multifaceted self-control procedure in the modification and generalisation of behavior in schizophrenia. Unpublished PhD thesis, Bowling Green University.

Gunderson, J. G., Frank, A. F., Katz, H. M., *et al* (1984) Effects of psychotherapy in schizophrenia: II. Comparative outcome of two forms of treatment. *Schizophrenia Bulletin*, **10**, 564–598.

Harrow, M. & Silverstein, M. L. (1977) Psychotic symptoms in schizophrenia after the acute phase. *Schizophrenia Bulletin*, **3**, 608–616.

Hartman, L. M. & Cashman, F. E. (1983) Cognitive–behavioural and psychopharmacological treatment of delusional symptoms: a preliminary report. *Behavioural Psychotherapy*, **11**, 50–61.

Hogarty, G. E., Schooler, N. R., Ulrich, R. F., *et al* (1979) Fluphenazine and social therapy in the aftercare of schizophrenic patients. *Archives of General Psychiatry*, **36**, 1283–1294.

Hole, R. W., Rush, A. J. & Beck, A. T. (1979) A cognitive investigation of schizophrenic delusions. *Psychiatry*, **42**, 312–319.

Jansson, L. & Ost, L.-G. (1982) Behavioural treatment for agoraphobia: an evaluation review. *Clinical Psychology Review*, **2**, 311–336.

Kingdon, D. G. & Turkington, D. (1994) *Cognitive–Behavioral Therapy of Schizophrenia*. Hove: Lawrence Erlbaum.

Liberman, R. P., Teigan, J., Patterson, R., *et al* (1973) Reducing delusional speech in chronic paranoid schizophrenics. *Journal of Applied Behavior Analysis*, **6**, 57–64.

Lukoff, D., Nuechterlein, K. H. & Ventura, J. (1986) Manual for the expanded Brief Psychiatric Rating Scale (BPRS). *Schizophrenia Bulletin*, **12**, 594–602.

Margolis, R. & Shemberg, K. (1976) Use of self-instruction for the elimination of psychotic speech. *Behavior Therapy*, **7**, 668–671.

MAY, P. R. A. (1968) *Treatment of Schizophrenia: A Comparative Study of Five Treatment Methods.* New York: Science House.

MEICHENBAUM, D. & CAMERON, R. (1973) Training schizophrenics to talk to themselves: a means of developing attentional control. *Behavior Therapy,* **4,** 515–534.

MEYERS, A., MERCATONS, M. & SIROTA, A. (1976) Use of self-instruction for the elimination of psychotic speech. *Journal of Clinical and Consulting Psychology,* **44,** 480–482.

MILTON, F., PATWA, V. K. & HAFNER, J. (1978) Confrontation vs belief modification in persistently deluded patients. *British Journal of Medical Psychology,* **51,** 127–130.

MOSHER, L. R. & KEITH, S. J. (1979) Research on the psychosocial treatment of schizophrenia: a summary report. *American Journal of Psychiatry,* **136,** 623–631.

NYDEGGER, R. V. (1972) The elimination of hallucinatory and delusional behaviours by verbal conditioning and assertive training: a case study. *Journal of Behavior Therapy and Experimental Psychiatry,* **3,** 225–227.

SILVERSTEIN, M. L. & HARROW, M. (1978) First rank symptoms in the post acute schizophrenic: a follow up study. *American Journal of Psychiatry,* **135,** 1481–1486.

SLADE, P. D. (1972) The effects of systematic desensitisation on auditory hallucinations. *Behaviour Research and Therapy,* **10,** 85–91.

—— (1973) The psychological investigation and treatment of auditory hallucinations: a second case report. *British Journal of Medical Psychology,* **46,** 293–296.

STANTON, A. H., GUNDERSON, J. G., KNAPP, P. H., *et al* (1984) Effects of psychotherapy in schizophrenia: I. Design and implementation of a controlled study. *Schizophrenia Bulletin,* **10,** 520–563.

TARRIER, N. (1987) An investigation of residual psychotic symptoms in discharged schizophrenic patients. *British Journal of Clinical Psychology,* **26,** 141–143.

—— (1991) Some aspects of family interventions in schizophrenia. I: Adherence to intervention programmes. *British Journal of Psychiatry,* **159,** 475–480.

—— (1992) Management and modification of residual positive symptoms. In *Innovations in the Psychological management of Schizophrenia: Assessment, Treatment and Services* (eds M. Birchwood & N. Tarrier), pp. 147–169. Chichester: Wiley.

——, HARWOOD, S., YUSUPOFF, L., *et al* (1990) Coping Strategy Enhancement (CSE): a method of treating residual schizophrenic symptoms. *Behavioural Psychotherapy,* **18,** 283–294.

——, BECKETT, R., HARWOOD, S., *et al* (1993*a*) A trial of two cognitive–behavioural methods of treating drug-resistant residual psychotic symptoms in schizophrenia: I. Outcome. *British Journal of Psychiatry,* **162,** 524–532.

——, SHARPE, L., BECKETT, R., *et al* (1993*b*) A trial of two cognitive–behavioural methods of treating drug-resistant residual psychotic symptoms in schizophrenia: II. Treatment-specific changes in coping and problem solving skills. *Social Psychiatry and Psychiatric Epidemiology,* **28,** 5–10.

TURNER, S., HERSON, M. & BELLACK, A. (1977) Effects of social disruption, stimulus interference and aversive conditioning on auditory hallucinations. *Behavior Modification,* **1,** 249–258.

WATTS, F. N., POWELL, G. E. & AUSTIN, S. V. (1973) The modification of abnormal beliefs. *British Journal of Medical Psychology,* **46,** 359–363.

Part III. Systemic and family therapies

Systemic approaches are difficult to define and differentiate from other therapeutic models. In his review of the field, Chris Evans (Chapter 10) defines some essential elements at its conclusion rather than at the outset, emphasising the necessity of an extended network of people, an insistence on the communicative content of all behaviour, and the importance of understanding this in a culturally informed way.

Conceptually, systemic approaches subsume all other models and stand 'meta' to them, offering a critique and commentary. Sometimes this critique draws on post-modernist ideas and deconstructs its own text, leaving unprepared readers, who expect a linear account of 'what is known', puzzled and disoriented. By its very nature, this approach to systems is difficult to express in terms of outcome research.

Evans' overview, which was commissioned for this volume to extend the systemic content, presents the approach as more than the application of other models in family or milieu settings. It is more than the application of systems theory to the understanding of severe mental disorder. Evans presents the reader with a dilemma; his opening caveat about not being expert in the field, by analogy with Bion (!), takes the reader by surprise. However, the next sections of this chapter deal with an important conceptual issue that is relevant to all the contributions. He describes how to dissect the levels of inference in a text, a process that he implicitly invites the reader to apply to Evans' own work.

Systemic approaches rely very heavily on the detection and 'use-in-practice' of boundaries, whether these are boundaries within the self, interpersonally, or within a family structure. Evans reviews the boundaries and definitions stated in psychiatric nosology and challenges the logical basis for some of its distinctions. In reviewing

149

the history of the concepts, he draws attention to some of the underlying themes in the conference. Should therapy be 'solution focused'? If so, how are the problem definitions of policy-makers, and indeed the family and carers, to be reconciled with the problems defined by the subject? The techniques of family systemic therapy, such as circular questioning, help to make explicit the basis upon which the problems are defined and agreed.

In practical terms, systemic analysis of the role of case managers is needed to make sense of the recurrent tension between resource allocation, public fears about safety and containment, the needs of the carer, and the rights of individual subjects to articulate their own priorities. The resolution of these tensions is sometimes seen as an issue to be pragmatically resolved by empirical research based on optimal outcomes. However, the systemic approach makes clear the inherent differences of position taken up by the various players. Analysis of the power relations inherent in psychiatric care is intrinsic to a systemic approach.

Systemic thinking is often allied with family approaches to psychotherapy, although the systemic approach within family therapy is by no means the whole of it. Many other strategies are possible that pay attention to wider human networks without sharing the systemicists' attitudes to communication. Evans explains how the systemicist would inevitably see these as based on a lower inferential level. As examples of such alternative approaches, Chapter 11 describes the Cassel approach to treatment of the whole family, and Chapter 12 a behavioural family approach to schizophrenia.

It could be argued that they would be equally at home conceptually in the previous two sections of this book, but it is evident from seeing them here how the latter especially has a distinct empirical basis that allows for organised observation and the testing of hypotheses. A clash similar to that between the 'nomothetic' and the 'idiographic' forms of explanation favoured respectively by Enlightenment and Romantic philosophies threatens to surface here. The difference between 'knowing' and 'knowing about' in the context of family therapy is acknowledged by Evans in his discussion of high- and low-level inference, respectively. As he points out, the assumptions made about the level of inference are crucial to developing an appropriate scientific method for evaluating treatments. He discusses the development of the highly influential, empirically founded system of work on 'high expressed emotion' in this light.

However, a further difficulty in the systemic literature concerns the extent to which purer systemic models are an approach to thinking about our models of illness, rather than the basis for treatment interventions. Evans reviews some promising routes by which systemic thinking may yet become more grounded in therapeutic practice, but their success remains to be seen.

10 Family and systemic approaches to psychosis: an overview

CHRIS EVANS

Introduction and personal experience: the empathic capacity

W. R. Bion describes how he explained to members of his early groups at the Tavistock Clinic his puzzlement that they, and the Professional Committee of the Clinic, appeared to think he knew how to run groups (Bion, 1961). In the same spirit, I must inform the reader of the gap between my qualifications and the faith the editors appear to have in me. I am not a qualified family/systemic therapist; I do not fulfil professional criteria for the label 'psychotic' (although I use, or think I use, two variants of such criteria when thinking and talking of others); finally, I did not attend the conference that stimulated this book. I suspect this disclaimer will irritate many, perhaps the editors themselves. However, I will hope that some readers will persevere and finish the chapter.

Bion wrote about "the differentiation of the psychotic from the non-psychotic personalities" (Bion, 1957) and he suggested that the distinction turned on "attacks on linking" (Bion, 1959). By this he meant attacks within the mind on links between "internal objects", that is, between images of others, parts of others, the self or parts of the self. I believe the systemic corollary of this is destruction of communication between people, specifically the destruction of the capacity to use empathic resonance as a mode of communication. Bion's remarkable insight into psychosis may have come from the extent to which his written, and I suspect his speaking, style can seem to attack conventional conversational patterns or linkages. This is beautifully clear in both his professional and personal writing. I have tried to create a very brief sense of this in these paragraphs so far. I start in this provocative way partly because most of us who have not been diagnosably psychotic have only two ways to experience this condition: the first when dreaming, particularly in a nightmare; the second when we find ourselves in an environment that destabilises our sense of what is 'real'. Like Kafka, Bion conveys some of this feeling. Some may argue that these 'normal' experiences are far removed from the experiences of people diagnosed as psychotic and may ask why I do not simply reference personal accounts of the experience of psychosis (*Lancet*, 1983; *British Medical Journal*, 1990; *British Medical Association News Review*, 1994; Chadwick, 1995). The answer is that to read others' accounts of their own experiences is not to experience something like it oneself, whereas to experience something related to their experience and to put it with their description is to move much further forward; this touches on the quintessentially human ability to empathise: to grasp intuitively the privacy and intentionality of the minds of others.

The issue of damaged or altered communication has already been mentioned; this author sides with Bion in regarding the systemic nature of psychosis as a particular set of alterations of interpersonal communication by attacks on generally accepted frameworks of meaning. These are brought about both by "attacks on linking" within the mind of the individual, and in the amplification of these attacks in the external world of relationships. This amplification of disturbance involves the communication between the individual and others, and, crucially, their response. The resonant nature of these interpersonal disturbances is an essential component of systemic thinking about psychosis. To have to strain to understand the thinking of the other is central to the experience of being with someone 'psychotic'. To respond to this strain by considering the communication meaningless or simply an epiphenomenon, a reflection of disordered neurology or biology, is to offer no personal route out of psychosis.

Case example 1

The index patient in the family was in his mid-20s. He had withdrawn from social settings since his mid-teens, having never been gregarious. He had not completed his college course and for the last three years had not left his room. He was brought to the hospital compulsorily after his parents and general practitioner requested a domiciliary visit from a consultant psychiatrist, who diagnosed schizophrenia on the basis of third-person auditory hallucinations, thought broadcasting and insertion, and paranoid delusional ideation. The family consisted of working-class parents, both in full-time manual jobs, an older sister who had married and left the family home, and two younger brothers still at home and both sociable and successful. Relations between the caring but exhausted and distressed family and staff deteriorated almost immediately as the patient developed very marked side-effects in response to neuroleptic medication, including drooling, an acute dystonia (easily cured by anticholinergics), Parkinsonian symptoms (not touched by the same medication), and then the appearance of a variant of the neuroleptic malignant syndrome (a life-threatening complication of antipsychotic medication) that necessitated medical treatment for some weeks. Nevertheless, given the previous improvement in the acute psychotic phenomena, and with the support of the general physicians, the neuroleptics were gradually reinstated as the patient's psychiatric state deteriorated. In desperation at the escalating staff–family battles, the family were referred for 'family therapy'. The parents and older sister attended reluctantly at the first session to meet their 'family therapists', who were, in fact, the social worker, psychologist and junior doctor from the general psychiatric team, none with any formal qualification in family therapy. We spent time listening to the distress of the three who attended the session and spent as much time explaining the medication, the side-effects and the absence of clear guidance available in the psychiatric literature. There were four more sessions after this, during which all the family except the patient attended at least three times. Together family and 'therapists' worked on reducing the family's expectations of the patient and countering their frequent attempts to place him in a state of cossetted invalidism. The final aim was to reduce their critical attacks on his laziness. Interestingly, this was done in response to the clinical situation, rather than as a planned response based on the literature on high levels of critical expressed emotion (see below).

There was a very marked change in the family atmosphere, the rest of the psychiatric team became able to deal with the patient and family amicably and creatively again, and the patient improved markedly and accepted a small dose of continuing medication, requiring only that the rationale was linked with his 'neurological vulnerability' shown by his neuroleptic malignant syndrome rather than with a psychiatric diagnosis. All did well for the next five years, contrary to initial prognostications.

Case example 2

The family, consisting of the index patient, aged 30, parents in their 60s, and an older sister, married and living away, were referred to a family therapy unit by a consultant psychiatrist after her domiciliary visit, requested by the general practitioner and parents. The patient had deteriorated markedly since the age of about 20, when he was falsely accused by the police of hooliganism with some black friends. The parents were from different East European countries, separate immigrants to Britain during the Second World War. The mother was Jewish, the father not, and they did not share a common language other than English, which both had learned since their immigration in their late teens. Their marriage had been opposed by both families and, although there had been some continuing contact with the extended family, meetings were fraught with tension, just as the parents' own marriage had always been. In contrast to his academically successful but nervous sister, the son had been gregarious and underachieving though clearly very able at school. As in the first example, he had dropped out of college and withdrawn to his room. He denied any acute psychotic symptoms, although acknowledged that he was extremely moody. However, his parents had concluded that his intermittent odd behaviour and conversation were only explicable on the basis that he was responding to auditory hallucinations. The psychiatrist thought that the patient was probably developing schizophrenia but was clear that there were no grounds for compulsory treatment. The psychiatrist noted the family's wish to change the situation, even though expressed oddly. The family therapy team consisted of trained and training members from a variety of mental health disciplines. One therapist conducted an initial session with the four family members, explaining the presence of a team behind the mirror and the possible advantages of using videotape. The two children talked about the strains of their ethnicity and religious background and of the parents' continual rows. The parents denied that the social stresses on them had been severe, pointing out that they were entirely normal given their backgrounds and explained, in bafflement, that the rows were markers of their affection and respect for each other and the guts that had enabled them to do well and love each other as they always had.

The team swapped places with the family (therapist going behind the screen with the family too) and talked about their different alignments with different members of the family. Great attention was given to the different sorts of courage shown, or perhaps the different fears that each was confronting, in coming to the clinic to see if anything could be done. Some members of the team noted their own childhood terror of parental rows; others picked up the difficulties they had experienced as parents dealing with the immense differences that can separate generations in ways of dealing with the world. Oddities in the son's behaviour, including sudden concern with the state of the window catches, were linked with his possible concern that opening the lid on all these things within a family can feel potentially explosive and uncontainable. This in turn was linked with hints of concern in the parents' conversation that suggested they might share some of the children's anxiety despite their overall air of confidence. These therapeutic themes continued for a year, during which the son made dramatic changes in his interactions with his parents, started a training course and tentatively attached himself to a country music group. There have been no further hints of hallucinations since the first session. The parents have softened their rows and much of the envy and jealousy between the children has disappeared. The family have agreed that they will come back to the clinic if they feel that there is a need in the future, but have not been in contact for over a year.

Diagnostic classification, labelling and the systemic perspective: 'levels of abstraction'

These vignettes raise a question that runs through systemic writing on psychosis: the question of 'level of inference'. The 'low level of inference' is based on the observation of behaviours that are thought to be common to patients described as 'psychotic'. The 'high level of inference', in contrast, suggests that interventions should be based on the assumed meaning of the behaviour within the mind of the patient. This level of inference will be based largely on our own personal experience and the way we harness this to understand the experience of the patient and the communication between us.

Clinicians and researchers subscribing to the low-level viewpoint do not argue that the experiences of the psychotic patient are trivial. However, they do not believe that understanding the experiences will be helped by drawing on their own personal experiences. Crucially, they would argue that more can be gained by understanding what is in common than by emphasising the exploration of individuality.

Family systemic therapy based on this view is widely given by non-specialist therapists as exemplified in the first case vignette. Sympathy with, and development of, such work has been the province of those who see systemic therapy as one of a number of therapeutic adjuncts to medication, analogous, for example, to a behavioural approach being added to help with medication-resistant hallucinations.

From this viewpoint the problem resides within the patient, and the diagnosis is an expert task for the clinician, who then prescribes a treatment, which is seen as external to, or applied to, that patient. The 'problem' is not seen as one facet of a complex, multipersonal system that includes the clinician.

The alternative, high-level inference emphasises empathic resonance between patient and therapist. This view, and the therapy based on it, has been widely accepted by psychodynamic psychotherapists since the 1950s, when systematic attention to countertransference began. In this context, countertransference can be seen as the use of high-level inference in the form of empathic resonance to the internal workings of the patient's mind. It is understood that the therapist's resonance to the patient changes the situation. However, such work is not fully systemic in its conceptualisation. The recognition of the interactivity and the dependence of the system on the impact of the observer is confined to the therapeutic dyad, and is not widened to the patient's social and professional system.

Implications for research

These differences in level of inference are not just issues for the clinician – they also affect the entire structure of clinical research. Most psychiatric research has traditionally taken a low-level position, arguing that the independence of researcher and researched is fundamental to the scientific method. Critics of this view have drawn attention to developments in other areas of science that challenge classical experimental design. The paradigms of science are thought to shift in a revolutionary rather than evolutionary way. Within experimental science there has been increasing awareness of the non-linear characteristics of even simple systems and the sensitivity to original conditions shown in chaos theory. For a fuller statement of this argument, making the case for empathic resonance, see Strauss (1994). Systemic models of therapy are based on the assumption that a 'problem' cannot be examined in isolation, but has to be seen as part of an interactive and recursive system. A crucial implication of this is the lack of any neutral position for a non-involved observer.

Definitions, theory so far and the specific application to psychosis

I have used the word 'systemic' instead of ugly combinations of 'family/systemic' in this chapter. However, much of the work described does draw a system boundary around 'the family' rather than around 'the neighbourhood' or 'the clinical team'. Both these alternative boundaries have their advocates, and the 'consultation model' relies heavily on isolating the team as a system requiring therapeutic attention. Work with large-scale networks analogous to a small 'neighbourhood' have been attempted. The choice of the boundary line is arbitrary, or can in some situations be selected for anti-therapeutic reasons, for example in the dismissive use of phrases like 'problem family'. As with the definition of all boundaries, the choice made here to concentrate on reviewing work with 'the family' has costs. In particular, it can push thinking toward a mythic or idealised conception of the family. It is clear that many of the psychological interventions reviewed below, and many of the systemic theories of psychosis, have their focus in 'the family' only for practical reasons.

Readers are invited to consider the arbitrary nature of the chosen boundaries when reading the review in the later part of this chapter, or indeed in the rest of the volume, or in the reader's own workplace.

Reducing the clinical and research isolation of the systemic perspective is a high priority if these ideas are to bear practical fruit. In this chapter, I have started with personal experience because any systemic view must take into account the act of viewing and the standpoints of the viewer. I have then argued that use of the clinician's or researcher's empathy and personal experience leads to methodology based on high-level inference, a method that is intrinsically different from that of conventional empiricism and the disease model. The distinction based on the level of inference will be shown later in the chapter to divide two almost completely separate developments in the systemic treatment of psychosis. I have also noted in passing that the systemic model involves serious attention not only to patient and clinician but also to the patient's and the clinical social systems as potential forces for change or stasis.

These are general principles that can be applied to many non-psychotic states. Is there anything specific to psychosis here? Psychotic experience is seen as so distant from the wider society and so damaging to the sense of self as to be greeted with powerful distancing mechanisms from the clinician. As a result, there is a fear of high-level inference – mapping from self to other and from other to self – when considering psychotic experience. The clinician is also inhibited from understanding how any intervention might actually worsen the situation. The fear of empathic resonance is less in non-psychotic conditions, and so there is often a compromise that the clinician allows contact with the non-psychotic aspects of the patient's experience.

As discussed earlier, the diagnosis of psychosis relies heavily upon the ability of the observing clinician to judge, as though through the eyes of another member of the subculture, whether an individual's beliefs are 'outside the normal range'. This requires at least a triadic, rather than dyadic, perspective, which is often neglected in the operational definitions of psychosis. The distancing and objectifying of psychotic experience can also be seen in the broader social system, for example in the discussion of 'schizo-phrenics' who commit violent crimes, or who are in need of 'containment'. The links between the narrow social system of the family and the broader societal system are important in any systemic approach to treatment, and the management of public systems, for example managing neighbourhood hostility to a new hostel ward, has become an essential part of the armamentarium of the social psychiatrist.

Diagnosis: a summary of the background

Psychosis is a markedly interpersonal, systemic concept, and a highly political one. Like any other diagnosis, or any personal adjective, a label is placed on one person by another which may or may not be helpful and has meaning only by virtue of location of the label, the labeller and the labelled within a social system. Like many psychiatric diagnoses, but unlike certain other labels, it is common to find that supporting criteria are themselves part of a complex social network of definitions.

History I: development of systemic theories (to about 1980)

There is a long history of interest in psychosis from within the systemic therapy schools. This may have arisen because the pioneers often worked with very deprived populations where only severe disorders reached therapists. There is also reason to believe that some therapists had an acute political awareness that to make progress in this area would establish the new systemic therapies far more rapidly than if only neurotic problems were tackled (Haley, 1975, 1986). The groundwork for a lot of systems/family thinking lies in the work of Harry Stack Sullivan (Aaltonen & Rakkolainen, 1994), particularly his interpersonal theory of schizophrenia, in which he argued for three levels, or modes, of experience:

(a) the prototaxic experience, occurring before symbols;
(b) the parataxic experience, characterised by private symbols;
(c) the syntaxic experience, conceptualised by exchangeable symbols likely to be similarly construed by others.

This had links with early semiology, particularly with the work of Charles Peirce, the American physicist and philosopher whose 'pragmatic epistemology' saw knowledge as capable of being evaluated only in terms of its utility (hence pragmatic). He believed that knowledge was built of:

(a) an 'icon' – an image or label;
(b) an 'index' – its connectedness with the individual object;
(c) a 'symbol' – an expectation that it will be interpreted as denoting the object in consequence of habit.

Sullivan suggested that the third level of representation and communication was possible only at his syntaxic level, but that prototaxic and parataxic levels prevail in schizophrenic and psychotic experience.

In Europe the terminology is different, but there are similar concepts to be found in the work of Bion, and also Klein and her followers' discussion of symbol formation (Klein *et al*, 1946; Segal, 1957). Work on the dyadic setting was extended into developments in groups and therapeutic communities. By contrast, the work of Fromm, Horney, Sullivan and many others in the rapidly changing social structures in the US led to even more externally focused theorising and thus to family theorising.

Early work included Bateson and his co-workers' ideas about the double bind: that schizophrenia might be produced by children repeatedly finding themselves on the receiving end of three separate messages. The first and second would contradict each other ("You're a very good baby!" said in tones expressing dislike or even hatred) while the third injunction would say that there is to be no resolution of the first two, that is, their mutual incompatibility was not to be questioned. This precludes the symbolisation and eventual resolution of disparate messages. The form of the injunctions is interesting: the first two injunctions were often reactive to the baby's actions and specific, but one was explicit and verbal ('digital') while the other was implicit and/or non-verbal ('analogical'). Finally, the third was essentially structural and abstract. This work was complemented by Bowen's notion of an "undifferentiated family ego mass" or "pre-existing emotional 'stuck-togetherness'". At about the same time Wynne and Singer were developing the concept of "pseudo-mutuality, pseudo-hostility and the rubber fence" to be found in families with schizophrenic members. Lidz developed the concept of "schism and skew" in the parental marriage (see Hoffman, 1981*a,b*, for a review).

This constellation of ideas culminated in the work of Laing on the 'schizophrenogenic' family and society (Laing, 1959, 1969). Some of these concepts were recast simplistically as the 'schizophrenogenic mother', an aetiological model that has been shown to be conceptually naïve. (The history of these developments is summarised by Hoffman, 1981*a*.)

Most of these theories about family functioning contained ideas about discordance between different levels of communication. These include discrepancies between verbal and other codings of affect and attachment. These theories have fallen into disuse and psychiatric textbooks often imply that empirical work has 'disproved' them. A fairer summary would be that attempts to operationalise the concepts have shown only equivocal differences between families with and without schizophrenic members, and, moreover, any differences that were observed could be plausibly related to the effect on the family of having a schizophrenic member.

The difficulty in researching family theories illustrates a recurrent problem related to levels of inference. Abstract models proffered by systemic theorists are reframed into tight linear, causal forms and subjected to survey research with poor operationalisation of the concepts. The researchers' largely negative findings are logically open to many interpretations as the empirical work was not able to address a causal sequence. The subtlety of the required analysis and interpretation of results tends to be missing in the eventual discussion, and particularly when the work is considered second-hand in a review.

British systemic therapists have not developed formal schools of theory or practice, although psychodynamic family work has been influential (Bennett *et al*, 1976; Skynner, 1976). By contrast, other countries developed schools of thought and schools of therapy. In the US, underpinned by, but apparently rejecting, their psycho-analytical trainings, structural and strategic modes of working were developed by Haley, Minuchin, Fishman, Ackerman, Framo and many others. In Italy, heavily influenced by the theoretical work of Bateson but again underpinned by psychoanalytic trainings, the Milan group (Selvini Palazzoli *et al*, 1978, 1980*a*) developed a particular method. Confusingly this is often labelled the 'systemic school', despite the fact that the strategic and structural groups were also influenced by general systems theory.

The 'three Ss' classification of systemically oriented work (strategic, structural and systemic) turns largely on the use of counterparadox or 'paradoxical injunction' in the strategic and systemic methods but not (overtly) in the structural; and on the deliberate use of therapist power and determination to move families in particular directions (acknowledged by both strategic and structural schools).

All these therapies led to the development of ways of working using teams, to active exploration of difference and change, and to the idea that small changes could produce long-term 'sleeper effects' going far beyond actual changes wrought in sessions. Creative use of 'reflexive questioning' and 'circular questioning' styles are well described in some hybrid strategic/systemic papers by Tomm (1987*a*,*b*, 1988) and Fleuridas *et al* (1986). Although at times major proponents of these developments talked about 'psychosis' or 'schizophrenia', their attitude towards communication and language tended to put these labels into a different philosophical frame from that of psychiatrists. Often they saw these as labels applied by people outside both the family and the family therapy, labels that might need to be subverted as they might seem to define and hence immobilise understandings of the problem (Selvini Palazzoli *et al*, 1980*b*).

History II: from around 1980 to 1995

The low level of inference: the emergence of 'expressed emotion'

Apparently quite independent of the early explosion in theories and practices of systemic therapy was the discovery, or description, of 'expressed emotion' (EE). This term was coined by Brown & Rutter (1966) and has come to describe families characterised by two things: 'emotional overinvolvement' and a high rate of critical comments about an index member (originally a member with schizophrenia; more recently the approach has been extended to a number of other disorders, both psychological and physical). Early work (*inter alia* Brown *et al*, 1972; Vaughn & Leff, 1976*a,b*; Kuipers, 1979; Leff & Vaughn, 1980, 1981) showed very different rates of early relapse in schizophrenic patients returning to high-EE families or in contact with them for at least 35 hours of the week. Later work (*inter alia* Leff *et al*, 1982, 1985; Tarrier *et al*, 1989; Rea *et al*, 1991; Randolph *et al*, 1994) has shown that systemic/family intervention can reduce or postpone relapse. Interventions used in these research studies have varied in philosophy from the psychodynamic to the behavioural, and in method from relatives' groups to direct family work or a combination of both.

More recent work has replicated some of the basic patterns of influence of EE, and even of intervention, across several cultures (e.g. Barrelet *et al*, 1990; Leff *et al*, 1990). Other work has demonstrated clearly that some of these results can be implemented by training routine clinical workers and does not appear to be confined to high-intensity research studies (e.g. Brooker *et al*, 1994) and there is some evidence that this form of intervention is markedly cost-effective (Tarrier *et al*, 1991). This opus is by far the largest contribution to the empirical literature, and has been widely reviewed elsewhere (for example, Kavanagh, 1992).

There are clear expositions of these methods of working (Smith & Birchwood, 1990; Kuipers *et al*, 1992; Leff, 1994). At the same time there is growing acknowledgement that the longer-term follow-up studies suggest that the effect of short-term interventions is definite but may wane with time, perhaps indicating a need for ongoing involvement with families. There is also increasing research evidence about the difficulty of engaging some families (McCreadie *et al*, 1991; Tarrier, 1991). One area of debate that has not been fully resolved in the literature concerns the choice between educating the family in the absence of the index patient or, alternatively, working with the family including the patient. There is both a pragmatic aspect to this question in terms of cost-utility and cost-effectiveness, but also a philosophical issue about the appropriate level at which to intervene. This requires further discussion.

High-level theorising: recent developments in systemic/family therapy

The rather crude 'three Ss' classification of systemic/family therapies has looked increasingly overstretched since about 1980. The Milan group of four split up, with Cecchin and Boscolo leading the development of what is sometimes referred to as 'post-Milan systemic' thinking (Cecchin, 1988; Cecchin *et al*, 1992) in which increasing emphasis is placed on 'neutrality' and less emphasis is placed on the particular steps to counterparadoxes in the family. This neutrality has two elements: firstly, there is likely to be uncertainty and/or disagreement within the family as to where the sympathies of therapist lies, and secondly, apparent disinterest in the direction of change.

Feminist thinkers have launched a welcome assault on naïve renunciation of the concept of power in systemic thinking (e.g. Goldner, 1988; MacKinnon & Miller, 1987) and have started to redefine language and its usages as being profoundly gendered by the time of adolescence (at the latest) in Western cultures (Gilligan *et al*, 1990, 1991; Brown & Gilligan, 1993; Gilligan, 1993).

Another theme has been linkage between family theorising and work on 'attachment' patterns (Byng-Hall, 1991), while other recent work has questioned the culturally restricted construction of independence as a positive attribute (Pedder, 1991; Tamura & Lau, 1992).

There has been a move towards short-term 'solution-focused' therapies (e.g. de Shazer, 1985, 1988; Berg, 1994). This theoretical movement, with its very practical accounts of therapy, moves away from 'problem-focused' work and from 'problem-determined systems' (Anderson & Goolishian, 1986). Others have argued that it is necessary to move further, to avoid focus even on solutions, as that too may restrict freedom for change in families and systems. This latter movement is sometimes known as the 'resource-focused' school of therapy (Ray & Keeney, 1993). The linguistics of therapy and links with post-modern epistemologies have led to models of systemic therapy grounded in narrative theory (Anderson & Goolishian, 1988; McNamee & Gergen, 1992) and story-telling. These use reversals and reflections of patients' and therapists' positions to illuminate the systemic patterns of the referred problems (Andersen, 1987, 1991; Epston, 1989; White, 1989; Inger & Inger, 1990; Epston & White, 1992).

This flowering of systemic writing is often at an extremely high level of philosophical abstraction, concerned with pattern, coherence and creative discontinuity rather than content. In the writing there is often an expression of equality with the client family which at times can feel disingenuous or even indifferent to distress. This efflorescence of writing is, with the exception of the largely qualitative work of Gilligan and her colleagues, almost entirely divorced from any conventional empirical research, and is difficult to formulate in terms of an evidence-based choice between therapies.

Eclecticism and the reunion of the psychodynamic and the family/systemic

No one reviewing the literature on systemic approaches to psychosis can have any doubts about the enormous gulf between the empiricism of the British and American-dominated research on EE and the other worldwide developments in systemic therapies and theories. However, various writers from continental Europe have synthesised the concepts of EE, psychodynamic theories and systemic theories. Examples include Ciompi from Switzerland (Ciompi, 1988, 1994; see Evans, 1989, for an earlier reaction to this synthesis) and authors from Scandinavia, whose work has been brought together recently (Aaltonen & Rakkolainen, 1994; Alanen, 1994; Lehtinen, 1994; Sorensen, 1994). This work involves a different relatedness to the patients and their families from that in the Anglo-American tradition of work on EE. Long-term attachment of families to clinicians is considered sensible; psychodynamic understandings of concrete or otherwise bizarre thought content and of hallucinatory experiences is thought to help clinical teams and families make links with the patient during the acute phase of psychosis; a gently respectful family orientation is assumed to underpin everything. All this is invoked at the same time as use of neuroleptic medication. The sense conveyed is that the biological approach to psychosis has become less separated from the social/psychological and that systemic interventions are widely respected. The other impression conveyed to this rigidly British thinker is of a thinly stretched weave of theories with frank willingness to avoid analysing inconsistencies between theories when the practice feels right.

Conclusions

A systemic conceptual approach requires three elements:

(a) consideration of more people than just the patient and therapist, that is, consideration of family, clinical teams and social matrix;
(b) recognition that psychoses, and all human thinking, are communicative functions: interactive, iterative, full of feedback loops and obeying non-linear dynamics;
(c) understanding of communications between the various protagonists in the social system within their cultural matrix.

There are two main schools of systemic work with psychosis separated by radically different 'levels of inference'. The low level of inference has wide implications for the definition of psychosis as a marginalised experience. The highly condensed overview of older and more recent publications on systemic work with psychosis highlights the radical separation of work at the two levels of inference, but reveals some work that attempts to integrate radically disparate theories and practices.

Despite this integrative work it is difficult to see the post-modern discursiveness of some systemic theories ever linking easily with traditional empiricism. However, some of the empiricists currently researching EE and the treatments derived from the concept are starting to recognise a need for links with other theories based on interpersonal attachment, communication, and the linguistic changes of psychosis.

References

AALTONEN, J. & RAKKOLAINEN, V. (1994) The shared image guiding the treatment process. A precondition for integration of the treatment of schizophrenia. *British Journal of Psychiatry*, **164** (suppl. 23), 97–102.

ALANEN, Y. O. (1994) An attempt to integrate the individual–psychological and interactional concepts of the origins of schizophrenia. *British Journal of Psychiatry*, **164** (suppl. 23), 56–61.

ANDERSEN, T. (1987) The reflecting team: dialogue and meta-dialogue in clinical work. *Family Process*, **26**, 415–428.

—— (1991) *The Reflecting Team. Dialogues and Dialogues about the Dialogues.* New York/ London: W. W. Norton.

166 Evans

ANDERSON, H. & GOOLISHIAN, H. A. (1986) Problem determined systems: towards transformation in family therapy. *Journal of Strategic and Systemic Therapies*, **5**, 1–11.

—— & —— (1988) Human systems as linguistic systems. *Family Process*, **27**, 3–12.

BARRELET, L., FERRERO, F., SZIGETHY, L., *et al* (1990) Expressed emotion and first-admission schizophrenia: nine-month follow-up in a French cultural environment. *British Journal of Psychiatry*, **156**, 357–362.

BENNETT, D., FOX, C., JOWELL, T., *et al* (1976) Towards a family approach in a psychiatric day hospital. *British Journal of Psychiatry*, **129**, 73–81.

BERG, I. K. (1994) *Family Based Services. A Solution-Focused Approach*. New York: W. W. Norton.

BION, W. R. (1957) Differentiation of the psychotic from the non-psychotic personalities. In *Second Thoughts. Selected Papers on Psycho-analysis* (ed. W. R. Bion), pp. 43–64. London: Maresfield Library (1984).

—— (1959) Attacks on linking. In *Second Thoughts. Selected Papers on Psycho-analysis* (ed. W. R. Bion), pp. 93–109. London: Maresfield Library (1984).

—— (1961) *Experiences in Groups and Other Papers*. London: Tavistock/Routledge.

BRITISH MEDICAL ASSOCIATION NEWS REVIEW (1994) Doctors suffer from manic depression too. *British Medical Association News Review*, **20**, 8.

BRITISH MEDICAL JOURNAL (1990) Reflections after manic depressive psychosis. *British Medical Journal*, **300**, 1597.

BROOKER, C., FALLOON, I., BUTTERWORTH, A., *et al* (1994) The outcome of training community psychiatric nurses to deliver psychosocial intervention. *British Journal of Psychiatry*, **165**, 222–230.

BROWN, G. W. & RUTTER, M. (1966) The measurement of family activities and relationships: a methodological study. *Human Relations*, **19**, 241–263.

——, BIRLEY, J. L. T. & WING, J. K. (1972) Influence of family life on the course of schizophrenic disorders: a replication. *British Journal of Psychiatry*, **121**, 241–258.

BROWN, L. M. & GILLIGAN, C. (1993) Meeting at the crossroads: women's psychology and girls' development. *Feminism and Psychology*, **3**, 11–35.

BYNG-HALL, J. (1991) The application of attachment theory to understanding and treatment in family therapy. In *Attachment Across the Life Cycle* (eds C. M. Parkes, J. Stevenson-Hinde & P. Marris), pp. 199–215. London: Routledge.

CECCHIN, G. (1988) Hypothesizing, circularity, and neutrality revisited: an invitation to curiosity. *Family Process*, **26**, 405–413.

——, LANE, G. & RAY, W. A. (1992) *Irreverence: A Strategy for Therapists' Survival*. London: Karnac Books.

CHADWICK, P. K. (1995) Learning from patients. *Clinical Psychology Forum*, **82**, 30–34.

CIOMPI, L. (1988) *The Psyche and Schizophrenia. The Bond Between Affect and Logic* (transl. D. L. Schneider). Cambridge, MA: Harvard University Press.

—— (1994) Theory of schizophrenia: comments. *British Journal of Psychiatry*, **164** (suppl. 23), 51–55.

DE SHAZER, S. (1985) *Keys to Solution in Brief Therapy*. New York: W. W. Norton

—— (1988) *Clues: Investigating Solutions in Brief Therapy*. New York: W. W. Norton.

EPSTON, D. (1989) *Collected Papers*. Adelaide: Dulwich Centre Publications.

—— & WHITE, M. (1992) *Experience, Contradiction, Narrative and Imagination: Selected Papers of David Epston & Michael White 1989–1991*. Adelaide: Dulwich Centre Publications.

EVANS, C. (1989) "The psyche and schizophrenia: the bond between affect and logic" by Luc Ciompi. *British Journal of Psychiatry*, **155**, 729–730.

FLEURIDAS, C., NELSON, T. S. & ROSENTHAL, D. M. (1986) The evolution of circular questioning – training family therapists. *Journal of Marital and Family Therapy*, **12**, 113–127.

GILLIGAN, C. (1993) *In a Different Voice. Psychological Theory and Women's Development*. Cambridge, MA: Harvard University Press.

——, LYONS, N. P. & HANMER, T. J. (1990) *Making Connections. The Relational Worlds of Adolescent Girls at Emma Willard School*. Cambridge, MA: Harvard University Press

——, ROGERS, A. G. & TOLMAN, D. L. (1991) *Women, Girls and Psychotherapy: Reframing Resistance.* New York: Harrington Park Press.

GOLDNER, V. (1988) Generation and gender: normative and covert hierarchies. *Family Process,* **27,** 17–31.

HALEY, J. (1975) Why a mental health clinic should avoid family therapy. Paper presented at the *Journal of Marriage and Family Counseling.*

—— (1986) The art of being schizophrenic. In *The Power Tactics of Jesus Christ and Other Essays* (ed. J. Haley, 2nd edn), pp. 57–80. New York: W. W. Norton.

HOFFMAN, L. (1981*a*) Early research on family groups. In *Foundations of Family Therapy. A Conceptual Framework for Systems Change* (ed. L. Hoffman), pp. 16–36. New York: Basic Books.

—— (1981*b*) *Foundations of Family Therapy. A Conceptual Framework for Systems Change.* New York: Basic Books.

INGER, I. B. & INGER, J. (1990) *Co-constructing Therapeutic Conversations. A Consultation of Restraint.* London: Karnac.

KAVANAGH, D. J. (1992) Recent developments in expressed emotion and schizophrenia. *British Journal of Psychiatry,* **160,** 601–620.

KLEIN, M., SEGAL, H. & MONEY-KYRLE, R. E. (1946) Notes on some schizoid mechanisms. In *Envy and Gratitude and Other Works 1946–1963* (ed. M. A. Klein), pp. 1–24. London: Virago Press (1988).

KUIPERS, L. (1979) Expressed emotion: a review. *British Journal of Social and Clinical Psychology,* **18,** 237–243.

——, LEFF, J. & LAM, D. (1992) *Family Work for Schizophrenia. A Practical Guide.* London: Gaskell.

LAING, R. D. (1959) *The Divided Self. An Existential Study in Sanity and Madness.* Harmondsworth: Penguin Books.

—— (1969) *The Politics of the Family and Other Essays.* Harmondsworth: Penguin Books.

LANCET (1983) Disabilities and how to live with them. A schizophrenic describes his recovery. *Lancet,* **ii,** 562–563.

LEFF, J. (1994) Working with the families of schizophrenic patients. *British Journal of Psychiatry,* **164** (suppl. 23), 71–76.

—— & VAUGHN, C. E. (1980) The interaction of life events and relatives' expressed emotion in schizophrenia and depressive neurosis. *British Journal of Psychiatry,* **136,** 146–153.

—— & —— (1981) The role of maintenance therapy and relatives' expressed emotion in relapse of schizophrenia: a two-year follow-up. *British Journal of Psychiatry,* **139,** 102–104.

——, KUIPERS, L., BERKOWITZ, R., *et al* (1982) A controlled trial of social intervention in the families of schizophrenic patients. *British Journal of Psychiatry,* **141,** 121–134.

——, ——, ——, *et al* (1985) A controlled trial of social intervention in the families of schizophrenic patients: two year follow-up. *British Journal of Psychiatry,* **146,** 594–600.

——, WIG, N. N., BEDI, H., *et al* (1990) Relatives' expressed emotion and the course of schizophrenia in Chandigarh. A two-year follow-up of a first-contact sample. *British Journal of Psychiatry,* **156,** 351–356.

LEHTINEN, K. (1994) Need-adapted treatment of schizophrenia: family interventions. *British Journal of Psychiatry,* **164** (suppl. 23), 89–96.

MACKINNON, L. K. & MILLER, D. (1987) The new epistemology and the Milan approach: feminist and sociopolitical considerations. *Journal of Marital and Family Therapy,* **13,** 139–155.

MCCREADIE, R. G., PHILLIPS, K., HARVEY, J. A., *et al* (1991) The Nithsdale schizophrenia surveys. VIII: Do relatives want family intervention – and does it help? *British Journal of Psychiatry,* **158,** 110–113.

MCNAMEE, S. & GERGEN, K. J. (1992) *Therapy as Social Construction.* London: Sage.

PEDDER, J. (1991) Fear of dependence in therapeutic relationships. *British Journal of Medical Psychology,* **64,** 117–126.

RANDOLPH, E. T., ETH, S., GLYNN, S. M., *et al* (1994) Behavioural family management in schizophrenia. Outcome of a clinic-based intervention. *British Journal of Psychiatry*, **164**, 501–506.

RAY, W. A. & KEENEY, B. (1993) *Resource Focused Therapy*. London: Karnac Books.

REA, M. M., STRACHAN, A. M., GOLDSTEIN, M. J., *et al* (1991) Changes in patient coping style following individual and family treatment for schizophrenia. *British Journal of Psychiatry*, **158**, 642–647.

SEGAL, H. (1957) Notes on symbol formation. In *Delusion and Artistic Creativity and Other Psycho-analytic Essays* (ed. H. Segal), pp. 49–65. London: Maresfield (1986).

SELVINI PALAZZOLI, M., BOSCOLO, L., CECCHIN, G., *et al* (1978) *Paradox and Counter-paradox*. New York: Jason Aronson.

——, ——, ——, *et al* (1980*a*) Hypothesizing – circularity – neutrality: three guidelines for the conductor of the session. *Family Process*, **19**, 3–12.

——, ——, ——, *et al* (1980*b*) The problem of the referring person. *Journal of Marital and Family Therapy*, **6**, 3–9.

SKYNNER, A. C. R. (1976) *One Flesh: Separate Persons. Principles of Family and Marital Psychotherapy*. London: Constable.

SMITH, J. & BIRCHWOOD, M. (1990) Relatives and patients as partners in the management of schizophrenia. The development of a service model. *British Journal of Psychiatry*, **156**, 654–660.

SORENSEN, T. (1994) The intricacy of the ordinary. *British Journal of Psychiatry*, **164** (suppl. 23), 108–114.

STRAUSS, J. S. (1994) The person with schizophrenia as a person. II: Approaches to the subjective and complex. *British Journal of Psychiatry*, **164** (suppl. 23), 103–107.

TAMURA, T. & LAU, A. (1992) Connectedness versus separateness: applicability of family therapy to Japanese families. *Family Process*, **31**, 319–340.

TARRIER, N. (1991) Some aspects of family interventions in schizophrenia. I: Adherence to intervention programmes. *British Journal of Psychiatry*, **159**, 475–480.

——, BARROWCLOUGH, C., VAUGHN, C., *et al* (1989) Community management of schizophrenia. A two-year follow-up of a behavioural intervention with families. *British Journal of Psychiatry*, **154**, 625–628.

——, LOWSON, K. & BARROWCLOUGH, C. (1991) Some aspects of family interventions in schizophrenia. II: Financial considerations. *British Journal of Psychiatry*, **159**, 481–484.

TOMM, K. (1987*a*) Interventive interviewing: Part I. Strategizing as a fourth guideline for the therapist. *Family Process*, **26**, 3–13.

—— (1987*b*) Interventive interviewing: Part II. Reflexive questioning as a means to enable self-healing. *Family Process*, **26**, 167–183.

—— (1988) Interventive interviewing: Part III. Intending to ask lineal, circular, strategic or reflexive questions? *Family Process*, **27**, 1–15.

VAUGHN, C. E. & LEFF, J. P. (1976*a*) The influence of family and social factors on the course of psychiatric illness. *British Journal of Psychiatry*, **129**, 125–137.

—— & —— (1976*b*) The measurement of expressed emotion in the families of psychiatric patients. *British Journal of Social and Clinical Psychology*, **15**, 157–165.

WHITE, M. (1989) *Selected Papers*. Adelaide: Dulwich Centre Publications.

11 Psychosis and treatment of the whole family

ROGER KENNEDY

Editors' comments

The approach taken at the Cassel Hospital draws on both the psychodynamic and the systemic traditions. Kennedy has written a personal account with examples drawn from current cases. In this chapter there is no attempt to evaluate the treatments against scientific criteria, nor to give a systematic overview of the conditions treated. The impact of the paper at the conference was considerable, largely because of the challenge to other psychoanalytically oriented practitioners to extend the range of applicability of the psycho-analytic method in in-patient treatment settings.

The reader may be interested in pursuing some of the clinical points raised by Roger Kennedy here primarily to exemplify the type of therapeutic intervention offered at the Cassel Hospital, discussed at length by Kennedy (1986).

There has been considerable recent work on the treatment of postnatal illnesses, and the implications of psychotic illness on the mother's ability to care for her child. Brockington & Kumar (1982) and Kumar & Brockington (1988) provide comprehensive overviews of the field of motherhood and mental illness and have chapters on the effect of postnatal illness in the mother on the mother–infant relationship (Margison, 1982; Melhuish et al, 1988).

Münchausen syndrome by proxy is described in greater detail by Bools (1996), and the assessment of risk in psychotherapeutic situations with forensic implications is discussed in detail in Cordess & Cox (1966), particularly in chapters by van Marle; Theilgard; and Cordess.

The work of the Cassel Hospital is put into historical context in the writings of Tom Main (Main, 1989), who describes the develop-ment of the therapeutic community approach.

References

Bools, C. (1996) Factitious illness by proxy (Munchausen syndrome by proxy). *British Journal of Psychiatry*, **169**, 268–275.

Brockington, I. F. & Kumar, R. (1982) *Motherhood and Mental Illness*. London: Academic Press.

Cordess, C. & Cox, M. (1996) *Forensic Psychotherapy: Crime, Psychodynamics and the Offender Patient*. London: Jessica Kingsley.

Kennedy, R. (1986) *The Family as In-patient*. London: Free Association.

Kumar, R. & Brockington, I. F. (1988) *Motherhood and Mental Illness 2: Causes and Consequences*. London: Wright.

Main, T. (1989) *The Ailment and Other Psychoanalytic Essays*. London: Free Association Books.

Margison, F. (1982) The pathology of the mother–child relationship. In *Motherhood and Mental Illness* (eds I. F. Brockington & R. Kumar), pp. 191–218. London: Academic Press.

Melhuish, E. C., Gambles, C. & Kumar, R. (1988) Maternal mental illness and the mother–infant relationship. In *Motherhood and Mental Illness 2: Causes and Consequences* (eds R. Kumar & I. F. Brockington), pp. 191–211. London: Wright.

Introduction

The main theme of this chapter is the treatment of very ill families as in-patients at the Cassel Hospital – a psychoanalytically based therapeutic community. Families with acutely psychotic members are rare, but we have had families in which one member has been manic–depressive, and some with schizophrenic parents. One clinical example outlines short-term work with a schizophrenic mother and her 10-year-old son. The Cassel family unit is sometimes a place where ill families can have a last chance to get help.

Typical reasons for referral include child abuse, severe depression, the after-effects of murder, Münchausen syndrome by proxy, and postnatal breakdown – all frequently complicated by severe social fragmentation. The unit provides a framework to help staff deal with the stresses and strains such work provokes. We can do this by looking in detail at transference and countertransference issues, and help staff to work with and tolerate some psychotic transference phenomena, often of a very destructive kind. The psychoanalytic training of the staff is a key part of the understanding that makes such work bearable.

Before presenting some clinical examples it is useful to conceptualise three different ways in which the concept of psychosis is being used in the work of the Cassel unit.

Psychotic anxiety, psychotic functioning and psychotic breakdown

In psychoanalysis the term 'psychosis' is used broadly and is not limited to specific conditions along the lines of the medical model of mental disturbance. Psychotic states vary in severity and patients may spend limited or extended periods of time in such states. Patients may reveal to us what is going on in their minds, but not infrequently we may have to guess what is going on, or make inferences from manifest behaviour. Some patients can conceal the manifestations of these psychotic processes. This can be for various reasons, such as fear of the consequences to their treatment, or concern that the professional may be unable to bear the emotional strain involved in tolerating psychotic states.

Several concepts are encapsulated in the psychoanalytic concept of psychosis. These include:

(a) use of primitive or developmentally early defence mechanisms;
(b) collapse of ego function or loose ego boundaries;
(c) loss or breakdown of psychological functioning, including –
    (i)   withdrawal from the social world,
    (ii) disturbance in reality sense,
    (iii) severe communication problems,
    (iv) severe problems in relationships,
    (v) a terror of relatedness,
    (vi) a sense of some inner catastrophe.

There is a quality of acute anxiety and of being despairingly alone and in the grip of some terrifying and maddening thought, of a sexual or other kind. Rather than a model of individual disease categories, a useful alternative are three descriptive (not aetiological) categories, which cover many of the features of psychotic states – psychotic anxieties, psychotic functioning and psychotic breakdown.

Psychotic anxieties are common, even universal, experiences. For example, in the large group, projective processes are widespread, and there is the attempt to rid oneself of unwanted thoughts and feelings by assigning them to others or requiring others to experience them in an intense way. As a result, the individual's own sense of identity becomes loose and persecutory anxiety abounds, as does a sense of feeling anonymous in the crowd. It is difficult to feel sane, easy to feel mad.

In the treatment of individuals or families, psychotic anxieties may be seen in a number of ways. At moments of approaching psychotic anxieties, you may find yourself feeling confused, unable to think, aware of fears about falling apart, in touch with an omnipotent denial of others, pushing towards merger with the other and aware of a blurring of personal boundaries. The therapist may even be anxious about his/her own sanity. Some families are particularly prone to flipping into such anxious states when under stress. Their children may become particularly vulnerable to abuse or neglect at such moments. The kinds of issue that are most potent in evoking psychotic anxieties include conflicts about dependency, closeness and intimacy.

By *psychotic functioning*, I refer to a more serious state of affairs, when one or more members of the family have a major disturbance in their relationship to the world. There may be episodes of losing touch with the world, or with the child; they may have delusional ideas about themselves, their body or their children, for brief or extended periods. In psychosis there is an attempt to remodel reality, to impose a view on others that may be unamenable to discussion. Social services may be seen as the source of all badness, while the parents feel themselves to be the innocent victims of the authorities, even when there is clear evidence of the parents having abused their child. Injuries to a child may be seen as only 'accidental' and not the result of the parents' violent attacks. Applying Bion's thought, there is a widespread attack on the linking of experiences (Bion, 1959). Workers, when dealing with such situations in the childcare field, may be forced to act, to provide a less delusional reality for a child. In treatment situations, it may be equally important to resist acting too soon.

Treatment of individuals and families who show psychotic functioning involves difficult judgements about risk, commonly leading to conflict between staff, splitting of the team and despair. Staff, despite feeling weakened, may be experienced as cruel and harsh authorities. There are often intense feelings of disappointment and failed hopes and expectations among both staff and patients when the psychotic core of illness of the patient is really touched. At such times, it is important to help staff to maintain a sense of separateness while they are dealing with the powerful projections from the patients. Also at these times, staff may be taken over by unrealistic wishes to cure the patients, so that the staff can go on and on attempting the impossible, pushing the patient into even more extreme psychotic states.

When does psychotic functioning tip over into *psychotic breakdown*? Breakdown refers to the situation when the ego, either in the individual or in the family group (the 'family ego') can no longer hold the personality, or the family structure, together. There may be a severe suicide attempt, delusional ideas may overwhelm the personality or the couple or the whole family. Projective systems in the family may be so intense and persistent that the family's whole pattern of living becomes unstable, as though the bricks and mortar of the family home had fallen apart.

The term 'breakdown' is used very loosely. Winnicott (1974) used it to describe "the unthinkable state of affairs that underlies the defensive organization". It includes both the external signs that something is wrong, and the subject's inner experience of bewilderment and chaos. A form of hatred becomes evident. On the one hand, there is the apparent hatred and rejection of reality, with a simultaneous hatred for unreality. There is an attempt, however desperate, to relate, to repair damage. Idealisation of destructive parts of the self also seems to be important to recognise in this context (Rosenfeld, 1987).

The Cassel family unit

To treat families where there is psychotic anxiety, psychotic functioning, and occasionally actual breakdown, a number of basic elements are needed. Firstly, a setting is necessary with therapeutic structures for patients and supervision structures for staff, which allow psychotic phenomena to be registered and reflected upon rather than leaving staff confused and anxious. Some confusion is inevitable, but the therapeutic environment needs to be protected from overload. Some safety structures need to be built in: areas where patients can function away from the heat of the transference. These are areas that build on the patients' ego strength. Ill people should not be treated solely by interpreting the transference. Ego strength can be built by interpretive and non-interpretive means, but a secure framework for treatment is needed before interpretation. Regression is inevitable during in-patient treatment, so it has to be carefully monitored. Regression can help to rework past conflicts, but 'malignant regression' (Balint, 1968) can be very destructive to both the individual and to the unit as a whole. It is important to know when to stop this type of treatment, particularly when staff have invested huge amounts of time and effort in a family. A realistic view of what can and cannot be achieved in therapy needs to be maintained. For this type of therapeutic work, the safety of the children and their welfare is the aspect of reality testing that guides treatment decisions. If at any time the children are seriously at risk, treatment will be ended, regardless of staff optimism. Staff need to be supported through the inevitable stresses and strains resulting from these decisions. It is stressful to have to bear primitive anxieties and face powerful destructive forces, but equally stressful to have to give up treatment after investing time and hope in a family.

The Cassel family unit can admit up to 13 families for assessment and treatment at any one time. The average stay in successful cases is about a year. The programme, which usually excludes the use of psychotropic medication, consists of detailed nursing work focused on family activities and parenting skills. Success in these develop the patient's ego strength, allowing individual, small-group, marital and family therapy to take place alongside. There is also individual and small-group therapy for the children, if they are old enough.

There is a focus both on family living skills and on individual needs and difficulties. The aim is to restore families to their communities so that they can either continue with life unaided, or use their local resources more effectively. 'At-risk' families need to be monitored very closely to make sure the children are safe. The 'safety net' requires detailed attention to what happens in a family from day to day as well as close liaison with the family's social work agency.

Meetings to see, hear about and discuss patients include daily meetings with patients, daily staff meetings, and regular reviews and supervision sessions. Safety is maintained by a network of staff relationships, from the nurse and therapist of a particular family across to the on-call duty team at night and at weekends. For the network of relationships to provide a secure, holding environment, there needs to be clear and effective transmission of information between workers. Each family has its own particular focus of work and nursing plan. The service does not provide long-term therapy; it has to be focused. The children cannot wait for years for their parents to make slow changes. The family's functioning needs to change quickly if the social services are to feel that the needs of the children are going to be met. Early in the stay, a family in which there has been abuse may be under particularly close supervision, with, for example, constraints on their freedom to go out of the hospital unaccompanied. If treatment proceeds satisfactorily, the restrictions are gradually relaxed, as the progress of the family is monitored through reviews (at which parents are present), supervision and case conferences.

Change is most likely to occur in families where abuse is either absent or at least openly acknowledged if it did occur. Mothers in families which change significantly are more likely to remember at least one good relationship from childhood and to establish good relationships with staff and fellow patients during treatment.

Postnatal depression

Family work at the Cassel began in the 1950s with the treatment of severe postnatal depression, although only the mother was admitted at that time. Now, if there is a father remaining in the family structure, he will also be admitted. There is commonly an underlying marital problem that needs to be incorporated in the treatment plan. In an emergency the patients can be admitted on the day of the assessment.

Pregnancy may be a pleasurable, if occasionally anxious, experience, for many women. But in some, the bodily and emotional changes are painful and frightening. The mother may turn back to the grandmother, or become identified with the foetus and later the baby. These shifting identifications can become major threats to the woman's mental health, particularly if there were inconsistencies in her own mothering. Then, instead of turning back to her own mother for support, she may turn too much to the baby for comfort. She may not be able to differentiate herself from the baby; she may feel irrationally that her own mother disapproves of her. The three generations – grandmother, mother and baby – can become confused in her mind. The child and adult elements of the woman's personality may become confused. There is an identification with the baby, but at the same time a loss of the mothering capacity. The baby comes to represent the mother, possibly in a psychotic way. Or, the baby may come to represent the life-giver for the emotionally dead mother. The baby can also then become the target of other and more sinister projections as part of this process of psychic splitting. If there is, in addition, an absence of other support, such as from a partner, then a woman may be tipped over into postnatal breakdown. It is important to differentiate borderline psychopathology from that of, say, schizophrenic mothers, who may well have quite different problems in looking after a baby.

In the family unit, the treatment of postnatal depression incorporates a detailed nursing plan. The patient with a reduced ego function needs a structure that will contain anxiety and provide support. Many women suffering from severe postnatal illness are in an acutely disturbed state, usually with psychotic functioning merging into breakdown. The nursing plan may include rotas of patients to help with the basic mothering tasks, until she can gradually take on more responsibility. Critical times such as bath times and feeding of the baby may then provide an important focus for nursing work.

There is often labile mood, fluctuating between suicidal depression and manic denial of emotions. Because of this, it is important to remain vigilant throughout the first week or two of admission, although one of the most dangerous times may be when the mother begins to feel less depressed. As some of the symptoms subside she may begin to feel pathologically guilty about being ill and not being able to attend to her baby. If the staff are not alert to the possibility of this change in mental state they may relax their attention at the very time when suicidal thoughts are predominant. Commonly, daily therapy sessions are provided (although they may initially be brief) as there is a need to monitor the situation from day to day as well as provide support. Involving the father is vital. Not infrequently, fathers come across as having tried everything possible to help, and yet on looking more closely there is a subtle attempt to locate all vulnerability and disturbance in the woman, perhaps extricating themselves from any responsibility for what has happened. Although the woman may go along with this state of affairs, it can result in her being overwhelmed by psychotic experiences. There is no safe haven, and breakdown may ensue.

Case example

A woman in her late 30s with a core identity problem, and whom we had successfully treated recently, was admitted as her local social services had poured in resources for her and her baby with minimal success. In fact, the baby, a few months old, was being looked after for half the week by professionals, at great financial cost. Her former partner had made it plain that he had wanted her to have an abortion, and when she decided to go through with the pregnancy he abandoned her and had nothing more to do with her. Her own mother was hospitalised for severe depression when the patient was a teenager, and also suffered from depression when the patient was a child. Her father was described as distant and unemotional. The patient had gone through periods of suicidal depression, but at other times was capable and held down a good job. She had a poor image of herself and was very sensitive to criticism. The nursing work focused on her mothering, through enhancing her practical skills. Although in part a capable mother, she had little awareness of the effect of her mood on her child. He was a lively little boy, in some ways too lively, constantly seeking her attention and interest and trying to be cheerful. He was one of those children who somehow learn to cheer up their mothers, whereas other babies may become depressed and morose themselves.

In therapeutic situations, the mother tended to identify with staff and made helpful suggestions to other patients, but she had difficulty in focusing on herself. In individual therapy sessions, much of the early work was focused on quite subtle shifts in the transference, when she quickly tried to avoid feelings of dependency by taking the therapist role, in part to avoid being overwhelmed by feelings of loss of control of psychotic intensity. The way she covered up her anger when it was seething underneath gradually became more amenable to exploration. Considerable work was done by one of the child psychotherapists on the mother–child relationship, with the aim of protecting the child from his mother's vulnerable mood states.

Münchausen syndrome by proxy

This syndrome describes the situation where a seemingly caring and concerned parent, usually the mother, brings a child to the doctor with fabricated symptoms or induced serious illnesses. We treated one case in which the mother, who had been sexually abused as a child, caused two previous children to go into coma by administering salt over a period of time; in another case, the mother administered aspirin and paracetamol to her child, which made her ill and present with blood in the urine. Another mother put her own blood in her baby's nappy in order to present to her doctor.

There is still much we not understand about this condition. People have emphasised the mother's use of the child to make a relationship with a doctor, in order to get care and concern in a perverse way. The child serves as a mere object to be used, or a mere vehicle for projections. The mother seems on the surface caring, but the therapist may experience a cold, heartless and ruthless quality in her. The emotional link between the mother and her children needs to be clarified in the paediatric history. The mothers have difficulty relating to the child emotionally. There is thought to be a false, hollow ring to their interactions. They feel they have the right as parents to do what they wish with their child, regardless of society's rules and taboos. They may feel that the child is an extension of themselves. The mothers we treated showed this quality at first, but were able to move to some extent into being more in touch with their denied dependency needs. However, this required a considerable amount of work, which often involved facing intense psychotic processes, usually of a destructive kind. Before the admission to the family unit, one of the mothers we treated had been admitted compulsorily, when her older children were removed from her. Workers around these families may be split into those who believe in the mother's good intentions, and those who are convinced of her dangerousness, which suggests that the mother is using defences of splitting. On closer examination, there may be a hypersensitivity to separation, with an associated fear of collapse and disintegration. The child, acting as a comfort object, is being used to maintain the mother's sanity. Once in treatment, the covert feelings of destructiveness become a major issue – perhaps with overt or covert attacks on the staff, or assaults on her own self. For example, two mothers we treated wished to have their uterus removed, although both were still in their 20s. A third mother, whom we are currently assessing, has had many somatic symptoms.

Our psychodynamic formulation suggests a mother with unstable or impoverished maternal representations. There may be a violent fantasy world, in which objects are controlled and then ruthlessly eliminated. However, it is very difficult for them to recognise their own hate and aggression. Like the doctors who see them at first, they themselves cannot believe how poisoning and destructive they can be. The workers are often left to experience the anxiety about the child; or alternatively may experience a delusional counter-transference, in which anxiety is denied and only the surface is recognised. In our treatment, we not only aim to tackle the internal dynamics, but pay considerable attention to the reality of the child, which helps to focus the treatment on what is essential if rehabilitation is to succeed. The marital situation may be a contributory part of the formulation. In one of the cases we treated, both mother and father had major difficulties, although the mother did the actual poisoning. The father had been badly abused as a child. The couple had virtually given up on communicating, except through their child's symptoms. In another case both father and mother shared a history in which they were abandoned by their own mothers as children and were then looked after by their fathers. In their own family, the mother was the one who put blood in the nappy and could not relate effectively to the child, while the father provided safety, thus unconsciously repeating their own family history of a mother who abandoned the child to the father.

Schizophrenic mother and child

Case example

This mother and her 10-year-old son were referred in order to clarify whether or not the mother could look after her son permanently, or whether he should remain in his long-term foster home. The boy, who had been removed from her care a couple of years previously because of her mental state and mothering difficulties, was placed in a foster home where he was subjected to sexual abuse. He was then placed with a safe foster family. The local authority felt that they had to make every attempt to look into the family situation and to assess fully the mother's capacities to care for her son in the long term. The mother, in her early 40s, had a long psychiatric history. As a child she was severely sexually abused. Her mother was a prostitute and the patient was involved as a child in pornography. She spent much of her childhood in care, and was also sexually abused in foster care. She began to cut herself around puberty, and as a result was placed in a variety of residential placements which could not contain her. She finally ended up in a secure unit. She had a history of alcohol and drug misuse, and was eventually diagnosed as having schizophrenia. She suffers from voices and delusions and has periods of acute breakdown, requiring admission. She was on depot injections of major tranquillisers on admission. She had lost previous children because of her problems.

In the month's assessment period, the mother was cooperative. In individual therapy sessions she came across as mechanical, emotionally cut off and fragmented at times. However, as the admission proceeded she was able to express more of her anger about the abuse of her son. Yet she maintained an unrealistic view of her capacity to look after him. In small-group sessions, she was, in contrast, surprisingly able to relate to the others and the situation, becoming at times the most insightful member of the group. But in general she was only just able to hold herself together by means of nursing support. She was out of touch with her child's needs. She described how she needed him to keep her boundaries. Her son was able to use the therapeutic situation well. He expressed in moving terms a deep sadness and a wish for stability. Memories of the sexual abuse kept breaking through. In fact, a decision was made that it would not be right to attempt further rehabilitation of mother and son, although we offered to do some focal work to help them to say goodbye. We also aimed to help the mother be able to maintain some limited access to the foster home. Up to then she was just angry with, and suspicious of, the foster parents, so that access had not been possible. While the son returned to the foster home, a further four months of treatment of the mother was begun. There were a few meetings with the son and with mother and son together; we also facilitated meetings between mother and foster parents. This was a very difficult time for the mother. She felt drawn again to her world of violent destructiveness, with drink, drugs and sexual promiscuity. She began to hear voices and to break down. However, we increased her major tranquillisers for a while, and were able to keep her going through this period. She found a 'voice' for herself with the other mothers, and also established a good relationship with her nurse. Her ability to talk more realistically in therapy sessions about her own abuse, her wish to destroy all men, and her ability to get into abusing relationships with the world, including social services, ourselves and dangerous men, was of crucial importance.

By discharge, she had a friendly relationship with the foster carers and arrangements were made for regular access visits. Her son was able to see how unrealistic it was to hope to live permanently with his mother and further psychotherapy was arranged for him. I think the treatment was successful because we kept to a focal task. We were not aiming to cure the mother, but to help her deal with the specific issue of letting her son go. This process of allowing separation needed inpatient treatment, because of her constant pull towards psychotic breakdown. In her own words she needed her son to keep her sane. Without the hope of him being there for her, she began to go mad again, and thus needed in-patient holding.

Summary

This chapter has focused on the methods developed to treat ill families as in-patients at the family unit of the Cassel Hospital, which provides a psychoanalytically-based therapeutic community approach. The work of the unit draws on the distinction to be made between psychotic anxieties, psychotic functioning and psychotic breakdown in order to bring some order into the complex field of psychotic states. While psychotic anxieties are universal, psychotic functioning and psychotic breakdown are terms that cover particular states of disturbance in the relationship to the world, leading in extreme cases to breakdown of the personality structure. The Cassel treatment programme attends to the psychotic states in patients, while also offering support both to the family members and to the staff involved. The three case examples illustrate some of the clinical points in the treatment of postnatal depression, Münchausen syndrome by proxy, and a mother with schizophrenia and her son.

References

BALINT, M. (1968) *The Basic Fault.* London: Tavistock.
BION, W. (1959) Attacks on linking. *International Journal of Psychoanalysis,* **40**, 308–315.
ROSENFELD, H. (1987) *Impasse and Interpretation.* London: Tavistock.
WINNICOTT, D. (1974) Fear of breakdown. *International Review of Psychoanalysis,* **1**, 103–107.

12 Behavioural family therapy approaches to the treatment of schizophrenia

GRAÍNNE FADDEN

The effectiveness of psychosocial or psychoeducational approaches to working with families of people with schizophrenia has been known for over a decade. A number of studies carried out in the US and in England in the 1980s, with follow-ups in the late 1980s or early '90s, showed consistently that relapse rates in schizophrenia were reduced to less than 10% nine months after the family intervention, compared with relapse rates of 40–50% for people who were maintained on medication but whose families did not receive any special help (Falloon *et al*, 1982; Leff *et al*, 1982; Hogarty *et al*, 1986; Tarrier *et al*, 1988). Follow-up studies two years after the intervention showed relapse rates ranging from 17% to 40% in those who had received the family intervention, compared with relapse rates ranging from 59% to 83% in those whose families who had not received the intervention (Falloon *et al*, 1985; Leff *et al*, 1985; Tarrier *et al*, 1989; Hogarty *et al*, 1991).

These approaches share a number of features. There is an adherence to a stress–diathesis model of schizophrenia, whereby a predisposition or vulnerability to developing episodes of schizophrenia is thought to be inherited, but that stressful events or situations in the environment are necessary before such an episode is triggered. The family of the person with schizophrenia is not implicated in the aetiology of the disorder, but can be helped in order to make the risk of relapse less likely. The attitude to the family on the part of the therapist is non-judgemental, non-blaming and supportive. It is felt that the family members are trying to do the best they can to cope with a difficult and stressful situation within the limits of their resources. There is an emphasis on providing information to families about schizophrenia, what causes it, what

181

are the main symptoms and treatments, and on how to recognise the early signs of relapse. The interventions all contain a skills-acquisition component, where families are helped to learn methods of coping with everyday practical problems. Other common features of these interventions are that the person with schizophrenia is maintained on medication, and that the family and schizophrenia sufferer are seen together at some stage during the intervention. Family interventions that do not contain these features have been found not to be effective in the treatment of schizophrenia (Kottgen *et al*, 1984; Vaughan *et al*, 1992). For those interested in reading more about these types of family interventions, a number of review articles are available (Strachan, 1986; Lam, 1991; Barrowclough & Tarrier, 1992).

In spite of the evidence regarding the effectiveness of family interventions in schizophrenia, a common complaint among families is that they do not receive information about what to expect or how to cope (Fadden *et al*, 1987; Hatfield, 1990). In fact, many families report feeling that professionals see them as providers of information, without offering them any help on how to cope. Examination of the numbers of families who are seen by professionals, the stage in the development of the disorder at which they are seen, and the kinds of help and information they are provided with reveals an interesting pattern (Fig. 12.1). Most families are seen when one family member develops a major mental health problem. The consultation is usually designed to provide information to the mental health professionals about when and how the disorder developed and to confirm the accuracy of the information provided by the 'identified patient'. Not all families are given information at meetings such as this, but a majority are told something about what is wrong. Some are told the name of the disorder and nothing else, and others are given a euphemistic term such as 'stress' to describe their relative's difficulties.

The proportion of families who continue to be seen after the initial stages and throughout the course of the disorder tends to diminish as time goes on. Few people are told what kind of behaviour to expect from their relative as a result of suffering from this disorder, and fewer still are told how they can deal with such behaviour. Very few families are offered an educational and skills intervention of the kind to be described here, and the majority of family members say that professionals do not inquire how they are getting on, or offer them help to deal with personal problems they develop as a result of dealing with the disorder in the family member. We therefore have a situation in relation to schizophrenia that could be described justifiably as unethical, where a particular type of family intervention

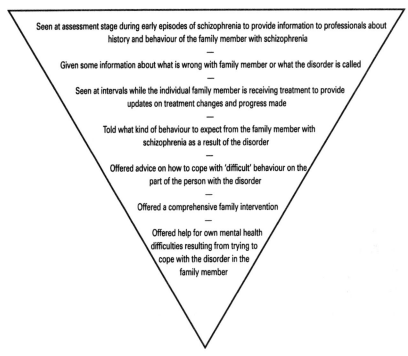

Fig. 12.1 Relative proportion (as width, decreasing from top to bottom) of families seen by professionals and types of help that they are offered.

has been shown to reduce relapse rates by half, but is not routinely offered to people with schizophrenia and their families.

The family approach that has been shown to be most effective at follow-up is the behavioural family therapy model developed by Falloon and his colleagues in California (Falloon *et al*, 1984). This approach is now used extensively worldwide, and is usually provided in the context of a comprehensive approach to mental health service provision (Falloon & Fadden, 1993*a*). Within this integrated approach to mental health care, the person with schizophrenia and the members of his/her family receive a range of different interventions in addition to family work, depending on their needs. One of the reasons why behavioural family therapy has been shown to be so successful is likely to be the fact that the intervention is not time-limited, and that families continue to receive help in the follow-up period, depending on their needs and their ability to cope with the difficulties they face. This chapter provides a summary of this approach; a more detailed account with numerous case examples can be found in Falloon *et al* (1993*b*).

Components of behavioural family therapy

Initial meeting with the family

The therapist meets with the family, including the family member with schizophrenia, to explain the approach, the rationale for using it and to provide information about its effectiveness. All family members are invited to attend, and they are usually the best judges of what constitutes the 'family' in their particular case. Often a grandmother or uncle can play as significant a role as more immediate family members. It is important also not to focus simply on those living in the same household. For example, siblings who have moved out of the family home are still affected by what happens at home and still play an important role in family life. The therapist works with whoever attends sessions, and continues to invite along those family members who are reluctant to attend initially. The members of the family who attend usually convey information back to those who have not participated, and frequently persuade them to come to subsequent meetings.

At the initial meeting, a number of issues need to be addressed. It is useful to check what experiences of therapy the family has had in the past. Some people will have had experiences of 'family therapy' which they found difficult and unhelpful and where they felt blamed for the illness of their family member. It is important for the therapist to reassure the family that she/he is not interested in attributing blame, but is concerned to help them to cope more effectively with a situation that can be difficult and stressful for all. The therapist usually needs to let the family ventilate feelings of anger, annoyance or frustration about aspects of the service, or the behaviour of professionals that they have found problematic in the past. It is important to acknowledge in a non-defensive way that the family may not have had all their needs met in the past and following this to focus on what is now being offered. It is helpful to describe what the approach involves, and to emphasise the fact that it focuses on practical, day-to-day problems, with the aim of making life less stressful for all family members. Families require practical information such as when and where sessions will take place, their duration and for how long they will continue to see the therapist. Some families are happy to engage in therapy straight away, while others need time to think before making a decision.

Assessment of individual family members

After the initial meeting, the therapist arranges to meet with each of the members of the family individually before seeing the family again as a group. These individual interviews have a number of goals.

(a) *To enable the therapist to establish a therapeutic alliance with every member of the household.* Family members appear to be far more likely to attend family meetings with the therapist when they have had a chance to meet with him/her on an individual basis, and to tell their story from their point of view.

(b) *To define each member's understanding of the nature and clinical management of their relative's disorder.* Members of the family may have differing views about what is wrong with their relative and what caused it. The therapist needs to be aware of these differences so that she/he can decide on the content and the information to be provided, and at what level to pitch this information.

(c) *To determine whether other members of the family are themselves vulnerable to any disorder, or have experienced difficulties in the past.* It is not unusual to find that somebody in the family is also experiencing mental health difficulties. These may be independent of the patient's difficulties, or may be related. It is now well established that caring for someone with an enduring mental health problem is extremely stressful, and that family members in this position experience a higher than average rate of mental health problems. The therapist needs to be aware if this is the case so that a decision can be made in an informed manner about how best to help all the family members.

(d) *To define the specific personal goals of each family member.* In families where one member has a severe and long-term mental health problem, the focus of everyone's attention is on that person. This is not helpful, either for the individual concerned, who feels that she/he is being observed all the time, or for the other family members, who forget their own ambitions and dreams in life. From this early assessment stage onwards, the therapist encourages the family members to think about their own personal goals, and what they would like to achieve for themselves. These goals must be realistic and achievable, and family members cannot set goals that depend on somebody else acting in a particular way. For example, saying "I would like my husband to be more supportive" or "I would like my sister to take her medication regularly" are not examples of personal goals, whereas saying "I would like to meet a friend for a drink once a fortnight" or "I would like to enrol in car maintenance evening classes" are examples of personal goals that family members may set. This process of family members setting goals for themselves takes the focus of attention away from the person with the disorder, and allows him/her more space within the family. Other family members regain a more balanced perspective on life as they begin to develop outside interests again.

(e) *To define specific problems that may need to be resolved for each person to achieve specific goals.* While family members cannot set goals for each other, the ability of individuals to achieve what they want for themselves will naturally be influenced by the behaviour of other members of the family. It is important therefore to identify what these issues are so that they can be discussed and resolved in family meetings. For example, one person may be unable to achieve a personal goal of enrolling for a night class because the family member with schizophrenia is unaware of dangers around the house, and frequently forgets to switch off the cooker after preparing a meal. The family will need to discuss how this situation can be dealt with in order to ensure that the family member can attend night classes without worrying about what is going on at home.

(f) *To define the strengths and weaknesses of each household member that may contribute to or detract from mutual problem-solving.* During the assessment stage, the therapist makes note of the particular strengths and difficulties of each individual in the family so that these can be used or addressed later. If one individual has particular strengths or abilities, for example is a good listener or is good at coming up with ideas, this person can model these skills for others in the family. On the other hand, if someone in the family has particular difficulty in expressing feelings, the therapist will need to pay particular attention to that person when training the family in this aspect of communication. The therapist should also check for literacy problems as participants will be asked to read and keep records as part of the approach.

A frequent question from professionals new to the behavioural family therapy approach concerns what they should do if people disclose information that they do not wish to share with other members of the family. The therapists must respect the wishes of the individual and ensure they do not share information told to them in confidence during individual meetings. Some information of this kind may have little bearing on the present difficulties experienced by the family, for example the fact that a husband or wife had a brief affair 20 years earlier. However, when information has immediate implications for the family, the therapist will encourage the family member to share it with the rest of the family, pointing out the consequences of not doing so.

Assessment of family communications and problem-solving

Skills

Once the therapist has interviewed the family together and individually, the next stage of assessment determines how the family functions as a group. In particular, it assesses their ability to communicate with each other and to solve problems together. This can be done in three ways.

(a) The therapist makes observations in a natural setting. The ways in which different members of the family communicate with each other are noted by the therapist whenever she/he meets with them or sees them interacting together.

(b) Reported problem-solving. The therapist asks the family to describe several recent examples of how they dealt with day-to-day issues or problems. This account is detailed, requiring descriptions of the setting, who was involved, how discussions were structured, and how the family arrived at a solution to the problem.

(c) Observed problem-solving. The therapist sets the family the task of discussing a relevant current problem. She/he observes how the family members communicate with each other and how they go about resolving this issue. The topic chosen should be one of family-wide concern rather than one that focuses exclusively on a particular family member. Care should also be taken that the issue chosen for discussion is unlikely to prove explosive and to precipitate a major family crisis.

The main purpose of the family assessment is to define the strengths and weaknesses of the household group as a problem-solving unit.

Formulation and summary

When all the assessments have been completed, the therapist meets with the family as a group, and summarises the results of the assessments. She/he agrees with the family what the main issues are, and what strengths the family possesses to help them to deal with the difficulties they face. Of course, the process of assessment continues throughout the time the therapist is in contact with the family.

Weekly family meetings without the therapist

The purpose of the behavioural family therapy approach is that the family will learn the skills necessary in order to solve problems effectively on their own, and that they will not remain dependent on the presence of the therapist in order to do so. Right from the start, therefore, the therapist invites the family to identify a time each week when they will be able to meet together to discuss household issues. The family is asked to begin these meetings straight away so that they have a forum for discussion of pertinent issues. These meetings are separate from the family meetings with the therapist.

Further work

The course of further work is determined by the assessments that have been carried out, and by the needs of the family at this point. Behavioural family therapy is not a 'package' where the same skills and information are provided to all families, but a modular approach. Different families are taught to acquire skills in the areas where they are deficient, but are not taught skills that they already possess. Similarly, the information provided is geared towards their particular needs and wishes.

Education

It is rare for this module not to be offered, as most families seem to have specific gaps in their understanding of the disorder, questions that they want answered, or particular areas of confusion where they seek clarification. Information is provided by the therapist in an interactive rather than didactic manner, and the amount of time spent on this section varies from family to family. The person with the disorder is seen as the expert on the disorder, and helps other family members to understand what the experience of schizophrenia is like. The therapist takes care to check the family's current understanding of the disorder, and gently tries to correct misconceptions, allowing the family time to assimilate new information. The therapist may not be able to answer all the family's questions, but endeavours to provide the answers, or to bring to the next session a colleague who can provide more detailed information on a particular aspect of care. Education continues throughout therapy, and the family may wish to return again and again to topics about which they are unsure. It is essential to help members of each family to recognise the early warning signs of relapse. Written material is provided so that families have the opportunity to go back over topics they are unsure of.

Communication skills training

Family members may need to acquire skills in some or all of the following areas:

(a) How to express positive feelings to each other.
(b) How to make requests of each other in a positive way.
(c) How to express unpleasant or negative feelings to each other in a constructive manner.
(d) How to listen actively to each other.

Each skill is introduced in a clear manner and is broken down into its component parts. The family is provided with instruction sheets which they can keep. For each skill, the following points are emphasised. Speakers should ensure that they get the other person's attention by making eye contact with them before saying anything. They should also make sure that the person to whom they are speaking is not distracted by other things such as radio, television, or by tasks in hand such as cooking. There is an emphasis on making comments that are specific rather than general so that the person listening is in no doubt about what is meant. Finally, family members are asked to take responsibility for their own feelings in relation to each of these communication skills, and to make 'I' statements rather than statements of the type "You made me feel...".

The component steps for each of these communication skills are listed below together with their rationale.

(a) Expressing positive feelings:
    (i)   look at person,
    (ii) say exactly what they did that pleased you,
    (iii) tell them how it made you feel.

This skill is seen as important because it helps to lift the atmosphere in the household, because people like having their efforts acknowledged, and because people are more likely to repeat actions that result in a positive response from others.

(b) Making positive requests:
    (i)   look at person,
    (ii) say exactly what you would like them to do,
    (iii) tell them how it would make you feel.

In making positive requests use phrases like: "I would like you to...", "I would appreciate it if you would...", "I would be pleased if you would...".

It is felt to be an essential skill in any household that family members are able to ask each other for things that they want, for help that they need, or for other members of the family to stop

behaving in a way that is upsetting for them. Asking in a positive
way is more likely to achieve success than nagging, shouting or being
sarcastic.

    (c) Expressing unpleasant feelings:
        (i)   look at the person and speak firmly,
        (ii) say exactly what they did that upset you,
        (iii) tell them how it made you feel,
        (iv) take responsibility for ensuring that your unpleasant
              feelings are resolved (e.g. arrange problem-solving
              discussions, or make positive requests for alternative
              behaviours).

It is seen as a natural part of family life that family members will feel
angry, annoyed or frustrated with each other. However, family
members often find it hard to express these feelings. This sometimes
results in angry outbursts after long periods of keeping things to
oneself, or in detrimental effects on the individual as a result of
keeping such intense feelings inside. Being able to express these
difficult feelings promptly and directly enables family members to
move on to take some actions to resolve the cause of these feelings.

    (d) Active listening:
        (i)   look at the speaker,
        (ii) attend to what is said,
        (iii) nod head, say 'uh-huh',
        (iv) ask clarifying questions,
        (v)   check what you heard.

Being able to listen to each other is a core communication skill for
all family members.

Problem-solving

One important skill that all families find useful is learning a
structured method whereby they can solve problems that arise, or
that can be used to structure their discussions when trying to work
towards particular goals. A six-point method of doing this is
introduced to the family as follows:

    (a) pinpoint the problem/goal,
    (b) generate potential solutions,
    (c) evaluate potential consequences,
    (d) agree on 'best' strategy,
    (e) plan and implement,
    (f) review results.

When families learn to use this method, they are then in a position to work out solutions to problems on their own, rather than depend on professionals or other people to come up with solutions for them.

How skills are introduced to families

Within the behavioural family therapy method, all skills are introduced in a similar format. The families quickly become used to it, and learning seems more rapid as a result. Its components are:

(a) the therapist elicits the rationale for the skill from family members;
(b) therapist summarises rationale;
(c) family members describe recent examples of use of skill or attempts at using it;
(d) therapist introduces skill in manageable steps;
(e) family members practise skill;
(f) family members receive feedback from each other and therapist;
(g) family members practise again if necessary using information from the feedback received;
(h) between-session practice is agreed;
(i) therapist checks that all family members understand what they are expected to do before next session.

Similarly, each session is structured in the same way, so that families know what to expect. Family members who have concentration problems seem to be helped by the familiarity of this approach, and find it easier to keep to a task. Those with schizophrenia also seem to favour the predictable nature of these sessions compared with therapy sessions that are unstructured and whose unpredictability leads to them feeling frightened and anxious.

The seven tasks of family sessions

These are:

(a) review of progress towards individual goals (2–5 minutes) –
  (i)   steps achieved,
  (ii) problems encountered,
  (iii) problem-solving/goal achievement efforts;
(b) review of family meeting (5–10 minutes) –
  (i)   structure of discussion,
  (ii) problem-solving/goal achievement efforts;

    (c) review between-session practice –
        (i)   worksheet reports of skills used,
        (ii) re-enactment of skills used;
    (d) revision of continuing deficits (5–10 minutes) –
        (i)   education (including use of early warning signs and current mental status),
        (ii) communication skills,
        (iii) problem-solving skills,
        (iv) specific behavioural strategies,
        (v)   crisis management, employing problem-solving method;
    (e) work on training modules (20–30 minutes);
    (f) assign between-session practice (5–10 minutes) –
        (i)   rationale,
        (ii) explain worksheets,
        (iii) use of prompt sheets,
        (iv) family meeting;
    (g) record-keeping (5–10 minutes after session) –
        (i)   therapist fills in own notes.

Ground rules are set for sessions from the start, for example that participants are punctual, and that sessions will be terminated if family members are abusive towards each other or if there is violence or threatened violence during sessions.

Common questions raised by therapists who are new to behavioural family therapy

How does the role of the therapist differ in behavioural family therapy from that in other forms of therapy?

Behavioural family therapists need to be active, energetic and enthusiastic, acting as a trainer or coach in helping families to acquire new skills. They have to prepare sessions carefully in advance, and to try to model in their own behaviour skills the families are expected to use. Therapists already familiar with a therapeutic style that relies on the family to raise all the issues, or where change can take years to come about, can find the active nature of this approach difficult to adjust to. Prompting people to do things such as expressing unpleasant feelings to each other may seem alien to therapists who wait for things to happen naturally. Once therapists have seen that the approach works, they are generally willing to risk changes in their style of working.

    The aim of behavioural family therapy is that families will eventually be able to sort out difficulties on their own without depending on the therapist. Other therapists new to behavioural family therapy can find it hard at times to sit back and let the family get on with solving problems, feeling that they are not being 'real' therapists because they are not doing anything. It can take time for the therapist to begin to get satisfaction from watching a family manage independently and to see this as successful therapy.

What are the expectations of families?

Families too have to be very active in behavioural family therapy, and to be prepared to work between sessions. Most families prefer this to sitting around talking, especially when they notice that change occurs quickly in those areas that are of concern to them. They also generally prefer the here-and-now focus of behavioural family therapy compared with approaches that emphasise the past.

How can a family who are constantly talking about their guilt be helped to move on?

When one of their members has schizophrenia, most families from time to time wonder if they have done something to cause this, and may express guilt about what they have or have not done. The first helpful thing the therapist can do is to provide accurate information about the aetiology of schizophrenia, so that families are not blaming themselves inappropriately. While it is important to give the family time to express their feelings of guilt, it is not helpful if families continue to do this, as behavioural family therapy sees guilt as a draining emotion that rarely results in anything constructive or positive. This too is pointed out to families, who are encouraged to shift their focus to current areas where they can have more effect.

What if the family is acting in a way that is unhelpful or damaging to the person with schizophrenia?

It is important here to distinguish between action and intent. In the behavioural family therapy model it is acknowledged that families may act in ways that are unhelpful but that it is not their intention to be unhelpful. It is felt that all actions on the part of the family are their best effort at that point in time to deal with a difficult situation within the limits of their resources. Often families act in unhelpful ways because nobody has shown them how to deal with problems in a more constructive manner. The behavioural family therapy approach does not make assumptions or interpretations about a family's behaviour, but concentrates on how to help them to improve their problem-solving efforts.

What if the family finds the approach 'artificial'?

Their feelings should be acknowledged, but the therapist will also emphasise the effectiveness of behavioural family therapy. Families may also be reminded that all change can seem uncomfortable, and that learning any essential new skill, such as driving a car, may have seemed artificial at the beginning. If possible, examples may be found of how the approach, although strange, has already helped with problems of concern to the family.

What if the therapist is reluctant to use the term 'schizophrenia' because of the stigma associated with it?

Some therapists hesitate to mention 'schizophrenia', fearing the effect it may have on the family. However, most sufferers and their families find uncertainty and lack of knowledge more difficult to deal with. They want to know what is wrong, and are relieved to have a name for it. Those professionals who are worried about schizophrenia being a 'label' often tell people what is wrong but offer them little else. Certainly there is little point in telling anyone they have schizophrenia if they are not going to be told anything else about it or offered help in dealing with the disorder and reducing the likelihood of relapse. The major issue is not whether the term 'schizophrenia' is used. It is what else is offered to people, and whether the service routinely provides the types of family interventions that have been shown to work with schizophrenia. The growth of user movements and government policies emphasising people's rights in recent years makes it unlikely that professionals will remain in a position to withhold information from families. Atkinson (1989) argues that there is no justification for not telling people that they have schizophrenia, on moral, clinical or practical grounds.

What if a family is reluctant to engage in therapy?

Families need to be given time to think, and several meetings may be necessary in order to identify and discuss their concerns with them. It is essential they understand what the approach involves, what will be expected of them, and that any unhelpful therapeutic experiences they may have had in the past are discussed. The effectiveness of the approach should be emphasised, with examples of how it could help them with their present difficulties. New families need to know that behavioural family therapy can help everyone in the family, not just the person with the disorder. Reading material can be helpful, as can a trial session to help them judge for themselves. Above all, the therapist should be enthusiastic, and should demonstrate that she/he believes that the approach is worthwhile.

References

ATKINSON, J. M. (1989) To tell or not to tell the diagnosis of schizophrenia. *Journal of Medical Ethics*, **15**, 21–24.

BARROWCLOUGH, C. & TARRIER, N. (1992) *Families of Schizophrenic Patients*. London: Chapman & Hall.

FADDEN, G., BEBBINGTON, P. & KUIPERS, L. (1987) The burden of care: the impact of functional psychiatric illness on the patient's family. *British Journal of Psychiatry*, **150**, 185–292.

FALLOON, I. R. H., BOYD, J. L., McGILL, C. W., *et al* (1982) Family management in the prevention of exacerbations of schizophrenia: a controlled study. *New England Journal of Medicine*, **306**, 1437–1440.

——, —— & —— (1984) *Family Care of Schizophrenia*. New York: Guilford Press.

——, ——, ——, *et al* (1985) Family management in the prevention of morbidity of schizophrenia: clinical outcome of a two year longitudinal study. *Archives of General Psychiatry*, **42**, 887–896.

—— & FADDEN, G. (1993*a*) *Integrated Mental Health Care*. Cambridge: Cambridge University Press.

——, LAPORTA, M., FADDEN, G., *et al* (1993*b*) *Managing Stress in Families*. London: Routledge.

HATFIELD, A. B. (1990) *Family Education in Mental Illness*. New York: Guilford Press.

HOGARTY, G. E., ANDERSON, C. M., REISS, D. J., *et al* (1986) Family psychoeducation, social skills training and maintenance chemotherapy in the aftercare treatment of schizophrenia. I. One year effects of a controlled study on relapse and expressed emotion. *Archives of General Psychiatry*, **43**, 633–642.

——, ——, ——, *et al* (1991) Family psychoeducation, social skills training, and maintenance chemotherapy in the aftercare treatment of schizophrenia. *Archives of General Psychiatry*, **48**, 340–347.

KOTTGEN, C., SONNICHSEN, I., MOLLENHAUER, K., *et al* (1984) Results of the Hamburg Camberwell family interview study, I–III. *International Journal of Family Psychiatry*, **5**, 61–94.

LAM, D. H. (1991) Psychosocial family intervention in schizophrenia: a review of empirical studies. *Psychological Medicine*, **21**, 423–441.

LEFF, J., KUIPERS, L., BERKOWITZ, R., *et al* (1982) A controlled trial of social intervention in the families of schizophrenic patients. *British Journal of Psychiatry*, **141**, 121–134.

——, ——, ——, *et al* (1985) A controlled trial of social intervention in the families of schizophrenic patients: two year follow up. *British Journal of Psychiatry*, **146**, 594–600.

STRACHAN, A. M. (1986) Family intervention for the rehabilitation of schizophrenia: toward protection and coping. *Schizophrenia Bulletin*, **12**, 678–698.

TARRIER, N., BARROWCLOUGH, C., VAUGHN, C., *et al* (1988) The community management of schizophrenia: a controlled trial of a behavioural intervention with families to reduce relapse. *British Journal of Psychiatry*, **153**, 532–542.

——, ——, ——, *et al* (1989) Community management of schizophrenia: a two year follow-up of a behavioural intervention with families. *British Journal of Psychiatry*, **154**, 625–628.

VAUGHAN, K., DOYLE, M., McCONAGHY, N., *et al* (1992) The Sydney intervention trial: a controlled trial of relatives' counselling to reduce schizophrenic relapse. *Social Psychiatry and Psychiatric Epidemiology*, **27**, 16–21.

Part IV. Integrative approaches to psychosis

The material in this final section shows ways in which the treatment of psychosis might be improved through two of the declared aims of the original conference: a preparedness to learn from the experience of more than one of the established traditions of psychotherapy, and a willingness to reintegrate areas of psychotherapeutic work within general psychiatry. There are many ways in which such an integration can be expressed, and this section can only illustrate a selection. In the first chapter, Margison and Mace look at the rationale and potential scope of integrative approaches to psychosis, and consider a very important historical example of psychotherapy that defies traditional classifications in this area, pioneered by Silvano Arieti.

Several examples of integrated work are then presented, namely: the care of victims of child sexual abuse on an acute psychiatric ward; the establishment of dedicated project wards for the group treatment of patients with psychosis within a traditional mental hospital; and the organisation of a coordinated national project for the care and aftercare of schizophrenic patients and their families. Each of these accounts clarifies ways in which the projects required the removal or realignment of old barriers and boundaries in ways that were not necessarily comfortable for those working on them, as well as for those who stood to gain directly from them. What each offers, therefore, is not only informative descriptions of some of the effects (and side-effects) that such work can achieve, but a good deal of practical experience that is likely to help others attempting a similar project.

The final contribution to this section comes from the final day of the conference. It also challenges some traditional and revered boundaries, particularly that between the understandable and the non-understandable. From his work on the meaning of psychotic delusions, Glenn Roberts illustrates how a relatively simple shift in perspective can prompt reappraisal not only of how, when and if to intervene, but of how those working with psychosis might best be trained to undertake this demanding task.

13 Integration and psychosis

FRANK MARGISON and CHRIS MACE

Up to this point, the three core traditions have been introduced in relative isolation. This may give the impression that increasing sophistication on the part of psychotherapists regarding the nature of psychosis has led to it being refracted through different lenses, creating images that are not always easy to reconcile. The contributions in this final section of the book illustrate ways in which attempts either to integrate insights from different approaches, or to adopt a more holistic approach that defies such easy categorisation, offer new directions for therapeutic endeavour. Indeed, it can be helpful to remember that psychotherapy's primary task is to help and relieve suffering, and that its theories are ultimately tested in responses to evident need. In looking towards the future of psychotherapy for psychosis, the example of medicine, whose own theoretical base has evolved continually in the service of clinical ends, may be useful.

Technology and differentiation in medicine and psychotherapy

Medicine has repeatedly been subject to two opposing forces: moves towards greater *differentiation* as technology develops; and developments in the provision of health care that promote greater *integration*. This is as true in the understanding and treatment of, say, diabetes as it is in schizophrenia. The ability to reclassify subtypes of disease which allows better 'targeting' of interventions is balanced against the need to treat the whole person, who is in turn part of a community.

Imbalances between differentiation and integration can themselves resemble the psychological features of psychosis. When differentiation is excessive, it is easy to lose any sense of a consistent overall perspective, as excessive focusing on individual elements blocks access to the picture as a whole. On the other hand, overemphasis on integration can lead to an illusion of wholeness that prevents discrimination of any separate elements (see Albeniz & Holmes, 1996).

Contributions in this book represent different attitudes to these opposing forces: some authors argue in effect that social and psychological interventions are part of the process of differentiation. Tarrier and co-authors (Chapter 9) and Kingdon and Turkington (Chapter 8) argue for an enlargement of the category of patients who can respond to carefully defined treatment interventions. Such interventions can be observed to work empirically and can be judged against other interventions in the same 'currency' as pharmacological interventions (effect sizes, compliance rates, relapse rates and cost-effectiveness).

This is not to argue that such interventions, once defined, cannot coexist with other treatments, but that the tradition from which they derive is hypothetico-deductive. Greater understanding is gained through increasing the refinement of research questions, and the boundaries of diagnostic groups are redefined on empirical rather than theoretical grounds.

A more integrative approach is implicit when the therapeutic perspective widens beyond that of the individual patient. In the preceding chapters, this is evident in the constructive interplay permitted by the therapeutic group (Walshe, Chapter 5; Pines, Chapter 6), and when the whole family is involved in treatment (Kennedy, Chapter 11; Fadden, Chapter 12). However, these represent only the start of the possibilities. What forms of philosophical as well as practical integration are currently possible?

The need for philosophical as well as practical integration was the 'accepted wisdom' of psychiatry only a couple of decades ago. The Meyerian tradition of integrating the social, the psychological and the physical was understood not merely at the level of the 'treatment package' from the multidisciplinary team, but as a way of describing and understanding the lifelong development of an individual in terms of these three coexisting and interweaving strands (Gelder, 1991). This outlook differs markedly from the essentially organic models of today, in which genetic predisposition is emphasised and experience has a place only in concessions that current life factors may influence the timing of onset of individual episodes of illness.

The integrative model of Silvano Arieti

There has been considerable criticism of eclecticism as a trend that blurs distinctions between different theoretical models and only dilutes their effectiveness. This is not the same thing as an integrative approach, in which complementary components of a hybrid therapy remain well defined and rigorously applied. One example of a carefully integrated and logical approach to treatment is to be found in the work of Silvano Arieti (1975). While he is not unique in taking an integrated approach to treatment, his writing is admirably lucid and his ability to convey the complexity of working systematically with problems at several levels is consistent with many comments by contributors to this volume. Arieti distinguishes four aspects of the therapeutic task, which broadly correspond to four different approaches:

(a) establishing relatedness (interpersonal);
(b) treatment of the overt symptoms (some of which is cognitive–behavioural);
(c) understanding and analysis (psychodynamic);
(d) general participation in the patient's life (systemic).

In establishing relatedness, he stresses just how contingent the therapist's approach must be in dealing with extreme withdrawal or excitement. He also stresses the importance of everyday human language rather than technical interventions, while being aware that some approaches (such as walking with the patient) may inadvertently generate a state of terror.

Arieti also describes how alienating and frightening direct questions can be (for example when interpreted as an attempt to take something away) and suggests talking about less highly charged topics initially, conveying a sincere attempt to reach the patient with 'no strings attached'. He suggests ways of talking empathically to, or remaining silently with, patients who are mute and catatonic. The therapist should not pretend to understand heavily distorted and thought-disordered speech, but sit and listen to the themes and the atmosphere of what is being communicated. At other times, with patients who talk incessantly about delusional preoccupations, the therapist might need to "detour his attention and re-establish his interest in the other aspects of life". The therapist, at times, needs to avoid implicit acceptance of the psychotic material by explaining that there might be reasons why things are being interpreted in particular ways.

Arieti's approach so far has been pragmatic and based on an equal and direct relationship with the patient. He also describes some of the specific techniques for removing symptoms, and these bear striking similarities to recent developments in cognitive therapy. He suggests "enlarging the patient's psychotemporal field" to help distinguish past events from the present and hence to reattribute meaning. He argues with the patient's tendency to take a 'referential attitude' and uses strategies to point out undue generalisation and inference as a way of reducing an undifferentiated threat to a series of smaller, concrete examples. He also suggests distraction and self-management strategies (although using different terminology).

Arieti draws heavily on some of the psychodynamic and psychoanalytic concepts discussed in Reilly's overview (Chapter 2). He points out that understanding transference and countertransference is crucial in any treatment approach. At the same time, the need to be involved more extensively in the systems of which a patient is a part represents an important theme that Arieti introduces. He comments that patients may develop depression as they become less overtly psychotic. He also points out that getting well 'for someone else' such as the therapist can be highly conflictual.

Arieti's integrative approach raises a general therapeutic issue about the *timing* and *context* of any intervention. Therapy can be used as prophylaxis against further breakdown or during an illness (either as a primary treatment or as an adjunct to other methods). He draws attention to the need for treatment to aid the recovery process, helping the patient to move on from habitual patterns of dependence after a long illness, or helping the patient to assimilate a terrifying experience after an acute psychosis.

There may also be coexisting difficulties that require attention in their own right. For example, a patient with a psychotic illness may also be dealing with current losses, such as bereavement, and losses that are partly linked with the illness, such as unemployment or the loss of a partner precipitated by the breakdown.

In this way Arieti's systematic, problem-solving approach is combined with both a systemic understanding (heavily influenced by Sullivan), and an approach that draws on psychodynamic thinking to understand what underlies the psychotic symptoms. While being pragmatic about possible resolutions, his approach is also interpersonal and pays considerable attention to the careful use of language. It has been summarised at some length because it exemplifies pragmatism, idealism and the integration of traditions which this volume seeks to foster.

The possibilities and problems of integration

Arieti's model of a more broadly based therapy has its counterparts in attempts to synthesise previous work in creating new forms of 'supportive' therapy for psychotic and borderline patients (Kates &

Rockland, 1994; Holmes, 1995). Glenn Robert's chapter at the end of this section moves from the importance of sensitivity to the particularity of psychotic speech eloquently surveyed by Murray Cox in Chapter 3, towards the reconstruction of 'narrative' from it as an intrinsically therapeutic endeavour. As he points out, the interest of researchers into attachment theory, who have used normative measures of 'narrative competence' as an index of attachment, has given a tremendous fillip to interest in the therapeutic potential of narrative. This interest has been reciprocated by systemic therapists (cf. Chapter 10) and is continuing to grow, with the likelihood that more narrative-centred therapies will be developed in the near future for use with patients often thought beyond the reach of explorative therapies.

Other approaches may be integrative by virtue of the way they are implemented within a more complicated system, whether this is a hospital ward, a hospital, or a national health-care delivery system. An example of initiatives at each of these levels that demanded new patterns of thought and work is provided in each of the three chapters that follow.

The impact of an integrative reorganisation is inevitably most graphic in the third of these, Pylkkanen's account (Chapter 16) of a nationally coordinated approach to the provision of psychotherapy that shows the importance of government policy in defining the delivery of complex services. In the UK, the equivalent responsibility for integration is devolved to local authorities and health authorities, who are instructed to integrate care at a bureaucratic level through such mechanisms as the Care Programme Approach; the linking of health and social care; and the management of risk to the community through the use of supervision registers. We are not yet at a sufficient distance to know whether these integrative forces are sufficiently powerful or coherent enough to achieve their objectives. There is also a general absence of any guiding vision in the UK that integrates the biomedical with the social–ecological view, or the social interactional view with individual psychology as Pylkkanen's chapter describes.

However, it is evident from each of these accounts that any concentrated move towards integration is bound to encounter resistance. Sarah Davenport (Chapter 14) presents a situation at some remove from attempts at national reform by addressing the difficult question of how wards need to operate so that some of their most disturbed occupants, whose sense of personal boundary has been violently damaged, will not have further harm done to them by the experience of being there. Active intervention is called for if a compulsive dynamic that would compound rather than relieve their sense of violation is not to be repeated. Dianne LeFevre and Frank Morrison

(Chapter 15) describe a project that is overtly ambitious, in the form of a therapeutic regime introduced for people traditionally believed to be unable to use it. The resistance of the beneficiaries is compounded by that channelled through staff and their colleagues. LeFevre records how such a struggle not only endangers the integrative project, but can endanger the health of those who identify with its success. It seems essential to be aware of such dangers in order to make use of the practical advice that these authors also provide. Even the immaculately designed programme that Pylkkanen describes in Chapter 16 was ended prematurely for non-clinical reasons. The future development of integrative approaches is likely to be assisted by analysis and classification of the blocks and barriers that seem to arise inevitably to hinder their progress.

Integration can also be seen as a strategy pursued by patients to deal with psychotic experiences. Using cognitive therapy techniques to assist the patient's struggle to integrate has been shown to be successful by Birchwood and colleagues (Drury *et al*, 1996).

Conclusions

While researchers may find it essential to isolate individual elements to test particular hypotheses, in clinical practice an integrated approach to any particular individual or family is likely to be beneficial. Greater integration seems required in the organisation of service developments than currently prevails, including the increasing integration of psychotherapists within multidisciplinary teams where a range of orientations is represented. Integration also needs to be far more apparent in the training of psychiatrists and others working with patients with psychoses.

References

ALBENIZ, A. & HOLMES, J. (1996) Psychotherapy integration: its implications for psychiatry. *British Journal of Psychiatry*, **169**, 563–570.
ARIETI, S. (1975) The psychotherapy of psychosis. In *American Handbook of Psychiatry* (4th edn) (ed. S. Arieti), pp. 627–629. New York: Basic Books.
DRURY, V., BIRCHWOOD, M., COCHRANE, R., *et al* (1996) Cognitive therapy and recovery from acute psychosis: a controlled trial. I: Impact on psychotic symptoms. *British Journal of Psychiatry*, **169**, 593–601.
GELDER, M. (1991) Adolf Meyer and his influence on British psychiatry. In *150 Years of British Psychiatry* (eds G. E. Berrios & H. Freedman), pp. 419–435. London: Gaskell.
HOLMES, J. (1995) Supportive psychotherapy: the search for positive meanings. *British Journal of Psychiatry*, **167**, 439–445.
KATES, J. & ROCKLAND, L. H. (1994) Supportive psychotherapy of the schizophrenic patient. *American Journal of Psychotherapy*, **48**, 543–561.

14 Pathological interactions between psychosis and childhood sexual abuse in in-patient settings: their dynamics, consequences and management

SARAH DAVENPORT

The problem

On Friday afternoon, you visit the ward to be greeted by the senior nurse, who tells you that the team all agree that Ms X's diagnosis should be regraded to personality disorder from schizophrenia. They claim evidence suggesting that she is manipulative and demanding of nursing input, and that all behavioural interventions have failed. The occupational therapist refuses to work with her, and her primary nurse has been off sick for the past week. The team want her discharged to residential care, organised by her social worker, as she is 'untreatable' and should not be occupying a precious in-patient bed. They blame the consultant for clinical ineptitude in admitting her in the first place, and point out just how much time they have wasted. Even the registrar agrees with the revised diagnosis and resents the medical time withdrawn from "more deserving patients" when he has to attend to her regular self-harming behaviour. The rage is tangible and demands a response. What should this be?

The thoughtful clinician may reflect for a while, before being drawn into the powerful dynamics being expressed. Reflection generates the following.

(a) Ms X was sexually abused by her mother's cohabitee between the ages of 5 and 15. He is serving a prison term but her mother refuses to believe that he is guilty, blaming her daughter for inventing a venomous lie. The staff team are also divided in their belief about this, just like Ms X's family.

(b) Ms X developed clear symptoms of schizophrenia at the age of 20, which respond to neuroleptic administration. However, she is frequently non-compliant, relapses, and is readmitted in crisis. During periods of relapse she appears regressed and highly dependent, but does not express florid positive symptoms; she often harms herself on the in-patient unit, making the staff feel angry, powerless and ineffective.

(c) Ms X has already had two other consultants and a variety of conflicting second opinions; she has not yet received a period of consistent care from one team for longer than six months – she has always been 'transferred', with an altered diagnosis, in contentious circumstances.

Even on a Friday afternoon, the thoughtful clinician may be able to reflect on the toxic re-enactment that is occurring here. Revictimisation within in-patient settings carries the risk of anti-therapeutic care for the survivor, and of harm (stress and burnout) occurring to the staff caring for the survivor, as those staff become caught up in the dynamic processes.

The preamble

The characteristic dynamics of abuse are primitive, salient and frequently overdetermined. The characteristic dynamics of psychosis are powerful, confusing and primitive, putting reality testing at risk for patients and sometimes for staff; they often excite considerable countertransference responses, which may or may not be objectively felt and understood as a communication. These dynamics interact with the large- and small-group dynamics of an in-patient setting, which is itself embedded in the institutional dynamics of the wider hospital. Interactions at each of these levels may occur to influence the care that is offered by staff and received by patients.

Surveys of psychiatric in-patients suggest that the prevalence of childhood abuse, sexual or physical, is as high as 57% (Jacobson & Richardson, 1987). Mullen *et al* (1993) reported that the severity of abuse correlated with severity of adult psychopathology. About half of any in-patient sample is likely to have elements within their psychopathology relating to that experience of sexual abuse. Those who are the most ill, including patients suffering from psychosis, may have some of the most severe manifestations of abuse. They may also be most at risk from disadvantageous interactions. It is therefore important to pay attention to the various ways in which these characteristic dynamics may interact to result in toxic re-enactment (or revictimisation). Understanding the potential for these interactions affords a way of improving the provision of therapeutic care, and suggests that more attention should be paid to staff support, clinical supervision and to facilitated staff groups.

Characteristic dynamics of abuse

Dependent children are powerless at the time of abuse to defend or protect themselves against physical and psychological violation. Their self is threatened with the anxiety of annihilation and their exterior is breached by the act itself. Primitive defences to protect the self develop, such as repression, denial, detachment of feeling, depersonalisation and dissociation. These may be adaptive for the child to survive the experience of abuse, but if they persist into adulthood, at the expense of more mature and flexible defensive functioning, these primitive defences become overdetermined and restrict the range and flexibility of interpersonal behaviour. There is a definite psychological cost to individuals with a rigid defensive style or inflexible personality function, as the opportunities for appropriate interpersonal support are limited and the risk of comorbidity high. The primitive defences that are self-preservative for the abused child usually persist. They subsequently distort adult defensive and personality style and result in major difficulties with interpersonal relationships. These can be summarised as follows:

(a) difficulty with establishing trusting relationships;
(b) difficulties with boundaries;
(c) difficulties within power relationships;
(d) revictimisation;
(e) low self-esteem, self-disgust and self-loathing;
(f) sexualisation of therapeutic relationships;
(g) transference difficulties;
(h) countertransference difficulties.

Difficulty with establishing trusting relationships

Sexual abuse of the dependent child by an adult usually occurs within a relationship where that child should have been able to trust the adult to meet dependency needs in a developmentally appropriate way. Where the needs of the child are not prioritised but exploited, the expectation of basic trust within the relationship is shattered, creating the repeated experience of disconfirmation of basic trust. In Bowlby's terms, the intimate attachment relationship that becomes the 'internal working model' for future relationships is one that is not to be trusted as it will result in personal violation. Where abuse is repeated and long term, and occurs in the absence of alternative protective relationships, the internalised model is salient and determines the quality and expectations of adult relationships. This may have a very damaging impact on the victim's ability to make and sustain therapeutic relationships, particularly where psychosis distorts interpersonal perceptions and expectations. Persecutory delusions, delusional perception, derogatory auditory hallucinosis and delusional mood will partially determine how a psychotic individual perceives the care environment. Where psychotic persecutory feelings fit with an internal working model that relationships are not to be trusted, the task of establishing a trusting therapeutic alliance is definitely uphill.

Many survivors of abuse will unconsciously test out relationships to determine whether their internal model of untrustworthiness is correct in the present case. This leads to repeated 'testing out' with carers. The repeated nature of the testing out may be necessary for the psychotic patient to disconfirm these expectations, but it may become very difficult for staff to tolerate, as it is in conflict with the ethos of their profession – that they are there to care and to be trusted. Care staff find it difficult to be distrusted; this often promotes irritation and frustration, particularly where the testing out seems to exclude all other potentially therapeutic interactions with staff.

Difficulties with establishing basic trust within a therapeutic alliance may also be compounded by a psychotic patient's lack of insight. Denial of illness, refusal to take medication and lack of trust may all conspire to produce an impasse in, or a breakdown of, the therapeutic process. This leads to demoralisation of staff and patient alike, but is potentially much more dangerous for the patient, who may become "malignantly alienated" (Watts & Morgan, 1994) from the treatment setting, and therefore at increased risk of suicide.

Difficulties with boundaries

Violation of the child's separateness, the use of the child as an object, or as an extension of the self of the perpetrator during the abuse, leads to long-term difficulties with understanding and maintaining personal boundaries. This is often expressed by the survivor in inappropriate questions about the personal life of a carer, excursions through social and professional boundaries (bursting into the office in the middle of a hand-over), confusion of personal boundaries (demanding that another patient is present during a key-worker session, or that a child is present during an adult transaction) and fragmentation and splitting of information and feeling states among the care team. These difficulties are augmented for the psychotic survivor, where the boundary between the inner and outer worlds is weak and confused. Intrapsychic conflict may be projected on to external figures, who may then become personifications of terror or anxiety. Symbolisation is often bizarre and concrete so that objects may become alive in the outside world to persecute or torture. Reality testing is poor and offers no protection. Care staff may be seen as personifications of internal feeling states and treated as such, that is, verbally or physically assaulted. The confusion of inner and outer worlds in psychosis is reinforced by the difficulties with appreciating and maintaining personal boundaries for the abuse victim.

Some attention must also be paid to the maintenance of safe physical boundaries within the care setting. Ward doors and windows may need to be secure, to contain an agitated psychotic survivor, who fears boundary intrusions and externalised persecutors. Time boundaries are also important in the form of regular appointments, secure from the intrusions of the telephone and the bleep.

Difficulties within power relationships

The relationship with the perpetrator is often one of the most important relationships in the abused child's life. Abuse occurs where there is misuse of the power relationship between dependent child and powerful adult. Misuse of this inequitable power relationship resulted in the child first being abused and then acquiring a restricted internal working model of an unequal power relationship. Survivors seem to be particularly sensitised to unequal power relationships, possibly because there is an overdetermined outcome from an unequal power relationship.

Survivors have great difficulty managing any inequitable power relationship, often shifting between the two polar positions of abused or abuser (by identification with the aggressor). There are no less salient, but more adaptive, models of interpersonal behaviour available to them. Rapid oscillation between the two polar positions also occurs.

Psychosis often robs sufferers of their personal power as autonomous individuals, and results in their placement in a care setting where power inequality between carer and cared-for is inevitable. This power inequality becomes much more tangible where compulsory admission and legal detention are issues. The opportunities for re-enactment are many, unless the dynamic interactions are thought about and at times explicitly interpreted.

Revictimisation

Child sexual abuse is a powerful predictor of victimisation in adult life. The synergism of difficulties with basic trust, boundaries and management of power relationships results in the potential for re-enactment within any interpersonal power relationship. The victim is likely to be abused again or the victim becomes the perpetrator within an exploitative relationship. This overdetermined revictim-isation interacts with the powerlessness of psychosis and the usual accompanying social disabilities, to result in revictimisation with many different themes. Psychotic sexually abused sufferers often find themselves at risk of further sexual revictimisation in in-patient settings, or may assume the role of the perpetrator with another victim of sexual abuse. Both these positions run the risk of the individual being labelled as 'promiscuous' in the first instance, or 'sexually coercive' in the second, and therefore becoming alienated because of staff disgust. Exploitation of some psychotic survivors by others for cigarettes and money is a further example of the synergy of abuse dynamics with those of psychosis as the cycles of abuse are perpetuated.

Low self-esteem, self-disgust and self-loathing

Some of the internal working models of the self held by the survivor of abuse are of low self-esteem (I am worthy of abuse), self-disgust (I am disgusting because disgusting things happen to me) and self-loathing (I am not loved, therefore not lovable and therefore must be loathsome). Survivors often believe that they are worthless and cannot be cared for, and so avoid care or demand it covertly. They may make wholly unrealistic demands for care that place carers in conflict with the ethos of their profession when they have to refuse.

Victims of abuse unconsciously seek situations that confirm their negative self-attributions or self-disgust. This may result in self-harming behaviours such as deliberate self-mutilation, or degrading behaviours such as eating from rubbish bins, faecal smearing, incontinence and wearing of soiled clothes. These behaviours may be left unchallenged as they induce disgust or revulsion in staff, and are a further risk factor for alienation from the treatment setting. These negative self-beliefs are often enhanced for the psychotic survivor by their disempowering experience of illness and by their delusional beliefs.

Sexualisation of therapeutic relationships

Survivors of child sexual abuse carry an internal working model of a relationship with an attachment figure (the perpetrator) that is highly sexualised and lacking in the other facets of a mature reciprocal adult relationship. The sexualised aspects of the relationship with the abuser may have been the only way in which care and recognition were received by the victim, who then becomes impoverished in the experience of being cared for in more appropriate ways. Hence victims may unconsciously recreate aspects of the original attachment relationship according to their own internal working model or 'script' with significant others, including their carers. These difficulties are compounded in psychosis, where sufferers may have very real difficulties with intimacy, communication, and loss of social skills, and may be severely socially isolated. The expression of needs in inappropriate or bizarre ways may enhance the likelihood of being misunderstood by care staff, and therefore increase the salience of a sexualised relationship. These aspects of the relationship may then be acted out by staff caught up in the dynamic and result in a very damaging revictimisation for the patient. There is much evidence reported from the psychotherapy literature of the high prevalence of sexual abuse of clients by therapists, and evidence from recent inquiries that sexual abuse of patients by staff occurs in a variety of different settings. The possibility of this occurring in any unit with any member of staff should never be discounted blindly.

There are also considerable risks for staff working with abused psychotic patients. The boundary between fact (or reality) and fantasy may be indistinct and confusing for the patient. Staff may find themselves meeting the needs of their patients inappropriately, and allegations of sexual misconduct may follow.

Transference difficulties

The feelings experienced by the survivor for significant attachment figures in the past, including the abuser, may be transferred on to current attachment relationships, notably those with carers. These feelings may be intense and may govern behaviour. For the psychotic patient, the distinction between internal and external objects and between good and bad may be confused as reality testing is poor. Behaviour may be regressed and impulse control less good than at more mature levels of functioning. Psychotic survivors may act out transference relationships and feelings within the care setting, sometimes putting themselves and staff at risk.

The patterns of transference may be complicated in an in-patient environment, and not necessarily restricted to the primary nurse or therapist/psychiatrist. The transference may also be split into, for example, 'good' and 'bad mother'. It is important to pick up on transference relationships established by psychotic patients early, to avoid the risk of dangerous acting-out or of transferred terror or fear. However, it is also important to avoid focusing on intrapsychic mechanisms at the expense of external reality when there are aspects or people within the setting that encourage transference.

Countertransference difficulties

> "However much he loves his patients he cannot avoid hating and fearing them; the better he knows this the less will hate and fear be the motives determining what he does to his patients."
> (Winnicott, 1947, p. 69)

Working with survivors of sexual abuse evokes very powerful feelings in their carers. These feelings are similar to the feelings experienced by the survivors themselves at an earlier stage of development, possibly at the time the abuse occurred. Like some of the feelings experienced by a young baby, these feelings are primitive, intense and frightening (e.g. fear, anxiety, rage, hatred, aggression and envy). These feelings are often projected by the survivor on to their carers, where they may become identified with intrapsychic conflict belonging to the carer. Countertransference, acting-out or retaliation then becomes likely unless the carer has some understanding of the situation. Psychotic patients often project hatred, anger and aggression on to ward staff, who find themselves irritable and angry with their patients, hating them back. Like the mother of a newborn baby, in Winnicott's terms, care staff have to be able to tolerate hatred without acting on it; the countertransference hate has to be brought into conscious awareness to detoxify it by thinking about it, and not acting on it. Hospital environments are not conducive to openness about hate, and such openness may be seen as professionally unacceptable in a carer. However, the consequences of failing to deal with countertransference hate may be anti-therapeutic care and a toxic ward environment.

Characteristic dynamics of psychosis

The psychoanalytic understanding of psychosis generates a model where the interactions between the psychotic patient and various other dynamic systems may be understood. The defences employed by the individual to deal with psychosis, and those arising as a result of abuse, both interact with those inherent in the social structure of the care setting, producing a particular dynamic outcome which may be good or bad for the patient concerned.

In psychoanalytic terms, psychosis occurs when the individual regresses to a primitive mode of defensive function, at the expense of a balance with more mature modes of defensive functioning. The primitive defences seen in psychosis are similar to those seen in the very early stages of normal psychological development (i.e. splitting, grandiose omnipotent defences and projective identification). In adult psychosis, regression to an early fixation point occurs and the balance of primitive with mature defensive functioning is disturbed, so that mature ego defences and reality testing become deficient. The quality of some of the primitive defences becomes changed, notably projective identification, which becomes pathological.

Psychotic regression results in the state of narcissism (Abraham, 1911), where the predominant pregenital impulses are aggressive and sadistic, and the predominant defences are introjection (oral taking in) and projection (anal expelling). This results in objects being taken into or expelled from the developing ego. These processes contribute to ego strength or weakness and the developing ego's experience of the internal and external worlds. Thus an awareness of these two entities develops as the personality continues to take in from the environment, and to expel what is intolerable. At this level, experience gives rise to an actual sense of taking in (e.g. feeding) or expelling (e.g. defaecating) that is associated with the relief of some unpleasant affect. In normal development this process is overlaid by symbolic thinking, which involves linking perception with thought, and the primitive link is superseded. However, these primitive meanings seem to live on in parts of the personality, and may be accessed in adult life during psychotic regression.

Klein (1930*a,b*) identified the sadism, which seems to characterise early stages of psychological development, where the world seems to be populated by potential persecutors; retaliation renders persecutors more rather than less harmful, as they are supposed in fantasy to be enraged further. This leads to a vicious circle represented by the paranoid state of hostility, where potentially good figures are regarded with intense suspicion. She also demonstrated that symbolisation was inhibited at this point, potentially distorting more mature ego development. Klein believed that this stage of psychological development was a 'fixation point' for psychosis, that is, these mechanisms achieved salience and that symbolisation (verbal linking) was inhibited during the profound defensive regression of psychosis.

Rosenfeld (1947) described the extreme degrees of splitting and fragmentation that may occur in psychosis; intolerable parts of the self are split off and located in external objects or within significant others, so that psychotic patients may experience part of themselves omnipotently located in, and so confused with, the object or person in which they were located.

Segal (1950) described the schizophrenia sufferer's difficulty in negotiating the depressive position successfully. Intolerable depressive affect is split off and projected into another, possibly a nurse, therapist or family member, so relieving the sufferer. (Klein believed that this explained why it is so difficult to detect affect in schizophrenia sufferers.)

In 1959 Bion described the difference between a normal and a pathological form of projective identification, the latter being present in psychotic illnesses, and the former a feature of normal psychological development (see Bion, 1967). This normal projective identification is the basis for an extremely primitive, non-verbal and non-symbolic communication between mother and infant. This has become known as 'containing' and is important in the treatment of disturbed people, who all need 'containment' of primitive pre-verbal anxieties as a part of the care offered. The pathological form of projective identification, seen in psychosis, is achieved with maximum violence and hatred, resulting in an invaded external object becoming suffused with retaliatory hatred, that is, a bizarre object. Bion also thought that the violence and omnipotence of the trajective psychotic processes disrupted the linking of thought and perception, resulting in thought disorder, and disordered interpersonal communication.

It is not difficult to see the mirroring of these psychotic processes in the interpersonal dynamics of abuse. The difficulties with personal boundaries can be explained by the use of primitive splitting and projection of parts of the self into others, leading to psychotic confusion between self and others. The countertransference difficulties directly relate to the use of primitive projective identification, whereby intolerable (usually negative) affect such as hate is split off by the psychotic patient and sadistically invades the carers as a violent non-verbal form of communication, which is expected to produce retaliation. This may then lead to the vicious cycle of hostility and suspicion encountered with psychotic patients.

Since these psychotic processes are mirrored in the dynamics of abuse, there is a risk of pathological synergism between the two, resulting in the failure of any treatment alliance and the provision of a toxic ward milieu. There is also the potential for institutional dynamics to act as a catalyst or synergist, increasing the risks of 'toxicity' for patients and staff.

Characteristic dynamics of institutions

Any in-patient setting is affected by the dynamics of the institution in which it exists. The characteristic feature of the social defence system of a hospital is its orientation to helping the individuals who work there avoid the experience of anxiety, guilt, uncertainty and doubt (Menzies Lyth, 1988). As far as possible this is done by eliminating situations, events, tasks, activities and relationships that cause anxiety or evoke unconscious conflict. Psychic defence mechanisms that give protection from the full experience of anxiety become incorporated into the socially structured defence system of the hospital. These are chiefly the most primitive defences, such as denial and projection, and it is to this primitive level of defence that individuals regress, when in stressful situations, such as caring for psychotic people. Individuals who are psychotic are often out of touch with reality, persecuted, hostile and highly dependent. They evoke pity, compassion, love, guilt and unresolved dependency needs; they may not respond to treatment and fail to improve, evoking powerlessness and envy of the care they are receiving. They may be violent, inducing fear and the wish to retaliate, in conflict with the caring ethos. They may perform acts of self-degradation, and induce revulsion and contempt. They face professionals with very strong and often mixed feelings resembling those present in infancy, so that primitive defensive functioning becomes built into the social and organisational systems of the hospital, where they play a part for good or ill in the care that is received.

The ways in which institutional dynamics shape individual staff–patient interactions within the ward setting can be summarised as follows:

(a) detachment and denial of feelings;
(b) ritualised task performance;
(c) collusive social redistribution of roles – 'scapegoating';
(d) avoidance of change.

Detachment and denial of feelings

Within any therapeutic relationship, it is necessary for the carer to develop and maintain adequate professional detachment and professional boundaries. This allows the carer to avoid excessive involvement and disturbing identifications that would interfere with the therapeutic process. The degree of detachment will vary with the defensive style of the carer and with the amount of conflict and anxiety that the patient presents to the carer. Where the anxiety and conflict evoked by a patient are significant and sustained, detachment and denial of feelings may become extreme (i.e. a self-preservative manoeuvre on the part of the carer). Translated into the dynamics of the hospital, this institutionalised defence is seen as sudden and frequent moves of nursing staff from one unit to the next, rotation for training purposes, high sickness rates and failure to follow through care plans, particularly those that require high face-to-face contact with the patient. Splitting up the nurse–patient relationship becomes built into institutions caring for very ill people, and psychotic survivors are both very ill and disturbed. The degree to which detachment of the nurse–patient relationship occurs should be addressed for each individual so that a balance can be found between the mental health needs of the professional and the patient's need to have a reliable, consistent therapeutic alliance. In many hospitals this issue has been addressed by the named-nurse initiative. However, unconscious forces frequently operate to limit anxiety-provoking situations, so that the relationship itself is avoided. Staff become detached from seriously ill patients, neglecting the essential empathy/emotional contact that is required to validate and 'contain' their distress. This feature of institutional dynamics interacts adversely with the dynamics of abuse, where the survivor has difficulty with basic trust and in making and sustaining attachment relationships. The suspiciousness of psychosis and the negative counter-transference response to people who are agitated, withdrawn or aggressive all increase the likelihood of countertherapeutic detachment and denial within the treatment alliance.

Ritualised task performance

Decision-making generates anxiety, particularly where the welfare of patients is at stake. Institutions often relieve anxiety by minimising the number and complexity of these decisions by standardising one procedure to achieve a particular task. This reduces the decision-making and substitutes ritual for tasks such as the giving of medication, attending to patients' personal hygiene or handing over. While some ritualised task performance is necessary to allow the system to function efficiently, excessive ritualisation promotes detachment and denial of personal responsibility for implementing a particular item of care. There are particular dangers in the interaction of these dynamics with those of child sexual abuse, if the care that is received is experienced as part of a ritual, where the patient is merely an object within an impersonal system. This interaction risks reducing them to the level of the object that they were, during the abuse, particularly if the abuse itself was ritualised.

Collusive social redistribution of roles – 'scapegoating'

All carers face a painful conflict over acceptance of the responsibilities of their role. Caring for dependent people evokes powerful feelings and a sense of responsibility which is discharged often at considerable cost. This responsibility is difficult to bear consistently and the temptation to give it up is considerable. Every carer also has wishes and impulses to behave irresponsibly, such as omitting boring or repetitive tasks. The balance of opposing forces in the conflict varies between individuals: some are naturally more responsible than others, and can usually be identified as such within the organisation. These individuals often act as the focus for projection during the institutional defence, which acts by externalising intrapsychic conflict as interpersonal conflict. People in certain roles are described as 'responsible' or 'irresponsible', and so carry for the unit those projected parts of others that are not currently tolerable. People tend to act on the roles psychologically assigned to them, so the defence may stabilise the system in an adaptive fashion, by locating responsibility with the most senior members of the organisation. However, it may lead to undue rigidity and scapegoating of certain individuals when other intrapsychic conflicts are played out in the same manner. Role rigidity and scapegoating of staff and patients may become the way in which the institution habitually deals with particular types of anxiety. These dynamics interact with the dynamics of abuse where psychotic survivors may be the recipients of disturbed psychotic projections, not tolerated by other patients or staff. They tend to be seen as 'the most disturbed' or 'the most psychotic' within a ward; they become 'the worst patient', being the object of multiple projections, and often the most disliked. This is a damaging position for any patient, but particularly so for victims of abuse, where their negative self-concepts are reinforced, and isolation and marginalisation from any group is re-enacted.

Avoidance of change

Change is inevitably an excursion into the unknown, where the outcome is uncertain and anxiety-provoking. Any significant change in a social system results in changes in existing social relationships and social structures; it also results in a change in the way that social system functions as a defence against deep and primitive anxieties. As such, change is unconsciously resisted, as it threatens a system of defensive operation that allows people to continue doing their job. It is therefore very difficult to change institutional practice, as familiar procedures are adhered to even when they are no longer relevant nor appropriate.

At present, all institutions within the National Health Service are working within a climate of change demanded by the transformation of a system of care into a market economy. Financial penalties exist for systems in which change has not occurred in the desired or contracted direction. This introduces real tension into a system inherently resistive to change, where even rational attempts to manage the change seem to be ignored. Conflict may ensue between different levels of management required to direct or respond to change, which in turn may demand input and time from staff involved in caring for patients. The net effect may then be to withdraw time from face-to-face contact with patients, so legitimising the detachment and denial of feelings that already exist within the system. These dynamics interact with those of abuse and of psychosis by minimising the opportunity to respond to survivors as individuals, and maximising the sense of that survivor being enmeshed within an unresponsive power structure that appears to be oblivious to individual differences and needs.

Implications for management

Understanding these dynamics and their potential for interaction and amplification within an in-patient setting is crucial, if the care offered is to be therapeutic.

Attention should be paid to the 'containing functions' of the ward and the staff who work there, by ensuring safe physical and personal boundaries. At times, particularly during the acute phase of a psychotic breakdown, security such as the locked door of an intensive care ward may be necessary. The use of medication may also be part of containing the psychotic patient in whom psychotic agitation or overarousal exists. The ability of all staff to contain primitive psychotic feelings and impulses should be supported by clinical supervision.

Acting out countertransference hate or unwittingly contributing to the synergism of primitive dynamics can make the care setting and the treatment alliance anti-therapeutic for the patient and toxic for the staff. There should be a forum in which the nature of the emotional burden that staff bear in the course of their work can be contained and explored. This should be in the form of regular staff support, preferably a staff group for all members of the multi-disciplinary team, facilitated by a psychotherapist. The weekly multidisciplinary team meeting is not generally an appropriate place to discuss and share emotional burden, or deal with intense counter-transference. The multidisciplinary team has many other functions and the agenda becomes confused.

The social structures of the ward and the institution, and the ward procedures, may contribute to the potential for re-enactment or revictimisation of the survivor, and detachment or disruption of the therapeutic relationship. Attention should therefore be paid to the allocation of a named nurse/key worker and consistency among the other professional staff. How to provide privacy, respect and dignity (and possibly single-sex accommodation) should all be considered in the care that is offered.

Education and training of all staff in the special skills required to work with psychotic patients who have also been abused in childhood should be mandatory, given the prevalence of the problem.

References

ABRAHAM, K. (1911) Notes on the psycho-analytic investigation and treatment of manic–depressive insanity and related conditions. In *Selected Papers on Psycho-Analysis*, pp. 137–156. London: Hogarth Press (1927).

BION, W. R. (1967) *Second Thoughts*. London: Heinemann.

JACOBSON, A. & RICHARDSON, B. (1987) Assault experiences of 100 psychiatric in-patients: evidence of the need for routine enquiry. *American Journal of Psychiatry*, **144**, 908–913.

KLEIN, M. (1930*a*) The importance of symbol formation in the development of the ego. In *The Works of Melanie Klein, Volume 1*, pp. 219–232. London: Hogarth Press.

—— (1930*b*) The psychotherapy of psychosis. In *The Works of Melanie Klein, Volume 1*, pp. 233–235. London: Hogarth Press.

MENZIES LYTH, I. (1988) The functioning of social systems as a defence against anxiety. In *Containing Anxiety in Institutions*, pp. 43–85. London: Free Association Books.

MULLEN, P. E., MARTIN, J. L., ANDERSON, J. C., et al (1993) Childhood sexual abuse and mental health in adult life. *British Journal of Psychiatry*, **163**, 721–732.

ROSENFELD, H. (1947) Analysis of a schizophrenic state with depersonalisation. In *Psychotic States*, pp. 13–33. London: Hogarth Press.

SEGAL, H. (1950) Some aspects of the analysis of a schizophrenic. *International Journal of Psycho-Analysis*, **31**, 268–278.

WATTS, D. & MORGAN, G. R. (1994) Malignant alienation. Dangers for patients who are hard to like. *British Journal of Psychiatry*, **164**, 11–15.

WINNICOTT, D. W. (1947) Hate in the countertransference. *International Journal of Psycho-Analysis*, **30**, 69–74.

15 The Hawthorn Project.
A group psychotherapy project
with chronically psychotic
in-patients

DIANNE CAMPBELL LEFEVRE and
FRANK MORRISON

"I used to be Alexander the Great and now I can't even get Dot to make the tea." (Hawthorn Project resident)

"I felt a cleaving in my Mind –
As if my brain had split –
I tried to match it – Seam by Seam –
But could not make them fit.

The thought behind I strove to join
Unto the thought before –
But sequence ravelled out of Sound
Like Balls – upon a Floor."

(Emily Dickenson, *c.* 1864)

Introduction and aims

The Hawthorn Project was an ambitious programme that ran for over five years in a large Victorian psychiatric hospital in east London. It sought positive change in patients, staff and the institution through the introduction of psychoanalytically informed psychotherapy. Initial attempts to rehabilitate a neglected group of patients had indicated pre-existing difficulties within the institution that a project of this kind would have to attempt to remedy if it was to fulfil its clinical aims. Other specific aims emerged with time; these

220

did not always fit neatly into a scientific paradigm, although the mature project incorporated research into social networks.

The form the project took reflected a number of decisive events. Firstly, the strong negative feelings shared by staff on the hospital's continuing-care wards had been impressed on us. Awareness of this as a countertransferential response to their work on those wards was a breakthrough that highlighted the need to look for an alternative model of care. Secondly, the nurse who subsequently became the project manager conducted a survey comparing staff views on patients' social networks with patients' views on their own networks. He found that staff who thought they knew patients well made remarkably inaccurate estimates. The differences between the staff and patients' views were statistically significant in the estimated number of contacts and highly significant in the identification of friends. When shared with the nursing staff, this finding came as a surprise to them. Thirdly, the introduction of 'care in the community' as a basis for policy and planning demanded some preparation of patients so that they could be moved out of the hospital. Fourthly, the hospital needed the approval of the Nurse Training Board to continue to train nurses. The establishment of a forward-looking project would improve the chances of gaining such approval.

These strange bedfellows gave birth to the Hawthorn Project. The uncomfortable countertransference feelings made us sensitive to the inadequacy of the current medical model and to the desirability of alternatives. The social networks experiment highlighted the gap in knowledge between staff and patients. The need to move many patients out of hospital altogether concentrated attention on reorganising the work of the hospital in order to achieve this. And the requirements of nurse training provided a lever to persuade management to support a project with research as well as service objectives.

Once this infant was born, the staff, like new parents, were fired with an enthusiasm and enormous energy that persuaded management and reluctant family members to let the baby live. This would be in the face of the envy, rivalry and opposition that often accompany the arrival of a new baby.

Description of the project

The institution

The institution was a large, century-old mental hospital whose patients were drawn from poor areas of east London. Many had been in hospital for decades. The hospital appeared to be run by the rigid application of institutional rules whose defensive functions have been described by Menzies Lyth (1970). Accordingly, patients were summarily moved to different wards and staff were often moved without warning either to themselves or patients. These practices, together with regimentation, staff uniforms, lack of privacy and a rigid shift system for the nurses, prevented therapeutic relationships from being formed. The research we carried out during the project supported our previous suspicions that this failure to form relationships was hindering patients' recovery. The 'Hawthorn Project' was the new name given to a group of what used to be called 'long-stay' wards in the hospital. The patients living there were often highly disturbed, just failing to qualify for admission to forensic units or special hospitals. The project wards were to be under the care of a single medical and nursing team, who were to introduce psychoanalytical psychotherapy groups as the unit's core activity. The understanding provided by a psychoanalytical viewpoint would serve as a reference point for everybody in the project. Other activities, such as training in general living, social skills and so on, were to revolve around the psychoanalytically oriented groups. Fig. 15.1 summarises this underlying organisation.

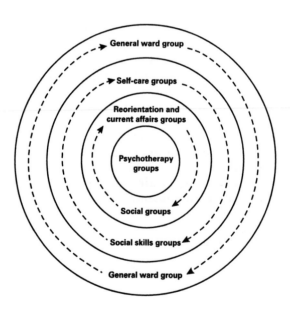

Fig. 15.1. Structure of the Hawthorn ward group model.

We knew that ward groups occasionally found in this type of institution were often disbanded through the actions of those staff and patients not involved with the group. We thought that this was because of envy and primal scene problems – "What are they doing in there, all alone and in secret?" By establishing psychotherapy groups at the centre of the project from the outset, we hoped to avoid such developments.

The staff and staff training

The staff associated with the project had all worked on the acute-care and continuing-care wards in the same institution and were qualified as either state-enrolled nurses or registered mental nurses. Those who were not attracted to the idea of a group-oriented unit moved to other wards within the hospital, and new nurses joined the project. Those who chose to work on the unit had worked in the hospital for between 6 and 25 years. None of the nurses had any training in psychotherapy, and most had never run a group before.

Frank talks with nursing and medical staff about the difficulties they had encountered in their previous work and about the current status of patients in this type of institution led us to the view that the extant medical model of management worked to reassure staff of their sanity and to perpetuate the madness of the patients. One of the first tasks we faced was to reduce the institutionalised barriers between these two groups of people in order to allow a different kind of relationship to develop. The very start of the project involved abandoning the shift system for nurses and staff uniforms, creating mixed-sex wards, and making the medical and nursing notes available to the patients.

In the absence of extra resources, we had to rearrange our expenditure and that meant taking risks. Having all patients in weekly groups made it possible to leave some wards without staff at night since we were able to monitor clinical changes that might have signalled dangerous behaviour.

Staff anxieties about facilitating groups were high at times, especially at the start of the project. It became clear that we would have to develop some kind of psychotherapy training for all the staff, whether or not they facilitated a psychotherapy group or some other group activity. We set out to value and assess each staff member's work from a psychotherapeutic angle. We hoped that this would reduce the envy and rivalry that often arises in institutions between staff. At the same time we energetically initiated arrangements to set up formal training in psychotherapy.

The consultant on the unit was the only staff member trained as a psychoanalytical psychotherapist. We were fortunate to find another trained psychoanalytical psychotherapist who was prepared to take an interest in this type of work and who continued to facilitate the work of staff throughout the project. The training started with weekly seminars covering basic principles of psychoanalytical theory. At the same time a weekly experiential group for all the staff on the unit was set up. The acute ward was part of the project when it started, and this is where a pilot study with the first of these groups was launched.

Weekly supervision throughout the life of the groups for all facilitators was obligatory, and staff from all the wards in the unit were expected to attend. It was a struggle to establish that time spent in training should be regarded as sacrosanct. This struggle persisted throughout the life of the project.

At ward rounds, patients were considered from a psychotherapeutic point of view alongside traditional discussions of diagnosis and management. Issues around transference, countertransference and resistance were explored in as much depth as time allowed. Countertransference needed particular attention as frank and open discussion of the therapists' countertransference feelings go very much against the grain of what is commonly imagined to be the acceptable attitudes of doctors and nurses. As confidence grew, the groups spread to the continuing-care wards.

Nurses had been carefully selected for the project by the project manager, not for their knowledge of psychotherapy (which was virtually non-existent at the start) or for their dedication (since harm can result if projected needs are disguised as dedication) but for their capacity for empathy and their ability not to act out despite sometimes intolerable frustrations. We discovered that staff who were secretive about the work they were doing with patients, or who refused any kind of supervision involving scrutiny of their work, were too destructive to remain working with the project. In practice, it was better to have staff who claimed no knowledge of psychotherapy than those who claimed experience but had no reputable training. We learned to seek a positive balance of staff who genuinely supported the idea of the group-psychotherapy orientation and who accepted the training requirements we had imposed.

Some staff felt that facilitating psychoanalytical psychotherapy groups was not for them. That was accepted and the other work they did in the project was respected and encouraged. What was not acceptable was a kind of envious destructiveness likely to lead to failure. The worst example of this was seen when, during the consultant's absence on leave, the visiting psychotherapist was told that she was no longer wanted and nurses were actively discouraged from attending supervision. The project on the acute ward had to be discontinued as a direct result. In normal working, the emergence of such currents within the staff team was usually first apparent in the staff group, where they could be addressed before real harm was done.

Patients

The hospital served two districts, one inner and one outer London. The patients in the project were mostly originally from the inner city. The study included 251 patients who were in hospital from 1986 to 1989. Thirty of these had weekly psychoanalytically informed psychotherapy and were part of the Hawthorn Project. The comparison group consisted of the remaining 221 patients. The patients in the comparison group lived under similar conditions in the hospital, having the same treatment interventions as those in the Hawthorn Project, such as social skills groups and occupational therapy, with active plans being made for their discharge to the community. However, they did not participate in any psychoanalytically informed psychotherapy groups, with all that that implied in terms of more intensive discussion of their progress within the staff team.

Of the 30 patients in groups, 24 had a schizophrenic illness, most with ongoing symptoms, and six had major affective disorder as classified in ICD–9 (World Health Organization, 1989). Of the patients in the project who were not selected for psychotherapy, three had brain damage and two refused to attend. The length of stay ranged between 3 and 60 years. The mean length of stay of the schizophrenic patients was 27 years, and that of the patients with affective disorder was 8.2 years. (The latter sample was biased by one patient who had been in hospital for 20 years.) There were 23 men and 7 women.

To give some idea of the patients' severity of disturbance, it may be helpful to quote from replies to the Twenty Statement Test (Yardley, 1987). This is a projective test in which patients are asked to write 20 statements under the headings "I am..." and "I am not...". SP, a 63-year-old man with a schizophrenic illness, in hospital for 30 years, said to "I am...": "I don't know. Sometimes I am a man – SC or SP – sometimes I think I am female, Alice or Ethel. I think I am eight or nine feet in shoes. I think I am a fat man. Made of fat. Not very clever. A silly sod for being in here." To "I am not...", he said, "I am not Henry the Eighth. I am not King Kong".

Clinical course

As the nurses gained confidence during their training, patients were assigned to groups following discussion in supervision meetings and ward rounds. The facilitators' views about whom they felt they could work with were given considerable weight, as were the staff's views about which patients might work creatively together. Patients who could not tolerate each other were not put together in the same group. Diagnostic categories did not influence where patients were placed. The number of group sessions offered varied between 32 and 126. The attendance varied from 65% to 94%. The groups took place for one hour per week and there were between six to eight patients in a group.

It is difficult to describe the process of these groups. They were always held at the same place and time each week. At the start, we explained to patients something about groups, in particular that they were places to talk about feelings. We were quite directive in that we made it clear that group members were expected to turn up on time and to stay for the hour. After a short while we had to ban smoking in the groups as the ritual surrounding cigarettes focused the kind of resistance we felt could have endangered the groups. At first patients did not turn up. The therapist sometimes sat alone or almost alone for the whole hour. We attempted in the early stages to take patients into the group. Later they turned up spontaneously and the attendance rate became unexpectedly good. It was very difficult for patients to sit in the same room together with others. Being in a circle was even more difficult. Initially some patients moved their chairs outside the group and others faced in the opposite direction.

A common theme in the groups was the rage and bitterness that so much of a lifetime had been wasted in hospital. This was evident when, 18 months after the start of the groups, the death of a member who had been an in-patient for over 20 years facilitated reality testing and mourning of the patients' loss of healthy life and their former selves.

Moves were felt as a persecution of the patients by the staff and were experienced by patients with extreme dread. One patient spoke of a group of birds being pushed out of the nest at such a time. The theme was taken up by other group members and related to previous losses and rejections. The staff were felt to be neglectful and abandoning by patients but new staff were dreaded.

More detailed examination of the groups subsequently indicated that they went through phases resembling bereavement. Searles (1979) has written of the schizophrenic patient's deeply repressed sense of grief, part reality based and related to the loss of self in the fragmentation process and correspondingly the loss of the chance of an integrated mother. The phases we noted within this were denial, rage, sadness, anxiety and reality testing. Each phase lasted about six months. As they progressed, there was a consistency of countertransference feelings between different facilitators at different phases of the groups (LeFevre, 1994).

In the course of these groups, transference psychoses, severe resistance and acting out were all observed. Resistance often took the form of leaving the group (to go to the lavatory, to make a cup of tea or for no reason), not turning up, psychotic outpourings, sleep, silence, continuous mumbling and so on. The staff dealt with these by pointing out first the usefulness and the purpose of the resistance, and second the power the resistance gave to the patient, as described so well by Cohn (1988). As Cohn reports, we found that this way of dealing with resistance brought a reassuring structure to the group and facilitated the next move.

All staff in the groups reported that they found it difficult at the start to interpret evidence of negative transference towards themselves (e.g. terrific hatred or murderous wishes towards group facilitators), feeling that to do so would drive the patients away. Instead, they concentrated initially on the positive transference to reinforce the therapeutic alliance. Negative transference was interpreted when it occurred in negative interaction between group members by pointing out the reason for the negative interaction and emphasising that this was an indication of how the patient attacked him/herself. This technique had similarities to Kernberg's (1980) modification of standard psychoanalytical procedures when working with borderline patients. In effect, the staff used insight-oriented as well as interaction-oriented approaches in the groups, following Kanas' (1986) discussion of group therapy for patients with schizophrenia. This helped in the transition from an initial position, when patients would relate only to the therapist (in a demanding, symbiotic fashion) to one where they could start relating to each other. Throughout, psychotic outpourings were not ignored but were understood as a resistance and as a mode of communication.

These groups remained outside the usual spectrum of analytic group therapy, where psychosis, when it emerges, does not dominate the process to the same extent (cf. Chapter 6). The staff had to cope with extreme disturbances for very long periods. To understand what was happening in them, in the absence of verbal cues, they had to rely heavily on countertransference. This was taken to include all feelings the analyst had towards the patient, as proposed by Heimann (1960). With such severely disturbed patients, using the primitive forms of defence described in Chapter 6, the countertransference can be overpowering and extremely difficult to deal with. Staff reported feeling 'done in' for a whole day or even two following a 'heavy' group. They were unable to stop talking about the groups when socialising after work. They reported that their spouses complained of the impact this was having at home.

To examine the countertransference, facilitators were asked to rank order their feelings in terms of frequency, powerfulness and importance, using their own words. Using the Delphi technique (Pill, 1971), the commonest feelings were: empathy (in the sense of feeling disorganised, confused and unable to think), feeling shattered, anxiety, sadness, happiness, hopelessness, and emptiness. Expressions also used were: "split in bits", "mind all in pieces", "lost the capacity to think", "dead", "crazy" and "wishing to run away".

During the lives of the groups, facilitators had repeatedly to take in and experience primitive idealisation before having to tolerate it plummeting to extreme depreciation, with the countertransferential feelings of impotence and shame this would bring. Still more difficult was having to hold feeling "in bits", absorbing the special non-human feelings described by Searles (1979) as the fear of disintegration; the cruel, metallic coldness and aloneness of the schizoid state; the terror of abandonment; the sadistic murderousness of envy on the rampage, and other emptying experiences that have no words at all.

If staff survived all this, they did so through a painful learning process, held to some extent by the supportive structures within the project. They learned to empathise with what were often painful and confusing states and then to step back without being overwhelmed for long enough to consider what they might say. (This might be seen as the substitution of normal projective identification for a pathological form in Bion's sense – cf. Chapter 6.) They felt that they developed greater ego strengths by doing so and, as the discussion of the project's outcome will describe, there was some evidence they were able to enjoy the benefits accruing from such strengths.

Social networks and research method

We have given a flavour of the clinical process that slowly took shape over months. Staff reported an awareness of movement in a therapeutic direction and became increasingly enthusiastic. It seemed pressing that we find some way of demonstrating the value of using group psychotherapy in this way.

An independent research team had measured the social networks of all the patients in the hospital in 1986 and did so again in 1989. There were 251 patients who were in hospital in 1986 and 1989. This provided an opportunity to look for changes in patients' networks and for differences between those who had received psychoanalytically informed group psychotherapy and those who had not.

'Social networks' refers to the number of friends, relatives, acquaintances and staff members named by patients. Morrison (1986) had found that those patients who were most ill tended to name the fewest people. Interestingly, patients with affective disorders named more people than those with schizophrenic disorders. Knowing that the more ill a patient was, the smaller the social network was likely to be, we assumed that improvement in the patient's intrapsychic state would be reflected in an enlargement of the social network. Improved ego strength and less recourse to primitive defence mechanisms would theoretically make it easier for patients to approach others.

From a practical point of view, obtaining an accurate picture of an individual's social network is not as easy as it may appear. Contrasting approaches have been based on either the quality or the quantity of the relationships. Basing the calculations on observing whom the patient sees is open to criticism, as not everyone we happen to see is actually part of our social network. Quantitative approaches can fail because people seen rarely might be much more important to someone than people who are seen more often.

In order to make an assessment of patients' networks, a series of semi-structured questions was used to elicit a set of names of people important to them, relying on their unprompted memory. This was followed by a wide variety of prompts to ensure as full a description of the networks as possible. Some examples of the prompts are: "Do you know any patients on this ward, other wards, or in occupational therapy? Do you visit anyone inside or outside the hospital?" This list is expanded until it is exhausted.

The interviewer then asked about the quality of the relationship to explore aspects of the social contact. "Can you tell me something about these people?" This was followed by further prompts: "How long have you known them? How often do you see them? What did you do? Where did you go? What do you talk about? How do you help each other? Is ... a friend or acquaintance? Would you mind not seeing...? What is the best/worst thing about...?"

In conducting the interviews, the ward staff introduced the researchers to the patients and the researcher explained the purpose of each interview before it began. We had previously found that networks measured by staff well known to patients yielded higher contact numbers than scores obtained from the same patients by testers hardly known to the patients. Measurements across the hospital were therefore always made by the same independent testers to ensure the validity of the results.

Results

The results are summarised below in terms of the social networks measurements, the outcome for patients, and the impact on staff, all with specific reference to the initial aims of the project.

Social networks measurements

In 1986, the 'overall contacts' in the Hawthorn Project started at a much lower level than for the comparison group. This may have indicated that the Hawthorn patients were a more damaged group at the outset. In 1989, the number of contacts for the Hawthorn patients had risen significantly ($P = 0.006$) while in the comparison group it had fallen (Fig. 15.2)

Contacts with professionals increased sevenfold in the Hawthorn group (Fig. 15.3). This gain ($P = 0.006$) was significantly larger than the 50% gain among the comparison group. These relative changes do reflect the different starting levels between the two groups and

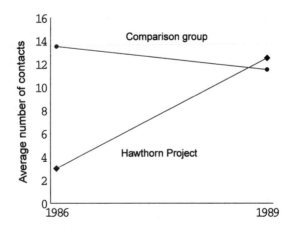

Fig. 15.2. *The average size of social networks (number of contacts) for the Hawthorn patients and those in the comparison group.*

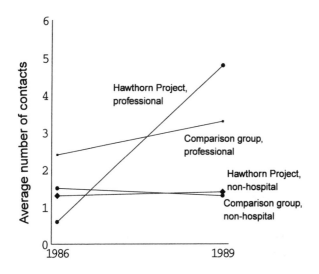

Fig. 15.3. Average number of non-hospital contacts and professional contacts among the Hawthorn and comparison groups.

the strategic increase in professional contacts that was part of the Hawthorn regime.

'Non-hospital' contacts represent mainly contact with relatives. Such contacts tended to stabilise over time. As expected, there was little change in either group.

'Same-ward' contacts increased in the Hawthorn sample by just under 50% to an average of about 5.6 contacts (Fig. 15.4). In contrast, there was a significant decrease in same-ward contacts in the comparison group, from 8.53 to 3.85. This may be the most significant finding of the research; as well as indicating that a predictable, but possibly transient, increase in contacts had been achieved among the project patients, it suggests that the consequence of ordinary care was a deterioration that had been prevented among patients in the project.

Clinical outcome

The social network measurements suggest it was easier for group members to relate more freely to others outside the group. This is reflected in the increase in their contacts on the same ward and on other wards and, to a larger but probably less meaningful extent, an increase in contacts with professionals. This implies that there had

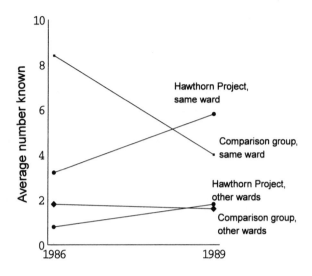

Fig. 15.4. Average numbers of same-ward and other-ward contacts among the Hawthorn and comparison groups.

been some positive intrapsychic change of a nature that is not detectable by doing the usual mental state examination. It may also have protected against some of the harmful effects of institutionalisation apparent in the comparison cohort.

Looking back and comparing the written-up sessions of the early groups with those a year or two later, there are remarkable differences. The patient who initially attended his group from behind the door or by looking in at it through a window was able to join the group for the full hour. Attendance rates increased. Instead of directing everything to the facilitator, patients were able to talk to each other about painful experiences. There was a shared theme, a coherency, enabling patients to think. The possibility of offering each other support became a reality that generalised to the process of sharing a house in preparation for the move into the community. This was particularly significant since group members did not necessarily come from the same house or ward.

We had hoped that one result of attending groups would be that the group members would find it easier to live out of hospital. Fifteen of the 30 Hawthorn patients moved out in 1989 and 1991. A further five moved out in 1994. None has been readmitted. While the small numbers in our own survey mean results must be interpreted with care, this compares well with the 20% annual readmission rates reported by the Team for the Assessment of Psychiatric Services (TAPS) (Thornicroft, 1991) for a similar population.

Impact on staff

The impact of the project on members of staff directly involved with it was both positive and negative. The obvious positive effect on staff was the increase in morale that was reported by staff and observed in them. The project manager kept a record of staff sickness and he noticed a decrease in the casual absenteeism that is so common in large, under-resourced hospitals. Beyond this, individual staff members achieved things they seemed unlikely to have attempted previously. For example, one member wrote a book, which has not been published but she said she would never have thought of doing so before. Two completed a BSc (Hons) with group psychotherapy as the subject. Both have gone on to do a masters degree, one in psychotherapy. Nurses read classic psychotherapy papers and willingly attended seminars and supervision outside their working hours.

Alongside this continuing positive impact on staff, there were serious negative effects that were of great concern to us during the life of the project. Of the six facilitators, four who were never ill before or after the project, developed severe illnesses requiring several weeks off work. One facilitator thought he would have to retreat into working half-time. All of the illnesses involved severe infections, suggesting an inadequate immune response as a result of stress.

A further negative effect concerned the staff's inability to document adequately the experience of the project while it was in process. One staff member described feeling as if he were "falling to bits in an attempt to get it all together, to integrate it". Both these developments may reflect the very powerful negative counter-transference that has already been described. Further evidence of this was provided by meetings organised to discuss the difficulties staff had with documenting the project. They spoke then of feelings of shame, at having so little to show, of a fear that even this would disappear, of emptiness and other feelings that mirrored those reported by facilitators when asked about their feelings following group sessions.

Our experiences during the project led us to believe that the effects patients have on staff in the therapy situation – countertransference – and vice versa are ill-understood and underestimated. The belief of the Prime Minister at the time that "there is no such thing as society, only individuals" may express a widespread lack of interest and awareness in the effects people have on each other. However, the kind of intersubjective experiences that have been described here in terms of transference and countertransference suggest an inevitable connectedness between individuals that is wholly compatible with the theories of modern (post-Newtonian) physicists. In particular, Powell (1991, 1993) correlates experimental physics with group experiences in a highly original way which may explain the profound and far-reaching effects that participation in this project appeared to have on staff. Sceptics about the effects of countertransference might find these ideas persuasive. They seem particularly relevant when working with patients who are as disturbed as ours were.

The institution

The immediate aim of regaining nurse training status for the hospital was fulfilled. Subsequently, the one-year psychotherapy training course for nurses developed for the Hawthorn Project staff was made available to the rest of the hospital. It ran as an independent course for about five years. This was to the benefit of the hospital, as trained nurses were able to take groups on wards outside the project. Because many of these nurses no longer received direct supervision from ourselves once they had completed the one-year course, we have been unable to assess fully the impact this has had on the working of the rest of the hospital.

Conclusions

We observed an increase in contacts in the patients' social networks and inferred that a type of psychic change had taken place that facilitated the capacity to relate to others and to negotiate the move out of hospital successfully.

It was difficult to know how much the psychotherapy groups in isolation contributed to this increase in networks. It does not seem possible to separate the effect of group attendance from the impact of the whole project's psychoanalytically informed style. Thus, the psychotherapy training, including introduction of the experiential group for staff, appeared to be crucial in raising staff morale on the project wards. Their contribution to diffusing staff anxieties and fears was the backbone of the project. This may itself have been decisive for the positive clinical outcome. We do believe our findings have been sufficient to demonstrate the need to duplicate the study in order to determine with more precision the 'ingredients' responsible for the changes we have reported.

Attention to the outcome of the project should not obscure the achievement represented by the fact that it survived as well as it did. At a recent talk on the Hawthorn Project an audience member stated that he had tried something similar but had abandoned it as it had failed. What he had tried was running groups on an otherwise unchanged ward – the kind of scheme that we decided at the outset of the project was doomed to failure and should be avoided.

In retrospect, it seemed that the project we were able to oversee had functioned as a whole, living organism and was more than the sum of its parts. Perhaps one of the most important factors that kept the project going was a united leadership able to resist splitting by other staff members. This in turn enabled staff to resist splitting by patients who, as a result, felt contained and safe. The leaders also kept the institution at bay, which was important in the ever-changing work environment and the climate of insecurity that prevailed at a time of imposed change.

The type of leadership we instituted had acted not by denying leadership roles but by 'leasing out' power. This somehow facilitated the ability to resist the abuse of power we believe to be commonplace and on the increase in the present-day National Health Service (NHS), to the detriment of staff and patients. All our staff members took on a lot of responsibility both in running the groups and in moulding the project. Inevitably, patients were also involved in some decision-making and in this respect the project functioned like a therapeutic community.

We remain convinced that one of the most important factors that made this sharing of responsibility and decision-making a functioning fact, rather than simply a good idea or plan, was the emphasis placed on the need for all staff members to enjoy the trust and freedom required for the countertransference to be discussed at all clinical meetings. Encouraging the irrational aspects of countertransference to be processed in a rational way helped to prevent acting out pathological countertransference towards both staff and patients. Hearing the consultant talking frankly about her own negative countertransference feelings was a great leveller among the staff team. Because it was done professionally and in the context of the psychotherapy training, it seemed to reduce envy without decreasing respect, while enhancing the awareness and tolerance of reality, however awful.

As for the project's financial cost, we were the second cheapest unit per capita in the hospital. Furthermore, performance indicators from the mid-1980s demonstrated that the hospital was one of the cheapest in the UK. This did not prevent the project being closed before its work was complete by dispersal of project staff to wards that were not part of the project. Although this move was ostensibly imposed in order to disperse the benefits of the project, it effectively represented a reversion to aspects of the hospital's previous rigid culture. This development reflected a series of attempts forcibly to curtail the work of the project, initiated at different times by different key professionals within the hospital, as well as from managerial subgroups. This result, which rendered the project non-viable, represented a fatal attack on it in the wake of many skirmishes. It highlights the effect on staff of an NHS whose style is, in our view, antithetical to working as a whole for the good of patients. A split and divided NHS, in which neighbouring trusts are instructed to compete and not cooperate, threatens to act, via its management, on itself and its staff like an auto-immune disease. This prevents creative activity, just as powerful pathological countertransference in a therapeutic interaction can overwhelm the therapist into acting out from a sense of self-preservation in a way that is no longer in an individual patient's interests.

The sort of destructiveness that resulted in the premature disbandment of our project was typical also of the primitive, regressed behaviour of demoralised staff in big, under-resourced institutions. In these institutions clinicians have to marry their functions as carers with those of business management. The envious destruction of something that is good for patients and that was good value for money by grandiosely creating a non-viable hybrid – planting a bit of the project on different wards – caused immense distress to the staff and patients working on the project. The fear and envy now so common in the NHS (*British Medical Journal*, 1994) results inevitably in abuse of power, often in the form of shaming. Sadly, creativity is likely to be destroyed in the process.

If, as we are proposing, a project of this kind is to be repeated, all these factors need to be taken into account. Staff undertaking comparable work will need to be supported adequately. What seems to be required is appropriate psychoanalytical training for the staff, active support from healthy management, adequate staff support, special attention to countertransference, and strong, resilient leadership. Whether this is possible in the NHS at the present time is debatable. We believe it is desirable and hope it will, in the not too distant future, become possible.

Acknowledgement

Paul Croucher was responsible for the statistics and was part of the independent team measuring social networks in the hospital.

References

BRITISH MEDICAL JOURNAL (1994) The rise of Stalinism in the NHS. *British Medical Journal,* **309**, 1640–1644.

COHN, B. R. (1988) Keeping the group alive. Dealing with resistance in a long-term group of psychotic patients. *International Journal of Group Psychotherapy,* **38**.

DICKENSON, E. (*c.* 1864) *The Complete Poems* (ed. T. H. Johnson), p. 439. London: Faber and Faber (1991).

HEIMANN, P. (1960) Counter-transference. *British Journal of Medical Psychology,* **33**, 9–15.

KANAS, N. (1986) Group therapy with schizophrenics – a review of controlled studies. *International Journal of Group Psychotherapy,* **36**, 339–351.

KERNBERG, O. (1980) *Borderline Conditions and Pathological Narcissism.* New York: Jason Aronson.

LEFEVRE, D. (1994) The power of countertransference in groups for the severely mentally ill. *Group Analysis,* **27**, 441–447.

MENZIES Lyth, I. E. P. (1970) *The Functioning of Social Systems as a Defence Against Anxiety.* London: Tavistock Institute of Human Relations.

PILL, J. (1971) The Delphi method: substance, context, a critique and an annotated bibliography. *Socio-Economic Planning Sciences,* **5**, 57–71.

POWELL, A. (1991) Matrix, mind and matter: from the internal to the eternal. *Group Analysis,* **24**, 299–322.

—— (1993) The psychophysical matrix and group analysis. *Group Analysis,* **26**, 446–468.

SEARLES, H. (1979) Counter transference and related subjects. In *Selected Papers* (chapter 18). Madison: International Universities Press.

THORNICROFT, S. (1991) *Team for Assessment of Psychiatric Services (TAPS).* Sixth Annual Conference.

WORLD HEALTH ORGANIZATION (1989) *International Classification of Diseases* (9th revision) (ICD–9). Geneva: WHO.

YARDLEY, K. (1987) *Who Are You, Self and Identity* (eds K. Yardley & J. Honess). London: Wiley.

16 The Finnish National Schizophrenia Project: a strategy for psychotherapeutic treatment and balanced deinstitutionalisation

KARI PYLKKANEN

Historical background

The Finnish mental hospital system was originally built in a very decentralised fashion. The government had already started a policy of regionalising all hospitals in the 1920s. Legislation promising considerable government subsidies for building and running hospitals encouraged the local authorities ('communes') to run their own hospital network. This policy reached its peak with the Mental Health Act of 1952.

The 1952 Act was unfortunately timed, coinciding with chlorpromazine coming on to the market and the beginning of a revolution in the treatment of psychoses. The law aimed to improve the quality of care for the mentally ill who lived in very poor institutional conditions. The methods it supported, however, reflected pre-war psychiatric know-how. The Act established an administrative framework for providing 10 000 new psychiatric beds during the next 20 years. While the industrialised world started having fewer patients in psychiatric hospitals, Finland, late to industrialise, kept building new mental institutions until the early 1970s.

The Finnish mental hospitals differed from those of most other countries in two ways. They were small in size and were run in a decentralised fashion. Each local authority wanted to get its share of the government subsidies by building a hospital of their own. As a result Finland had 60 psychiatric hospitals for its 5 million population at the end of the 1970s. No hospital had more than 1000 beds.

Finnish society is based on a high level of local autonomy: the 455 independent local authorities all collect their own taxes and run the health service jointly with their neighbours. Until 1993 the government controlled the use of its subsidies for health care (about 45% of total cost) by setting certain quality standards and by maintaining equal access to care through legislation and administrative orders. For this purpose there was, until 1991, a government health directorate, the National Board of Health.

At the end of the 1970s Finland had up to 4.2 mental hospital beds per 1000 population. International comparisons with this figure are, however, complicated because there is no standard definition of 'mental hospital bed'. Nursing-home beds were included in the Finnish statistics for mental hospitals until the late 1980s.

Attempts by the National Board of Health to promote out-patient care had proven rather unsuccessful. In 1979 an initiative of the Association of Mental Hospitals developed a model for care of schizophrenia following the example of somatic health care. It offered an option for starting something quite new. An expert group was set up by the National Board of Health to outline a National Schizophrenia Project in 1980. This draft project had a dual strategy: to meet the interests of the mental health service purchaser, the central government health authority, and those of the providers, the local hospitals. The former wished to decrease the number of institutional beds; the latter wanted the government to instigate an ideal model of the treatment of schizophrenia for the providers to follow (Pylkkanen, 1990).

The aims of the National Schizophrenia Project

When set up by the National Board of Health, the project had numerical and measurable aims.

The first aim was to decrease the number of old long-stay and new long-stay patients in mental institutions by 50% over 10 years by applying new research and innovations. Old long-stay was defined as two years or longer in hospital, and new long-stay as one to two years in hospital. Both figures could be obtained from the annual census. Every patient found registered for only the second time in the census was a new long-stay patient.

The second aim was to develop, both qualitatively and quantitatively, community-based out-patient activities in order to enable the treatment system to reduce the number of long-stay patients. The activities could be measured by collecting statistics about existing care practices. Also, a questionnaire survey was conducted in 1992 to evaluate the qualitative and quantitative changes. Evidence of success would imply a balanced and controlled process of deinstitutionalisation.

These aims could not be achieved without changing both the hospital and out-patient structure and activities. If the programme were successful, the tradition of long-term hospitalisation of schizophrenic patients would end, to be replaced by a new culture of treatment.

The starting year was 1982, when assessments of the initial situation were made. Two follow-up years were selected. The first was 1986, halfway through the project. The final follow-up date was 1992. Both the patient population and the system of care were surveyed in order to measure how far the aims had been realised. The project started at a time of great economic expansion; it ended during the period of heavy recession that began in 1990.

Organisation

The National Board of Health appointed three committees to carry out the project. The Steering Committee was chaired by the Director General of the National Board of Health, Dr Matti Ruokola. In it the purchasers were represented. The Expert Committee represented the providers, including all relevant professional groups. The chairman was Dr Kari Pylkkanen, Director of Mental Health Services at the National Board of Health. The Planning Committee was chaired by Professor Yrjo Alanen, who was also the director of the whole project

Local project organisation was established in all 21 mental health districts. Each district had a project chief responsible for carrying out the project activities in that district. Twice a year a biannual seminar was held for all those participating in the local activities.

The project's organisation was run down in 1988. The idea was that the tools for carrying out the task should be developed during the first years. The final outcome of the project, reflecting the new orientation and methods, would then be assessed during 1988–92.

Commitment was a key word in organising the project. Every provider in the country was asked to participate and 70% of mental health districts did take part.

Funding

This project was cheap in terms of extra budget money invested in it. Only 5.5 million Finnish markkaa were allocated through various channels. The actual work completed was much more. Most of the cost was absorbed through changing working practices in the publicly funded health service. About 300 professionals made extra efforts for the project over six years without extra pay. They were responsible for coping with the problem of schizophrenia in their district. They developed their practices according the guidelines of the project. All this was possible only through the support of the district leadership.

Strategies and methods: the four main subprogrammes

The key strategies followed guidelines developed by Professor Yrjo Alanen and his co-workers in Turku. The aim was to create an integrated approach to the treatment of schizophrenia all over the country and to develop new, psychotherapeutically oriented activities. Alanen differentiates five basic approaches to schizophrenia: biomedicine, individual psychology, psychology of interaction, social–ecological and integrative approaches (Alanen *et al*, 1991).

The project aimed at a reasonable integration of these approaches. There was a desire to develop practical applications using the integrative approach and to avoid the split within psychiatric practice into competing, separate and non-communicating schools.

The new schizophrenic patients: new approaches and five-year follow-up

Professor Yrjo Alanen and his co-workers had developed over many years at Turku University Clinic a model of care for psychotic patients (Alanen *et al*, 1991). This model emphasised a psychotherapeutic, needs-adapted approach. It guided new approaches for the new schizophrenic patients for the whole country. The practical goals in developing the treatment were listed as guidelines for practitioners:

(a) Plan your treatments.
(b) Make your treatment out-patient oriented and community-based.

(c) Make your treatments integrative, individual and needs-adapted. Treatments must be followed and plans changed when needed.
(d) Take the psychotherapeutic and family-oriented approaches as starting points in your treatment plan.
(e) Make an interactive intervention at the very beginning of each treatment. Invite the patient, family members and those near to the patient to a meeting at which your team also participates.
(f) Keep the doses of medication minimal.
(g) Think of rehabilitation from the very beginning.

Alanen defines needs-adapted care under four points (Alanen, 1993):

(a) Therapeutic treatments are planned individually to meet the needs of patients and of the people nearest to them.
(b) The psychotherapeutic attitude, with efforts to try to understand what has happened and happens to patients and those near to them, characterises the treatment.
(c) Different therapeutic activities must support, not counteract, one another.
(d) The treatment is a developmental and interactive process.

A five-year follow-up of new schizophrenic patients was carried out in six districts, which had all implemented the treatment model. The material of this study comprised all new cases seen in one year in a total population of almost 1 million. DSM–III criteria (American Psychiatric Association, 1980) were used in diagnostic assessments. Follow-up was done six months, one year, two years and five years after first contact.

The incidence and follow-up study was carried out by Salokangas *et al* (1991). It investigated 227 newly diagnosed schizophrenic patients in the six districts. The annual incidence of new schizophrenic patients met in psychiatric services was 16–19 per 100 000. There was no significant regional variation in this figure. This finding was very interesting because simultaneous study of the prevalence of long-stay patients revealed a fourfold variation (National Board of Health, 1988). It seemed that iatrogenic factors had more impact on the outcome of schizophrenia than the illness itself.

The prevalence of schizophrenia is two times higher in eastern and northern Finland than in southern and south-western parts of the country (Lehtinen *et al*, 1989). As there was no difference in the incidence of new cases, this difference must be explained by greater chronicity of the illness in north and east Finland.

TABLE 16.1
Prognosis of the new schizophrenic patients (n = 226) at five-year follow-up (%)

Prognostic indicator	First contact	2 years	5 years
No psychotic symptoms	7	50	46
Full working ability	–	40	38
Worked the whole year	44	25	29
Received a pension	2	33	41

Adapted from Salokangas *et al* (1991).

In 70% of the follow-up cases, early intervention had been carried out with the patient, with at least one family member participating. In 90% of cases both neuroleptic drugs and psychotherapy were assessed to be necessary components of the treatment plan.

The use of hospital decreased gradually during the five-year follow-up. During the first year, 77% of cases were treated in hospital. At two-year follow-up, 29% of patients had been hospitalised during the last year, and in the five-year follow-up 23%. The prognosis of the new schizophrenic patients is presented in Table 16.1. About half the patients had recovered from the psychotic symptoms during the follow-up. Only 10% of the patients were so well recovered after five years that no psychiatric diagnosis could be given to them. Two-thirds of the patients received a diagnosis of psychosis at the five-year follow-up.

The acute psychosis teams (APTs)

The early studies on incidence and prevalence had pointed out that psychosocial factors have a major influence on the prognosis of schizophrenic patients. Therefore new developments were thought necessary at the time of first contact and intervention. The key ideas of the project were to be implemented at the very beginning of the patient's career. The APTs were developed for this purpose. The APT can be characterised as follows. Each team:

(a) serves a population of approximately 80 000;
(b) consists of three or four specially trained persons (psychiatrist, psychologist, special nurse, social worker trained in psychotherapy);
(c) is the usual recipient of referrals from general practitioners for acutely psychotic patients (appointments are given for either the same or the following day);

(d) makes the initial, interactionally oriented investigation of all psychotic patients in the catchment area;
(e) supervises the family- and milieu-oriented activities in the district;
(f) arranges follow-up visits to the patients;
(g) gives consultation in problem situations.

Several reports have been published of the experiences of the APTs. Vartiainen *et al* (1994) have reported eight years' experience in Kuopio, where this model was first tested in 1986. The Kuopio team has three members: an experienced psychiatrist, a psychologist and a psychiatric nurse. All members of the group have a grade 1 training (Finnish psychotherapy training standards) in either psychoanalytic individual psychotherapy or family therapy.

For six years Kuopio had one team for a population of 85 000 in the catchment area, managing 12–16 patients at one time. Thus these three professional people actually took care of the patient population of one former psychiatric hospital ward. Any doctor can refer a patient to the team if he/she thinks the patient may be psychotic and does not think that admission is urgently needed. All health-care professionals in the area are informed about the team.

The first appointment will always be given within the same day or the next day. The patient is always told who recommended the referral. The family will be asked to participate in the first session. The patient is told that the aim of the team is to work, in cooperation with the patient, to overcome the crisis in an out-patient setting. During the first week sessions may be held daily. The key concepts of the work are keeping the appointments, keeping the promises given, and the availability of the team. The team applies psycho-analytical concepts in its thinking.

On average patients made eight visits to the team. In 1989 the team met 80 patients; 72 (90%) were sufficiently psychotic to meet all the legal criteria for involuntary admission. All these severely psychotic patients would have been admitted ten years ago, but now 63% were treated in an out-patient setting over the crisis period.

Rehabilitation programme for the old long-stay schizophrenic patients

The key ideas for the rehabilitation model for the old long-stay patients were developed by the Sopimusvuori Therapeutic Communities in Tampere. Thanks to the initiative of Professor Erik

Anttinen, this privately founded community had gained 20 years' experience in rehabilitation (Anttinen & Ojanen, 1984).

The Sopimusvuori communities were small. All patients had an individual rehabilitation plan and participated from the very beginning in the planning of their own rehabilitation. A graded model of rehabilitation was used (Ojanen, 1988).

Two main sectors in rehabilitation were differentiated: housing and activities. In both sectors the stepwise approach was seen as very important. Patients moved along the steps towards more demanding activities. They could also move a step backwards.

A four- and nine-year follow-up of rehabilitation of old long-stay patients in eight districts was carried out by Professor Markku Ojanen. One hundred and thirty-nine patients were followed up from all steps of the programme. Twenty-three patients died during the nine years, five of them suicides. The patients had spent an average of 11.8 years in hospital; the longest stay was 33 years. The average age at outset was 41.8 years.

Seven levels of rehabilitation were used in the follow-up assessment (Ojanen, 1988):

(a) treatment in an ordinary hospital ward;
(b) rehabilitation ward in a hospital;
(c) rehabilitation home in a hospital;
(d) rehabilitation home in the community;
(e) daily rehabilitation;
(f) supported housing;
(g) home, own flat.

Patients on the higher levels are supposed to be in a more advanced stage in their rehabilitation programme. In 1983 none of the patients were on the seventh level. In 1992 a third of the patients (45) had reached this step. The average rehabilitation level was 3.4 in 1983. In 1992 it was 4.7.

Three types of change in patients' rehabilitation status can be differentiated: advanced, no change, or regressed. During the follow-up 65% of the patients had advanced, 17% had made no change and 18% had regressed. It was judged that 76% of the rehabilitation efforts had proved to be successful and 24% failures.

During the nine years of the follow-up, the patients spent an average of 2.1 years in hospital. As this compares with a 12-year average hospital stay before the project, the result is very good. While 23% of the patients did not return to hospital at all and 49% spent less than half year in hospital, 10% of the patients stayed practically the entire nine years in hospital.

Balanced deinstitutionalisation

In the early 1980s, Finland drafted a national programme as part of the World Health Organization's Health for All by the Year 2000 Strategy (Ministry of Social Affairs and Health, 1987). The original document from the World Health Organization was based on very crude, morbidity-linked quantitative data. The Finnish version allowed space for secondary and tertiary prevention in psychiatry to be emphasised. The project's work was coordinated with the national mental health strategy. Mental health issues were considered a major challenge in public health.

Formerly, the key quantitative indicator for describing psychiatric care had been the use of mental hospital beds. This involved very inadequate oversimplifications. The Finnish 'Health For All' programme applied two numerical aims to the development of the psychiatric service system:

   (a) the number of psychiatric staff allocated to community care had to be increased to 6.5 community-based mental health workers per 10 000, from 2.5 per 10 000 in 1983;
   (b) the number of psychiatric beds would be gradually reduced by 50% while the community-based resources were increased simultaneously.

The government committed itself to annual, earmarked resource changes concerning psychiatric community care. Guidelines for community-based resource allocation were given in the annual government budget guidelines for the local authorities over 1983–89.

Ten years after

A follow-up of changes in the treatment system during the 10-year period 1982–92 was carried out by Dr Timo Tuori (Tuori, 1994). A questionnaire with 105 questions was sent to all 67 catchment areas. The response rate was 79%. The questions aimed to find out whether one aim of the project, developing care in the community to such an extent that it was able to care for the deinstitutionalised patients, had been realised. Standard statistical data were also collected in the follow-up.

Staff allocated to community-based care

The aim of investing heavily in out-patient care was reached. By the year 1992, out-patient staff had doubled from 2.5 per 10 000 to an average 5.1 per 10 000. The overall increase in community-based out-patient resources was 104% in ten years. Regional variations had diminished remarkably. The highest staffing level in community-based care in a district in 1992 was 8.4 per 10 000 and the lowest 3.9 per 10 000. The almost fourfold difference between the best and worst districts in 1982 had narrowed to a twofold variation in 1992. The reduction of regional differences seems to indicate that the importance of allocating personnel resources to community care was generally accepted.

A third of the catchment areas had decided on further increases in numbers of psychiatric out-patient staff. The trend that began ten years ago seemed to be continuing in 1993, but in only a third of the districts.

Psychiatric beds and the frequency of admission

The number of patients in psychiatric hospitals fell by almost 60% in the ten years, from 3.6 per 1000 in 1981 to 1.5 per 1000 in 1992. The project seemed to be rather successful in reaching its quantitative goals here. The changes in the hospital system were very rapid. Regional variations in the use of hospital beds also diminished. The expansion of out-patient settings took place a bit earlier than the most radical cuts to the hospitals.

Numerical targets were set for the optimal developments expected. According to the formula for balanced deinstitutinalisation, the provision of out-patient staff in 1992 should have been as high as 6.6 per 10 000 to meet the decrease in hospital capacity. It was 5.1 per 10 000. The main trend was positive in terms of controlled change. The running down of hospitals, however, was less well controlled than the development of new out-patient structures. The overall outcome was that the increases in community-based resources were insufficient to balance the lost hospital capacity.

Use of APTs

The APT was part of the service in 16 districts during the follow-up, while three districts had no APT. Out of the 67 catchment areas, 44% had an APT of their own. Altogether, 58 new APTs had been established in 31 catchment areas by 1992 (i.e. in the five years since the publication of details of the new approach). The size of the APTs varied from two to four persons. Five professional groups were working in these teams: 42 psychiatrists, 35 psychologists, 74 nurses, 26 mental assistants, and 14 social workers.

Since 1991 Finland has suffered from very severe economic recession and 20% unemployment. The APT approach needs a large amount of resources. The teams could be expected to be under severe economic pressures at a time of heavy cutbacks. This did not appear, however, to be the case. Only three groups reported being under economic threat.

Number of trained psychotherapists and use of the project model

One of the early findings in 1982 was that there was a lot of psychotherapy activity and interest. Public-sector health staff, however, seldom had adequate training in psychotherapy. In the early follow-up study (Laakintohallitus, 1985) of the new schizophrenic patients, only 20% of the therapists who practised psychotherapy with schizophrenic patients had adequate recognised training in psychotherapy.

In the 10-year follow-up, the Finnish Psychotherapy Training Guidelines (Pylkkanen, 1989) were used to measure changes in the numbers of trained psychotherapists in the districts. In these guidelines, grade 1 training consists of at least 2.5 years' training in some mode of psychotherapy; grade 2 training takes five to six years. In 1992 every district was employing psychotherapists who met the training criteria of at least grade 1 level. Twelve districts also had grade 2 trained therapists while seven were still without. The attitude to psychotherapy in the treatment of schizophrenia had also changed. Only 5% of the catchment areas reported no change in their psychotherapy practices. More family orientation was reported by 91%, and more individual psychotherapy by 51%.

The project model for treatment of schizophrenic patients was published in 1987 as a book (Laakintohallitus, 1987). The *Nordic Journal of Psychiatry* also published the model in English (Alanen *et al*, 1990).

The treatment model presented two key interactional principles that were supposed to be followed in any treatment of a schizophrenic patient:

(a) the patient must be present in all situations where he/she is concerned as often as possible;
(b) the family and those people important to the patient must be met continuously, from the first intervention on.

Adherence to these principles was assessed in the follow-up. In the early 1980s only 45% of the patients had participated in the staff meetings where their treatment plan was discussed. Ten years later, the relatives participated at least in some of the meetings dealing with the patients in 87% of the catchment areas. The family was met within the first week in 75% of the catchment areas. The attitudes of the patients and relatives were reported to be very positive. The staff reported that relatives found the model positive slightly more often than the patients. In four catchment areas out of five the impact of the model was regarded as very great or rather great (Tuori, 1994).

The follow-up of the long-stay patients

Two follow-ups of old and new long-stay patients were made: one in 1986 and one in 1992. It is interesting to note that the original calculations at the starting point (1982) for estimating changes in the numbers of long-stay patients appeared to be wrong. The concept of new long-stay was more complicated than thought originally. The idea of collecting the data from standard annual statistics did not work. The reason for this was the 'revolving-door syndrome'. A third of the original (1982 analysis) new long-stay patients did not actually meet the given criteria, because they did not stay in hospital over one year for the first time. The annual standard statistics could also register them as new long-stays when they stayed in hospital for over a year for the second or third time in their life. A new category of long-stay, 'revolving-door long-stay patient', had to be developed. The changes are presented in Table 16.2. The original aim was to cut down the number of both new and old long-stay patients by 50% in 10 years. This aim was reached. The new long-stay numbers came

TABLE 16.2
Changes in numbers of new and old long-stay patients, from 1982 to 1986 and 1992

	Aim, as change from 1982	1986	1992
Patient indicators			
New long-stay	-50%	-14%	-60%
Old long-stay	-50%	-22%	-68%
RDNLS[1]	Not specified	-4%	-31%
Resource indicators			
Increase in community-based staff	Not specified		+104%
Fewer beds	-50%	-16%	-55%

1. RDNLS: revolving-door new long-stay – second time or more registered as new long-stay (over one year in hospital). The aim for this category of patients was not specified in the original design of the project.
Based on Tuori (1994) and National Board of Health (1988).

down by 60% and the old long-stay numbers by 68%. Also, the number of patients having several hospital admissions over a year in length came down by 31%. Community-based services developed following the design created by the project.

A good indicator for measuring changes in the rate of institutionalisation is the time interval between first-ever admission and the first admission leading to the new long-stay status. In the first follow-up (1986) almost a quarter of all newly admitted schizophrenic patients remained as new long-stay patients. In 1992 this figure was 3%. The overall number of new long-stay patients had dropped by 65% and simultaneously the time interval from first admission to first new long-stay registration had become remarkably longer for those who finally became new long-stay patients.

To sum up, the two main original aims (reducing the number of old and new long-stay patients, and developing community-based services) were reached in the ten-year follow-up.

Balanced deinstitutionalisation – is it possible?

The incidence of first-time hospital admission of schizophrenic patients did not change during the follow-up over 1988–92. Practically all schizophrenic patients were still admitted at some phase of their illness. The reduced use of hospitals was due mainly to shorter periods being spent in hospital after admission. We cannot claim that patients could be cared for by the community-based service alone. The fairness of the balance between the resources and capacity of community-based care and the hospitals plays a crucial role in evaluating whether or not deinstitutionalisation was properly controlled.

It seems that Finland managed to increase community care steadily while reducing mental hospital capacity until 1990. In 1990 the general health policy of the government changed. In order to improve decentralisation in the health service, the government gave up almost all control of health-care resource allocation and quality control. After this change, the growth in resourcing community-based care slowed down considerably. Simultaneously, the run-down of hospitals accelerated much more than the project plan had predicted (Table 16.3). Table 16.3 does not provide a very optimistic view for the future. The original idea was to make a real change towards community care by increasing information through service-based research. The aims of the project could, however, be reached only as long as the government centrally controlled the development of community-based resources by setting national quality standards.

TABLE 16.3
*Changes in hospital capacity and community-based resources in 1988–90
and 1990–92 in Finland*

	Psychiatric beds	Resource in community
1988–90	-15%	+22%
1990–92	-21%	+11%
Sum change, 1988–90 to 1990–92	-40%	-50%

Based on Tuori (1994).

The steps towards totally local resource control from 1990 onwards changed the balance radically. Deinstitutionalisation became 40% faster than before, and the development of community care was cut to half of its previous level (Pylkkanen, 1994).

A complicating factor in interpreting developments over 1990–92 is the economic recession, which became evident during 1991 in Finland. It affected public services more slowly than business. When excess hospital capacity was to be cut in the 1990s, it was not expected that the psychiatric hospitals would suffer the worst of these cuts, given the 60% reduction in beds they had already seen, but they did. Patient needs would dictate that any further cuts in hospital capacity would require new provision in the community. Retrospective transfer of former hospital resources would have been needed to make money follow the patients. This did not happen.

Is a controlled and balanced deinstitutionalisation possible using the knowledge we have? I think the answer is yes, but only under certain favourable organisational conditions. Finland managed to carry out a rather balanced process for eight years (1982–90). The key factors contributing to this success were (Pylkkanen, 1994):

(a) quality standards controlled by a centralised purchaser (the government);
(b) successful coordination of the project's aims, with general health politics by the central health directorate (the National Board of Health);
(c) government commitment to the project's aims;
(d) commitment of the mental health professionals;
(e) commitment of the autonomous psychiatric providers at district level;
(f) a growing national economy.

Since 1991 all these factors have changed very rapidly. The government commitment and central quality standards ended in 1990, when active government participation in mental-health resource allocation ceased. As part of this decentralisation process the National Board of Health was abolished in 1991. From the beginning of 1991 the previously independent psychiatric providers (mental health districts) were financially and administratively integrated to district general hospitals, which took over the economic and administrative leadership of psychiatry. Since then several community-based services have been transferred from the district control to the local health centres providing primary care. The Association of Mental Hospitals, whose initiative to the National Board of Health started the project, was abolished in 1991. The growth of the national economy ceased in 1990–91, when the heavy economic recession started in Finland.

The only success factor that remains unchanged is the commitment of the professionals, which seems not to have been enough for balanced deinstitutionalisation to continue under the new economic and administrative structures. Under the present organisational and financial conditions, Finland could hardly have begun successfully to carry out a national schizophrenia project.

The project remains a historic effort in Finnish psychiatry. It contributed remarkable changes to psychotherapeutically oriented interventions in the treatment of schizophrenia. Having started, the changes seem to be continuing. The First Finnish Consensus Conference on Psychiatry was held in 1987 on the treatment of schizophrenia (Suomen Åkatemien, 1987). A remarkable change in attitudes of the mental hospital staff took place. An element of hope was introduced. The primary task of psychiatric hospitals, treatment of the most severe psychoses, was gradually given its due recognition (Pylkkanen, 1993). This was reflected in the positive changes in the milieus of acute and long-stay psychiatric wards.

Schizophrenia and the health market

Schizophrenia will remain the core responsibility of psychiatric care. Fair prioritisation of its treatment in the health market is a challenge for all health-care systems – and differs as a task from prioritisation of other treatments. The Finnish experience of the National Schizophrenia Project points out clearly that the treatment system of severely disabled schizophrenic patients cannot be subject to the same decentralisation and open-market conditions as other health-care activities without risking irreversible damage to it.

It is the ethical and moral responsibility of the whole society to prioritise the care of schizophrenic patients. Care for schizophrenia is part of the basic package of health care. Its finance should not be left to be decided by market forces alone. Governments should take responsibility for ensuring that minimal standards for the care of schizophrenic patients are met. Professionals and voluntary organisations should keep on reminding society about the necessary preconditions for good care for schizophrenic patients by speaking out about what they know. Hopefully the Finnish experience will encourage others to design new programmes for the treatment of schizophrenic patients to meet the challenges of rapidly changing cultural and economic conditions.

References

ALANEN, Y. (1993) *Skitsofrenia. Syyt ja Tarpeenmukainen Hoito.* Juva: WSOY.

——, ANTTINEN, E., KOKKOLA, A., *et al* (1990) Treament and tehabilitation of schizophrenic psychoses. The Finnish treatment model. *Nordic Journal of Psychiatry*, **44** (suppl. 22).

——, LEHTINEN, K., RAKKOLAINEN, V., *et al* (1991) Need-adapted treatment of new schizophrenic patients. Experiences and results of the Turku Project. *Acta Psychiatrica Scandinavica*, **83**, 363–372.

AMERICAN PSYCHIATRIC ASSOCIATION (1980) *Diagnostic and Statistical Manual of Mental Disorders* (3rd edn) (DSM–III). Washington, DC: APA.

ANTTINEN, E. & OJANEN, M. (1984) *Sopimusvuoren Terapeuttiset Yhteisot.* TaMpere: Lege Artis Oy.

LAAKINTOHALLITUS (1985) *Skitsofrenian Hoidon Valtakunnallinen Kehittaminen.* Helsinki: Valiraponti. Valtion painatuskeskus.

—— (1987) *Skitsofreniaan Sairastuneen Hoito ja Kuntoutus.* Helsinki: Hoitomalli. Valtion painatuskeskus.

LEHTINEN, V., JOUKAMAA, M., JYRKINEN, T., *et al* (1989) Mielenterveyden ongelmat ja hairiot. In *Terveys, Toimintakykyja Hoidon Tarve Suomessa* (eds A. Aromaa, M. iAello'vaara, O. Impivaara, *et al*). Helsinki: Kansanelakelaitoksen julkaisuja, AL:32.

MINISTRY OF SOCIAL AFFAIRS AND HEALTH (1987) *Health for All by the Year 2000. The Finnish National Strategy.* Helsinki: Government Printing Centre.

NATIONAL BOARD OF HEALTH (LAAKINTOHALLITUS) (1988) *Skitsofreniaprojekti 1981–1987. Skitsofrenian Hoidon Valtakunnallisen Kehittam Isohjelman Loppuraportti.* Helsinki: Valtion painatuskeskus.

OJANEN, M. (1988) *Pitkaaikaispotilaiden Hoidon ja Kuntoutuksen Kehittaminen. PSP – Projektin Seurantatulokset.* Helsinki: Psykiatrian tutkimussaatio.

PYLKKANEN, K. (1989) Quality assurance programme for psychotherapy. The Finnish experience. *Psychoanalytic Psychotherapy*, **4**, 13–22.

—— (1990) En forandringsstrategi four psykiatrisk halsovard. Skitsofreniprojektet Finland. In *Strategi, Okonomi Forsog* (ed. F. K. Jorgensen), pp. 133–143. Kopenhamn: Dansk Institut four Klinisk Epidemiologi.

—— (1993) Promoting commitment for psychotherapeutic treatment approach. Experience of the Finnish National Schizophrenia Programme 1981–1991. In *Crossing the Borders* (eds S. Haugsgjerd, B. Sandin, K. Pylkkanen & B. Rosenbaum), pp. 82–89. Ludvika: Nordic Association for Psychotherapy of Psychoses.

—— (1994) The Finnish National Scizophrenia Project 1982-1992. *Psychiatria Fennica*, **25**, 169–183.

SALOKANGAS, R., RAKKOLAINEN, V., STENGARD, E., *et al* (1991) *Uusien Skitsofreniapotilaiden Hoito ja Ennuste: 5 Vuoden Seuranta.* Helsinki: Psykiatrian tutkimussaatio.

SUOMEN AKATEMIAN (1987) *Skitsofrenian Hoito,* Konsensuskokous 26.-28.10. Publication no. 611987. Helsinki: Finnish Academy of Science.

254   *Pylkkanen*

Tuori, T. (1994) *Skitsofrenian Hoito Kannattaa.* STAKES raponteja 143. Jyvaskyla: Gummerus Oy.

Vartiainen, A., Vartiainen, H., Kalliokoski, M.-L., *et al* (1994) Akuutin psykoosipotilaan avohoito mielenterveyskeskuksessa. *Suom Laak Lehti,* **49**, 560–564.

17 Meaning and madness. A narrative approach to psychopathology and treatment

GLENN A. ROBERTS

The problem of meaning is central to the care and treatment of people with psychotic disorders. This paper is basically concerned with stories as carriers of meaning and the use of story in sickness and in health. I shall argue that constructing narrative sequences, story-making, is a fundamental way of organising understanding inside and outside madness, and an appreciation of the dialogue between illness and healing narratives is essential for clinical care and involvement with psychotics. As such I am not saying anything new but seeking to pick up a strand of emphasis that runs throughout psychiatry and psychotherapy.

I would like to acknowledge from the outset a heavy debt to an American psychiatrist, James Phillips (1991), who has spoken on narrative dimensions in psychopathology and introduced me to a quotation of Peter Brook's that can serve as a guiding text for this paper:

> "Our lives are ceaselessly intertwined with narrative, with the stories that we tell and hear told, those we dream or imagine or would like to tell, all of which are reworked in that story of our own lives that we narrate to ourselves in an episodic, sometimes semiconscious, but virtually uninterrupted monologue. We live immersed in narrative."

The word 'story' has somehow acquired a softness, a triviality – "it's only a story". We seem to have lost an awareness that story is how we express and carry meaning, it is what we constantly form and reform when we talk about our lives. It may have been lost or obscured in our enthusiasm to be scientific; if so, we may have lost something of great value. As Satish Kumar observed:

"Our preoccupation with facts creates an obsession with measurement, but the truth cannot be measured. Facts are only the body
of the truth, the spirit of the truth comes with the story." (*The
Independent*, 9 May 1992)

There appears to be a growing emphasis on restoring the meaningful and personal. It is extraordinary that an editorial in the *American
Journal of Psychiatry* (November 1993) entitled "Understanding the
experience of schizophrenia" should feel a need to state "There is
no substitute for encouraging expression and for listening to what
patients have to say". The fact that patients want this too may be
supported by a survey published by MIND that reviewed the experiences of more than 500 service users and continued to criticise the
impersonality of psychiatric approaches, which were referred to as
"mechanistic and dismissive of individuality".

These comments find an echo in Satre's criticism (in Sims, 1988)
that "Psychiatry is too quickly satisfied when it throws light on the
general structures of delusions and does not seek to comprehend
the individual concrete content of the psychosis".

The problem can be illustrated with a case.

A paranoid doctor came into hospital to "take a holiday" in a protected
environment. He brought with him a massive document that he had
been working on for the previous year describing in fine detail the
conspiracy against him. He had written on the top of it "the whole
story" and spoke of his own sense of heroism at doing battle with
such wicked men, and his satisfaction at getting all the evidence in
order. He had taken to carrying a large knife in his briefcase for he
felt the time would come soon when he would need to take action
first, before his partners acted to destroy him. He also expressed a
grudging admiration for the subtlety of their plot as he readily
conceded that to any ordinary person he would appear mad.

We could have stopped there but he could also respond to the
question, "What would you have to think about if you were not so
taken up with the conspiracy?" and he listed the collapse of his career
and the frustration of his professional ambition, the failure of his
marriage, alienation from his children and his recently recovered
memories of being sexually abused by his father, who was also his
headmaster. He was later able to speak of the emptiness, frustration
and futility of his life before these delusional developments.

He could tell two separate stories and initially could see no
relationship between them; our subsequent work focused on telling
them both fully and allowing them to illuminate and reveal the
significance of each other. Eighteen months later he was substantially
well; he had lost his practice but taken up other work and had a sense
of regained pride and optimism. He continued to believe the
conspiracy was true but in his words he had "cocooned it" and it now
took up very little of his attention or concern. We may take an

interesting double meaning from 'cocooned' in that the beliefs are both protected from him and for him.

The link between meaning and madness is not always appreciated and there are some major concerns that must be faced if this is to be anything more than an interesting discussion. Ciompi (1989) has warned of a "disastrous splitting" between understanding and treatment of schizophrenia. This points to a fault line that has been drawn in many ways: mind/brain; female/male; right/left; heart/ head; art/science; subjective/objective; imagination/reality. The risk of mindless psychiatry or brainless psychotherapy has been noted.

It may still be that trainees are poorly prepared to understand their patients. Yorke (1988) has cogently argued that there is a widespread "defect in training" that denies trainees the confidence that can come from understanding their patients from a psychological point of view, whether those patients are psychologically treatable or not. Roth (1970) emphasised that the structure of professional training, with its rapid changes of post and emphasis on resolution of acute symptoms, may result in the trainee failing to gather a longitudinal perspective of the person adapting to the complexities of an illness, which in turn inhibits consideration of the meaning of the illness.

A further split, of equal importance, may be the division between purchaser and provider, which appears to be separating skilled and trained staff from face-to-face contact and devalues the cultivation of a personal relationship. Psychiatric social workers bemoan the detachment of care management from caring contact and many, perhaps most, patients with chronic psychotic disorders are cared for by community nurses with excessive case loads or untrained care staff in increasingly dispersed community services.

All these conceptual, professional and organisational factors conspire against a service substantially committed to long-term supportive and therapeutic relationships and the ready development of meaning and understanding. It is into this comparatively infertile soil that any renewed emphasis on the psychotherapy of psychosis must take root.

It might be asked, 'what is needed?' Contemporary care for the long-term mentally ill has been described as ideally based on "an individualised assessment of need and a sensitive understanding of the person's inner world" (Holloway, 1988). However, it is by no means clear to a general psychiatrist how to achieve this sensitive understanding. I think it may be helpful to remember where we have come from and to realise that it has not always been like this.

Bleuler's observations leading to the modern concept of schizophrenia (Bleuler & Bleuler, 1986) arose from intimate and continuous contact with his patients. Bleuler was 29 when appointed Chief of the Clinic Rheinou, a converted eighth-century monastery forming an island community on the Rhine. For 12 years he was:

> "working with them (in agriculture), organising their free time (for instance, hiking with them, playing in the theatre with them, dancing with them).... During his life with the patients, Bleuler had always a memo-pad at hand, where he noted what touched and interested him in his patients' behaviour. He frequently noted in shorthand what the patients actually said.... He was eager to describe their symptoms in an objective scientific way and to suggest at the same time the importance of understanding the personal psychodynamic life of the individual." (Bleuler & Bleuler, 1986)

He did, of course, also work in close cooperation with Carl Jung.

Few, if any, psychiatrists today practise their work in such an intimate fashion and we may similarly find Bleuler's conclusion inaccessible, that "the schizophrenic is not unintelligible, and that we can develop empathy for him". However, the costs of failing to find this understanding may be considerable, for, as Jaspers (1963, p. 310) commented, everything understandable is given a sense of value and worth, while "in contrast we do not value the ununderstandable". The chronically psychotic as some of the least understood, are also some of the least valued.

Story as a ubiquitous source of meaning and understanding

If understanding is desirable but difficult to access, we perhaps need reminding that "understanding proceeds primarily by story" (Romanshyn, in Cox & Thielgaard, 1987) and that story is an ancient and ubiquitous carrier of meaning.

The storiographer Richard Bowman (1989) has commented on the significance of story:

> "people tell stories to each other as a means of giving cognitive and emotional coherence to experience, constructing and negotiating a social identity investing the experiential landscape with moral significance. Not only do we have story telling minds but we become social beings through story telling."

Holmes' (1993) discussion of the link between storytelling ability or 'narrative competence' and secure attachment underpins this discussion with a developmental perspective.

We shall see later that the association between secure attachment and story can work in both directions, such that the securely attached tell coherent, well-shaped and salient stories, and those who can place their lives within the framework of such stories, even if they are delusional, may adopt some of the benefits of secure attachment.

The drive to generate stories appears particularly enhanced in desperate circumstances. A particularly vivid and well studied example is the evolution of a species of unfounded gossip called 'bobards' among the inmates of concentration camps (Bravo *et al*, 1990). These were elaborate stories of military activity and political developments; the authors comment that "at the heart of these accounts we find a resource of the human mind which impotent in the face of overpowering force, instead drew on mythical hopes". They go on to comment, "But that is not so different from so much of human hope and human thinking".

Some ancient stories have survived centuries of interpretation and continue to inform, inspire and guide, acting as narrative icons that offer windows and perhaps doors into a greater reality, stories to live by, sacred tales.

Laurens van de Post (cited in Cox & Theilgaard, 1987) has commented on the social and existential significance of stories: "Without a story one had no class or family; without a story of one's own, no individual life; without a story of stories, no life giving continuity with the beginning and therefore no future".

Illness narratives

There appears to be a renewed interest in storytelling in medicine with the recent publication of books such as:

(a) *The Man Who Mistook his Wife for a Hat* (Sacks, 1985);
(b) *The Illness Narratives* (Klienman, 1989);
(c) *Toscanini's Fumble...* (Klawans, 1988);
(d) *The Boy Who Couldn't Stop Washing* (Rappaport, 1990);
(e) *Doctors' Stories* (Hunter, 1991).

And clinicians have always had much in common with oral historians who value the individuality of each life story and instead of regarding it as an awkward impediment to generalisation, consider it as a vital document in the construction of understanding.

Kathryn Montgomery Hunter (1991) spent two years eavesdropping on medical activity and concluded that physicians habitually tell stories, such that their case conferences, case reports, theorising and model-making all have a narrative structure, and "how else," she asks, "is the individual to be known but by a narrative account of his case?" She considered that where medicine de-emphasises case story in preference for something more objective, of greater scientific standing, it loses something of fundamental importance: "The loss of story making and telling has its impact on failure to care for the long term, chronically ill and incurable patient."

Hillman (1983) has offered essentially complementary views in his exploration of case history as a form of fiction. He likens psychological theorists to storytellers, selecting and moulding their patient material to support the plot:

> "A case history no matter how outer its style is also a mode of imagining ... we can respect case history for the genre of fiction that it is, one cast in literalisms that necessarily does not recognise itself as such."

Winnicott (in Holmes, 1993) described psychotherapy as an extended form of history-taking. The patient comes with a story, however tentative and disjointed, which is then worked on by therapist and patient until a more coherent and satisfying narrative emerges. This provides an explanation of the patient's difficulties and a means of linking inner and outer experience.

Treatment or therapy is therefore seen as a battle of stories, a contest of singers, a collaboration between fictions, a revising of the story into a more intelligent, more imaginative plot.

A narrative approach to psychopathology

I shall limit this discussion for the most part to the development of delusions, and present it in three sections:

    (a) meaning of delusion – narrative process in origins;
    (b) meaning in delusion – the relationship between delusional contents and life story;
    (c) meaning through delusion – the acquisition of meaning and purpose through delusion belief.

Some have considered that psychosis illustrates the limits of a narrative approach as it represents a departure and a discontinuity. So let us first consider the origins of delusion.

Meaning of delusion

A general model of delusion formation is presented in Fig. 17.1 (Roberts, 1992). Most theories of delusion formation pivot around the appearance in consciousness of some unaccountable, unpredictable anomalous experience, which may be seen to arise from antecedents or occur as a primary phenomenon. Many psychopathologists have described this prodromal and decompensatory phase as predominantly affective and extremely unpleasant. Roth (1970) refers to it as turmoil and Arieti (1964) as prepsychotic panic.

Cutting (1989) considered this early stage as the key to understanding delusional development, an unknown disruption fundamentally altering the patient's knowledge of the world. And drawing on Conrad and Matussek, he states that it could best be regarded as a breakdown of gestalt perception, a disintegration and fracturing of previous meaning patterns accompanied by an uncanny sense of strangeness and significance – the delusional mood.

There may then be two adaptive phases.

(a) *The attribution of meaning to experience.* Although psychosis is inaugurated by a destruction and dissolution of meaning, the fracturing of gestalts, the reparative forces brought to bear on this rent in the psychic fabric include the powerful disposition to narrative construction, and from this position of anomalous experience and perceptual novelty a narrative transformation takes place. Meanings are drawn from reservoirs of personal meaning, often calling on images of the powerful unknown in popular science and religion, and biographical material of great personal salience. This crystallising out of symptoms may be attended by "psychotic

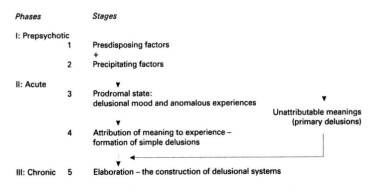

Fig. 17.1. A general model of delusion formation.

insight" (Arieti, 1964) and the relief provided by these explanations may foster their perpetuation.

(b) *Elaboration to form systems of belief.* It seems characteristic of the chronically deluded that the more extensive the delusional system, the more comprehensive a reconstruction of their life story is involved. Dupre (in Arthur, 1964) expressed an early view along these lines, that "delusions of the imagination" are due to the tendency to invent stories through a pathological activity of creative imagination, which he called 'mythomania'.

Once established, the delusional system, like any comprehensive system of belief, is protected from erosion, and subsequent discrepancies between delusional and real world perspectives are likely to be resolved either by further elaboration of the beliefs, so as to incorporate the new information, or withdrawal and adjustment of life circumstances so as to protect the beliefs from challenge; delusions are therefore self-reinforcing.

Perris (1989) has described the development in health and sickness of basic cognitive schemata which consist of a coherent, integrated set of ideas and thoughts providing the fundamental intellectual resources for labelling, classifying, interpreting, evaluating and ascribing meaning to objects and events. These schemata continuously structure our experience and are structured by it. He holds these to be broadly equivalent to belief systems, rules of life, meaning structures, basic assumptions, working models and assumptive worlds. They also appear equivalent to the basic stories we tell about ourselves and others. Once acquired (constructed) they tend in health and illness to be stable and self-reinforcing; psychotic reorganisation can be seen to represent a reconfiguring of this core meaning structure resulting in a dysfunctional schema. These core schemata or stories of stories are then relatively enduring aspects of cognitive organisation, stories that nest in each other, anthologies we live in, and are collected or recollected according to stable organising principles that encourage the preservation of confirmatory information.

Patients' stories are full of such attempts to affirm their own beliefs. For example, a patient of mine believed himself to be the Messiah and positioned himself in church so as to receive the priest's bows and genuflections. Another, who believed there was a tunnel in his roof through which his neighbours invaded his house at night, shut his cat in his attic and when, after several days, it stopped scratching to get out, he concluded it must have escaped through the roof tunnel, but did not check.

Jaspers (1963) spoke of delusional systems being derived from the psychology of creativity, and this might be expressed as stages in story-making, as an adjustment to psychotic dissolution and a creative adaptation to fragmentation by creating new meaning structures and elaborating these to construct and reconstruct the life story. This brings us to the pivotal question of considering what kind of stories arise in these circumstances, with what benefits, and what may be the implications for approaching such patients clinically.

Meaning in delusion is not so difficult to find

"Much madness is divinest sense
To the discerning eye."
(Emily Dickinson, 1862)

Freud (1939) underlined the therapeutic potential of finding a 'kernel of truth' in delusion as providing common ground upon which psychological treatment could occur. But this poses the question of how to search and where to look for this kernel of truth.

The Vienna group (Berner *et al*, 1986), in presenting a multi-axial classification of delusional states, included an axis recording specific contents and concluded that the specific circumstances in the personal history are frequently of great importance in the choice of delusional theme.

Kaffman (1984), in a study of 34 families in which at least one member had developed a delusional system, concluded that there was always a basis in historical reality for the contents and that this may support the incorrigibility of these 'false beliefs' – in a transformed and distorted way the individual is telling the truth.

Jim was a dapper 48-year-old man, estranged from his wife, who came into hospital on his first admission with a huge bundle of papers. He described a complex series of interconnected beliefs centring on being a linguist and prophet with the ability to write in numerous unlearned scripts (undoubtedly a diner at the "great feast of languages"). His bundle of papers consisted of transcriptions of his voices, which he believed to be of great significance for mankind.

He had several other remarkable skills, being able to receive and transmit Morse code by clicking his teeth and relay messages via British Telecom satellites. He was in a constant communication and battle with benign and hostile forces and periodically published books by reading them aloud in front of the television; he was very angry that he had never been paid.

He was an only child, shared his father's interest in cricket and played for the county team. His father died when he was 11 and he said, "ever since then something was missing". His school performance deteriorated, he truanted and was very unhappy. He was expelled later and joined the army, where he stayed until 42, when he was obliged to leave. He had lived exclusively within the barrack community and travelled extensively throughout Europe and the Far East as a storeman. Life changed dramatically when he left the army. He felt lost, aimless and his marriage broke down. "When I left the army I tried very hard to get a job until I gave up – 22 years in the service seemed for nothing – totally wasted – I'd been totally wasted." A series of failures followed, including falling in love with his young pregnant niece. Then the languages began: "It was a totally abrupt change. I felt there was something right to do about this – I found out who I really was I'm Solomon now [i.e. solo man – alone and Solomon the wise]. It's a pity I'd not been writing before – I'm totally dedicated to the way I see things – I'll never get bored."

When asked he was easily able to rewrite the languages in plain English. This illustrates a number of features: that patients can back-translate and decode apparently cryptic material if asked; that it is not that hidden in any case; and that psychopathology in a different register can be seen as an expression of the literary resources of the intact psyche.

Among his papers there was a sheet on which he seemed to express his dilemma:

> "Ego – Alta Ego
> Is it better to exist in a state of non reality or be non existent in a state of reality?
> Am I always going to have a two sided problem?"

The delusional contents, instead of being regarded as obfuscating and meaningless, thus provide a route if not a royal road into making sense of individuals and their predicament in life.

Meaning through delusion

I have described elsewhere (Roberts, 1991) an extensive study of 17 patients with long-standing elaborate delusional belief systems who were compared with a carefully matched control group of previously deluded patients in remission. Their responses to a shortened version of the Beck Depression Inventory (Beck & Beck, 1972) and the Purpose in Life Test (Crumbaugh & Maholick, 1964) demonstrated that the possession of an elaborate delusional belief system protected against depression and was accompanied by an enhanced sense of meaning and purpose in life (Fig. 17.2).

Summary

A narrative approach to psychopathology emphasises the search for understanding of delusional contents in the biographical past and considers delusions as arising from the healthy, intact parts of the person, attributing meanings to anomalous experiences and, for some, compensating for significant losses, traumas and destructive

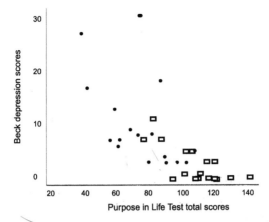

Fig. 17.2. Relationship between Beck depression scores and scores on the Purpose in Life Test. •, *previously deluded patients in remission;* □, *currently deluded.*

events. Some go on to elaborate alternative life stories built up into delusional systems, and as such it is possible to see people using their storytelling, narrative capacities to cope with psychosis. There appear to be considerable benefits associated with attachment to some psychotic narratives constituting a transformation of the personal world.

There is a paradox to be considered, for there are two patterns of healing through the creation of story, and they are in exactly opposite directions to each other. The progression from psychosis to sanity, illness to health, is accompanied by a recovery of the 'real' life story, and therapy may be directed at this process of recovery of information, organisation, understanding and telling – a process of leaving behind the psychotic ideas and experiences, and attempting to make sense of them, to integrate or ignore them, from the standpoint of sanity. This leads to recovering a story and a way of telling it that is intelligible and acceptable to others.

It would also seem possible that psychotic people may achieve similar therapeutic benefits through the creation or recreation of their life story within psychosis. Hence they achieve a form of pseudo-sanity, accompanied by psychotic insight, understanding and integration, but at the cost of isolation, although even that may be compensated for by experientially residing in a psychotic pseudo-community that gives a satisfactory explanation of the strange, altered world and a basis for doing something about it. As Cameron (1959) stated, "it reestablishes stable object relations though on a delusional basis, and thus makes integrated action possible". But, as Cameron neatly concluded, "This is his victory and his defeat".

The implications of a narrative approach to treatment

I would assume from the outset that the standard treatment of psychotic disorders is based upon careful use of medication and some form of psychosocial rehabilitation. However, this is seldom completely successful and is in any case insufficient. Chronically deluded patients are often lost to follow-up, refuse medication and preserve their beliefs even when treated against their will, although they often realise the wisdom of ceasing to talk about them. It follows that beyond giving appropriate medication, any treatment is dependent on developing a relationship. It is difficult if not impossible to build a relationship with someone who cannot be understood.

Our case histories are the basic text we work from, and every effort needs to be made to build up a full and comprehensive clinical biography for every patient. Patients with chronic psychoses are often eclipsed by their disorder. They have lost their stories. Frequently their psychiatric notes, perhaps documenting a decade of treatment, are relatively empty and offer little evidence of an attempt to understand the individual. Recovering a biographical perspective may help to reinstate an awareness of the person within the patient and foster respect. There are parallels with reminiscence therapy, for both patients and staff.

The construction of this story may in turn shed light on the meaning of some of the psychotic contents, which will start to dismantle the unknowable quality of these patients and facilitate empathy. These meaningful associations may then open up some common ground and help to orient a therapeutic relationship.

The intractability of delusions may be less puzzling if their explanatory power is acknowledged. As coping mechanisms they are understandably protected from challenge. Engagement may be assisted by a form of therapeutic collusion, respecting these belief structures as meaningful and valuable to the patient, and seeking to build trust more than "beat the drums of logic" (Huszonek, 1987).

There is an interesting relationship between medication and meaning. Diamond's (1985) review of medication and quality of life drew a distinction between effective medication and the patient genuinely doing better. He emphasised that objective goals, such as reduced hospital attendance and reduced symptoms, may be poorly correlated with subjective properties such as happiness and contentment. He commented:

> "Anti-psychotic drugs clearly decrease positive symptoms, but many patients are left withdrawn, apathetic, asocial and depressed ... some may welcome or even invite their psychosis as a way of escaping a world that is objectively miserable."

Support for this view can be found in Van Putten *et al*'s (1976) study of drug-refusing schizophrenic patients, which showed that non-compliers characteristically had a resurgence of 'ego-syntonic grandiose delusions' after discontinuing their medication.

Working towards recovery

Most authors who write of psychotherapeutic effort with psychotic people consider that the recovery and construction of the 'real' life story is a major component in the healing process.

Cox & Theilgaard (1987, p. 60) spoke of this as "a complete story – intelligible, constituent and unbroken is the theoretical, created end story, ... at the end, at the successful end – one has come into possession of one's own story".

In this we are asking our patients to take the same steps as the eldest princess in A. S. Byatt's (1992) short story of the same name. She tells the tale of a young woman who leaves her castle and gets into increasing danger until she meets a wise old woman and realises that she is living out a narrative: "You are a born story teller," said the old woman, "You had the sense to see you were caught in a story and the sense to see you could change it into another one".

Hillman (1983) speaks of "therapeutic fictions" and sees the essential task as helping patients to formulate a new story or to reconnect with their old one and hence recover their 'sustaining fiction', or, as Ibsen (1965) put it, their "vital lie". If delusions are adaptive and meaningful, then it follows that loss of these beliefs, recovery, may be viewed as a threat and experienced as painful.

> A patient sought help after he found himself waist deep in water while believing he could walk across the River Taw. He recovered from his messianic delusions, which hampered his life in many ways, but with considerable regret. He explained to me how he prayed that God would allow him, in his words, to go mad again: "Every day was a happy day, I didn't have to think about drinking, eating, sleeping and money". He described how in his former state he had felt looked after by God and had an enhanced sense of compassion for all the people around him, mostly because he saw them as inferior creatures who lacked his superior qualities.

There is a striking similarity between some of the suggested mechanisms by which patients may benefit from their delusions and the therapeutic factors in psychotherapy. The construction of elaborate delusions has been described as serving this same purpose, constituting a form of attempted self-healing through narrative reconstruction – storytelling – and the risk for some is that recovery represents a deconstruction of this healing fiction.

When we tell our stories we give away our souls (Hillman, 1972); there may be re-entry problems.

A recovering schizophrenic wrote (*American Journal of Psychiatry*, 1986):

> "There are days when I wonder if it might not be more humane to leave the schizophrenic patient to his world of unreality, not to make him go through the pain that it takes to become part of humanity. These are the days when the pain is so great, I think I may prefer the craziness until I remember the immobilising terror, the distance and the isolation that keeps the world so far away and out of focus. It's not an easily resolved dilemma."

Andrew Sims (1988) has expressed it like this:

> "As the delusions fade the patients gain insight and regard them as false beliefs 'due to the illness'. Such a person needs help in accepting himself as a fit repository for his own self confidence once more. He may feel himself to be damaged, vulnerable and untrustworthy and suffer a massive loss of self esteem."

This all points to the need to remain vigilant and to seek to preserve contact on recovery, to work actively with those patients able and willing to understand and incorporate their psychotic departure back into the narrative continuity of their lives, so that it becomes a story that can be told from the standpoint of sanity, or what Jaspers called "digesting their psychosis".

A narrative approach may also contribute to understanding the unresponsiveness of post-psychotic depression to standard treatments because for some it is an existential depression in a crisis of losing delusional compensations and facing reality again. Similarly, the high rate of suicide in remission serves to re-emphasise the struggle and vulnerability that may accompany recovery with the need to let go of the new story and incorporate into the old story the reality of insanity, with all the compound losses that may entail.

Working with the chronically deluded

Restoring a biography, seeking to decode and understand delusional speech, remains valuable. It may be that working to establish trust and understanding with those who inhabit castles in the air may enable the portcullis to be raised, not so that the individual can come out, but so that the worker can enter in. There are numerous examples of chronically deluded patients sustaining fruitful relationships, often with unqualified staff, so that some of their needs can be met in non-delusional ways. It must be the case that it is easier to sustain involvement with and commitment to a delusional patient if a worker feels a sense of understanding and has a way of constructing a story that makes sense. Cameron's (1959) view that in these circumstances the primary focus should not be on the delusional structures but on understanding what has made them necessary, and seeking to reduce anxiety, seems particularly appropriate:

> "As anxiety and the threat of disintegration subside, paranoid certainty becomes less necessary to personal survival – the patient can begin to entertain doubts and consider alternative interpretations... in this way the conceptual structure of the pseudo-community (delusional system) may be gradually replaced by something approaching the structure of social reality."

This emphasis on gradual replacement appears particularly appropriate, as it allows the possibility of introducing opportunities for patients to meet their needs in non-delusional ways while accepting that they may continue verbally to assert the same delusional convictions.

Conclusions

Speaking as a general psychiatrist, our professional training has conspicuous flaws and omissions. The obsession with measurement and statistical truth, if unalloyed to the personal and individualistic, presents us with a dehumanised abstraction. This carries a spurious air of precision and derails psychiatric thought and practice from being the most holistic and humane of medical disciplines. At the heart of this is a devaluing of face-to-face contact, time spent together, and a redundancy of relationship. This carries a risk that psychiatrists may again become alienists and may lack, and painfully feel the lack of, a strong and tender healer heart to complement their well developed physician brains.

Fundamentally there is a need to heal the 'disastrous split' and work towards some form of integration of psychotherapy and psychiatry in ordinary psychiatric settings where most psychotic patients are treated. This could emerge as an outcome of implementing the new training guidelines, which have otherwise been called idealistic, but could go a long way to enhancing the narrative capacity of future generations of psychiatrists.

There is a need to anthologise psychiatry again, drawing together its biological, psychosocial, psychodynamic and spiritual dimensions, so that the containment and control of severe disorder is seasoned by a healing pattern of understanding and a rich awareness of the conditions that patients live in.

The fact that increasing numbers of people suffering from chronic psychotic disorders will be cared for 'in the community' by staff with minimal training underlines the need for a sufficiently approachable and robust therapeutic strategy to understand, value and hold them, within the warm embrace of a sustained and sustainable relationship. There is a need to hold an attitude that the inner world of psychosis can be rendered substantially understandable, to teach this and model it in our day-to-day work, however constrained we are by the limits of time and quantitative demands placed upon us.

There appears to be a growing interest in cultivating an attitude of mutual respect between psychotherapy and psychiatry, and perhaps by extension between the healer and the scientist. I have argued that a basic strand of emphasis is to be found in recovering the freedom and facility of the storyteller, reappraising a narrative approach to psychopathology and treatment, and the search for meaning in madness.

A note on confidentiality

The people described in this paper are either disguised (the first case) or have been previously written up as part of an MD thesis (*Meaning and Purpose in Delusional Belief Systems*, G. Roberts, 1991, University of Bristol) with their consent.

References

AMERICAN JOURNAL OF PSYCHIATRY (1986) 'Can we talk?' The schizophrenic patient in psychotherapy. *American Journal of Psychiatry*, **143**, 68–70.

ARIETI, S. (1964) *Interpretation of Schizophrenia.* London: Crosby Lockwood Staples.

ARTHUR, A. Z. (1964) Theories and explanations of delusions: a review. *American Journal of Psychiatry*, August, 105–115.

BECK, A. T. & BECK, R. W. (1972) Screening for depressed patients in family practice. *Postgraduate Medicine*, December, 81–85.

BERNER, P., GABRIEL, E. & KIEFFER, S. (1986) Paranoid psychosis: new aspects of classification and prognosis coming from the Vienna Research Group. *Psychopathology*, **19**, 16–29.

BLEULER, M. & BLEULER, R. (1986) Books reconsidered: Dementia Praecox die Gruppe der Schizophrenien: Eugen Bleuler. *British Journal of Psychiatry*, **149**, 661–664.

BOWMAN, R. (1989) *By Word of Mouth – The Revival of Story Telling* (eds D. Jones & M. Medlicott). London: Channel Four Television.

BRAVO, A., DAVITE, L. & JALLA, D. (1990) Myth, impotence, and survival in the concentration camps. In *The Myths We Live By* (eds R. Samuel & P. Thompson). London: Routledge.

BYATT, A. S. (1992) The story of the eldest princess. In *Caught in a Story: Contemporary Fairy Tales and Fables* (eds C. Park & C. Heaton). London: Vintage.

CAMERON, N. (1959) The paranoid pseudo-community revisited. *American Journal of Sociology*, **65**, 52–58.

CIOMPI, L. (1989) The dynamics of complex biological psychosocial systems. *British Journal of Psychiatry*, **155** (suppl. 5), 15–21.

COX, M. & THIELGAARD, A. (1987) *Mutative Metaphors in Psychotherapy*. London: Tavistock.

CRUMBAUGH, J. C. & MAHOLICK, L. T. (1964) An experimental study in existentialism: the psychometric approach to Frankl's concept of noogenic neurosis. *Journal of Clinical Psychology*, **20**, 200–207.

CUTTING, J. (1989) Gestalt theory and psychiatry: a discussion paper. *Journal of the Royal Society of Medicine*, **82**, 429–431.

DIAMOND, R. (1985) Drugs and the quality of life: the patient's viewpoint. *Journal of Clinical Psychiatry*, **46**, 29–35.

FREUD, S. (1939) Constructions in analysis. *Standard Edition, Volume 23*, pp. 255–269. London: Hogarth Press.

HILLMAN, J. (1972) *The Myth of Analysis: Three Essays in Archetypal Psychology*. Evanson: North Western.

—— (1983) *Healing Fiction*. New York: Stanton Hill.

HOLLOWAY, F. (1988) Day care and community support. In *Community Care in Practice* (eds A. Lavender & F. Holloway), p. 182. Chichester: Wiley.

HOLMES, J. (1993) *John Bowlby and Attachment Theory*. London: Routledge.

HUNTER, K. M. (1991) *Doctor's Stories: The Narrative Structure of Medical Knowledge*. Princetown: Princetown University Press.

HUSZONEK, J. J. (1987) Establishing therapeutic contact with schizophrenics: a supervisory approach. *American Journal of Psychotherapy*, **41**, 185–193.

IBSEN, H. (1965) The wild duck. In *Four Major Plays*. London: Signet.

JASPERS, K. (1963) *General Psychopathology* (transl. J. Hoenig & M. W. Hamilton). Manchester: Manchester University Press.

KAFFMAN, M. (1984) Paranoid disorders: the core of truth behind the delusional system. *International Journal of Family Therapy*, **6**, 220–232.

KLAWANS, H. L. (1988) *Toscanini's Fumble and Other Tales of Clinical Neurology*. London: Bodley Head.

KLIENMAN, A. (1989) *The Illness Narratives. Suffering, Healing and the Human Condition*. New York: Basic Books.

PERRIS, C. (1989) *Cognitive Therapy with Schizophrenic Patients*. Cassell: Guilford Press.

PHILLIPS, J. (1991) Narrative structures in psychopathology. Paper delivered at the joint conference of the European Society for Philosophy of Medicine and Health Care and the Philosophy Group of the Royal College of Psychiatrists, St Catherine's College, Oxford.

RAPPAPORT, J. (1990) *The Boy Who Couldn't Stop Washing*. London: Collins.

ROBERTS, G. A. (1991) Delusional systems and meaning in life – a preferred reality? *British Journal of Psychiatry* (suppl. 14), 20–29.

—— (1992) The origins of delusion. *British Journal of Psychiatry*, **161**, 298–308.

ROTH, S. (1970) The seemingly ubiquitous depression following acute schizophrenic episodes: a neglected area of clinical discussion. *American Journal of Psychiatry*, **127**, 91–98.

SACKS, O. (1985) *The Man Who Mistook His Wife For a Hat*. London: Duckworth.

SIMS, A. (1988) *Symptoms in the Mind – An Introduction to Descriptive Psychopathology*. London: Balliere.

VAN PUTTEN, T., CRUMPTON, E. & YALE, C. (1976) Drug refusal in schizophrenia and the wish to be crazy. *Archives of General Psychiatry*, **33**, 1443–1446.

YORKE, C. (1988) A defect in training. *British Journal of Psychiatry*, **152**, 159–163.

Afterword

CHRIS MACE and FRANK MARGISON

The grouping of psychotherapeutic interventions into three main traditions that has been adopted in this book looks set to stay. While they may never be fully compatible with one another at a theoretical level, all three types of psychotherapeutic work have their place in providing a comprehensive service for psychosis. Growing points in each of the traditions have been identified in the book, and they provide essential resources from which innovative therapeutic models are likely to be derived.

The way in which psychotherapies from any of these traditions are implemented is likely to be of enormous importance in the future. A recent report (NHS Executive, 1996) has summarised three chief ways in which any of the psychotherapies discussed here may be implemented within the National Health Service. Psychotherapy may be one component of a broader care plan; different models may be integrated within a single therapeutic intervention; or a psychotherapy may be administered in 'pure' form.

Each of these brings with it a distinct challenge that will have to be addressed for some of the hopes expressed in this book to be realised. They will be discussed in turn.

Psychotherapy within a complex care plan

Some psychological interventions are part of a complex multidisciplinary care plan. An individual might simultaneously need to have neuroleptic medication to reduce positive symptoms and reduce the risk of relapse, help with compliance and early recognition of relapse, a key worker to help negotiate accommodation and occupation, respite care, and specific help to increase social contacts. Interleaved with these social and pharmacological approaches there might be help with reducing family conflict, and concurrent cognitive–behavioural therapy to enhance the ability to cope with intrusive psychotic experiences. A multitude of such combinations might be planned as part of a care programme.

Having psychotherapy as one component of a care plan brings a struggle to integrate a service in the face of interdisciplinary and interagency rivalries. The challenge here is to coordinate all these components within an interagency system that retains a human, responsive face rather than reducing the individual to a series of components, each of which is treated by a different bit of the organisation.

Integrating different models within one therapy intervention

The second type of psychotherapy delivery might involve only one worker who draws from a variety of approaches to produce an integrated treatment plan with agreed goals. This is integration at the level of a single treatment intervention. The challenge to one professional providing a hybrid intervention is the conceptual task of integrating a treatment plan based on several theoretical models that can be delivered by an individual therapist. The therapist is challenged to draw together the best evidence available while avoiding the temptation to shift chaotically from model to model as a response to the chaos experienced by the patient.

The pure model

Finally, the third type of psychological intervention is delivered by someone expert in that approach with attention primarily to treatment 'fidelity' rather than integration across methods. The challenge here concerns our ability to maintain a consistent approach within a model. An example might be the patient who requires the consistency and reliability of an analytic setting in order to explore the meaning and history of a symptom which at a superficial level seems 'non-understandable'. The task in this case is not primarily to keep tuned to the chosen mode (although this can be difficult enough) but to remain sensitive to the patient's needs instead of acting from a sense of therapeutic omnipotence.

Provision in the National Health Service

These challenges, which follow any attempt to practise psychotherapy within the complex system that is the National Health Service, are not unique to work with psychosis. Some others have been discussed in Chapter 13 where, after advocating the potential benefits of integrated treatment approaches in this area, some of the difficulties of integration were considered. However, there may be particular difficulties that arise when psychosis is the focus of therapeutic endeavours. These reflect the depth and the breadth of the concern that it engenders.

The unusual depth of this concern would reflect the fact that the experience of psychosis represents an involuntary dislocation in reality that is profoundly disturbing and that moves others to replace it, often forcefully, with something that seems more familiar and preferable. The breadth of concern reflects the way in which psychosis, equated with 'severe' mental illness, is an acknowledged social priority, upon which many people, apart from clinicians, feel a responsibility to act. Inevitably, these individuals' own versions of reality, whether they be politicians, purchasers or publicists, make themselves felt in ways that challenge clinical certainties developed in a different era. (In Chapter 10, Evans referred to a move from problem-based therapy through solution-based therapy towards resource-based thinking among systemic therapists that probably has parallels across the psychotherapeutic spectrum.)

There is a danger that the relatively intense concern that psychosis can engender is met with professional and managerial responses that themselves risk being, in John Walshe's sense (cf. Chapter 5), psychotic. These involve assertions that we all know what the priorities are, that being involved with this group of patients is worthwhile irrespective of what we do, that we know what is *really* going on here, and so on. As Walshe's discussion indicates, self-sustaining beliefs of this kind are common in the face of overpowering anxiety, when they enjoy widespread assent, but this is no guarantee that they are justified in any other sense. (Some damaging professional consequences of such inappropriate beliefs are discussed by Wessely, 1996.) In working with psychosis, when tendencies of this kind are at their most powerful, it seems especially important to have a well grounded sense of what is real and what is true.

The reader will find references to many kinds of truth in this book, including appeals to figures, to forms, to feelings, to facts, and to faith. In practice, none of these has had a monopoly in determining what is done on behalf of patients with psychosis. The failure to make family therapy widely available, despite strong evidence of its value in treatment and relapse prevention (Chapter 7) is one glaring example of a failure to respect the evidence of research (cf. Anderson & Adams, 1996). Conversely, the routines of 'case management', and potentially neurotoxic new drugs for schizophrenia, have been widely introduced with a minimum of evidence concerning their benefits.

Psychotherapeutic research in this area, as in many others, is far better placed to influence practice now than even ten years ago. The technical difficulties of researching psychotherapeutic practice have been well rehearsed (Aveline & Shapiro, 1995) and all the difficulties apply with added potency in the field of psychosis. Treatments need to be particularly clearly specified as therapists are likely to drift out of mode in response to the challenge of treating an illness that is fundamentally about fragmentation of experience. Selection of homogeneous groups of patients in classic group-design studies is difficult given the problems of diagnosis alluded to earlier in this volume. Desired outcomes are not straightforward to define, given the often differing priorities of patients, families and clinicians. Psychotic patients might also be particularly sensitive to the inevitable intrusions of the researcher into the therapeutic space. Given these limitations, a schema of Howard *et al* (1993), which distinguishes the three phases of remoralisation (the return of hope), remediation (the removal of symptoms) and rehabilitation (return to optimal function), provides a particularly useful framework to guide future research into the psychotherapy of psychosis.

At the conclusion of the York conference, we were left with considerable optimism that psychological treatments would have a substantial role in treating psychosis in the future. For this to be realised, however, there would not only need to be a major reappraisal at both service and governmental levels of the advances that have already been made and of their potential, but significant changes in the training of psychiatrists preparing for practice in the next century.

What can be said about these? Certainly, more attention needs to be given during training to increasing practitioners' sensitivity to patients' communications and language. Familiarity with the concepts and methods of the three main therapeutic approaches through teaching and supervised clinical practice would also help trainees personally to integrate the principles illustrated here alongside the knowledge of psychopharmacology, genetics, virology and neuroimaging that is so often impressively in evidence. But greater awareness too of the irrational and countertherapeutic consequences of some institutional dynamics on the one hand, and the capacity to critically evaluate apparently objective evidence on the other, seem essential components of training if future clinical services are to be led and organised in ways that realise their full therapeutic potential.

References

AVELINE, M. & SHAPIRO, D. A. (1995) *Research Foundations for Psychotherapy Practice.* London: Wiley.

HOWARD, K. I., LUEGER, R., MALING, M., *et al* (1993)A phase model of psychotherapy: causal mediation of outcome. *Journal of Consulting and Clinical Psychology*, **61**, 678–685.

ANDERSON, J. & ADAMS, C. (1996) Family interventions in schizophrenia. *British Medical Journal*, 505–506.

NHS EXECUTIVE (1996) *NHS Psychotherapy Services in England: Review of Strategic Policy.* London: HMSO.

WESSELY, S. (1996) The rise of counselling and the return of alienism. *British Medical Journal*, **313**, 158–160.

Index

Compiled by CAROLINE SHEARD

ACI 133
acting out 227
acute psychosis teams 243–4, 247–8
aesthetic access to personality 37–9,
    43–4
aesthetic imperative 37, 43–4
aetiology 49–50
analytical psychology 6
Antecedent and Coping Interview 133
antidepressants 13
antisocial behaviours 102–4
APTs 243–4, 247–8
arbitrary interference 119
Ashworth Inquiry 91
attachment 203
    and family systemic therapy 163
    and narrative competence 259
aversion therapy of hallucinations 99

Beck Depression Inventory 264, 265
behaviour, modelling 91
behaviour modification 7
behavioural family therapy 108, 181–3
    assessment 184–7
    communication skills training 188–90
    components 184–91
    education module 188
    expectations of families 193
    formulation and summary 187
    further work 188–90
    and guilt feelings 193
    initial meeting 184

problem-solving 190–1
    questions asked by new therapists
        192–5
    with reluctant families 194–5
    role of therapist 192–3
    skill introduction 191
    tasks of family sessions 191–2
    weekly meetings 187–8
behavioural psychotherapy 6–7
belief modification 132
betrayal 17–18
Bleuler, E. 6
bobards 259
borderline empathy 83–4
borderline personality disorder/
    organisation 25–6
borderline phenomena in groups 77–87
boundaries 149–50
    and sexual abuse 208–9
Brief Psychiatric Rating Scale 143–4

care plans, psychotherapy within 272–3
Care Programme Approach 203
Cassel family unit 170, 173–4, 180
challenging behaviour 102
change avoidance in institutions 217–18
Chestnut Lodge Follow-Up Study 21, 25
children, safety of 173–4
chlorpromazine 13
cognitive–behavioural interventions 8,
        89–91
    in non-schizophrenic psychoses 93–5

schema-based techniques 120–5
in schizophrenia 95–110, 115–27,
  133–45
Collaborative Treatment of Depression
Research Programme 93
communication skills training 188–90
community care 61, 102, 221
  Finland 246–7
confrontation 132
containment 214
context of intervention 202
contingency management 131
coping strategies
  definition 134
  in hallucinations 100
coping strategy enhancement (CSE)
  101, 134–8
  evaluation 138–45
countertransference 19, 214, 221, 224,
  227–8
  in groups 80–1
  and sexual abuse 212
CSE *see* coping strategy enhancement

deinstitutionalisation, balanced 246,
  250–2
delusion
  cognitive–behavioural interventions
    96, 98–9, 118–25, 133–45
  development of psychological
    interventions 131–3
  inadequacy of pharmacotherapy 130–1
  meaning of 261–5
  model of formation 261
  and narrative 260–5, 268–9
  and normality 117–18
démence 2
denial 215–16
depression
  cognitive–behavioural interventions
    125–6
  post-psychotic 268

detachment, in institutions 215–16
developmental disharmony 23–4
diagnosis 49–50, 159
dialect, regressed 40
differentiation in medicine 199–200
direct analysis in schizophrenia 116
double bind 6
double-density dialogue 41
downward arrow technique 122–3
dysmorphophobia 94

eclecticism 200–1
EE 107–9, 162–3, 165
Einheitpsychose 2
empathy 152–5
empathy resistance 32
experience, levels of 159–60
expressed emotion 107–9, 162–3, 165

failure in psychotherapy 20
family ego 172–3
family systemic therapy 149–51, 165
  application to psychosis 157–8
  and attachment 163
  case studies 154–5
  definitions 157–8
  development 159–64
  and eclecticism 164–5
  feminist theories 163
  level of inference 156–7, 161, 165
  post-Milan theories 163
  research 157
  resource-focused 163
  schools of 161–2
  solution-focused 163
  three Ss classification 161, 163
family theories 159–62
family therapy 107–10
  see also behavioural family therapy;
    family systemic therapy
fantasy 65

Finnish National Schizophrenia Project
(FNSP) 20, 252–3
    acute psychosis teams (APTs)
        243–4, 247–8
    aims 239–40
    balanced deinstitutionalisation 246,
        250–2
    funding 241
    historical background 238–9
    new patients 241–3
    organisation 240
    rehabilitation programme for long-
        stay patients 244–5, 249–50
    subprogrammes 241
    ten year follow-up 246–9
    treatment model 248–9
Finnish Psychotherapy Training
    Guidelines 248
FNSP *see* Finnish National
    Schizophrenia Project
fragmentation 214

goal-setting 185–6
government policies 203
group leader
    functions 77–8
    libidinal attachment to 73
group therapy, Hawthorn Project 220–36
groups
    borderline phenomena in 77–87
    countertransference in 80–1
    equality within 69
    feelings of omnipotence 69–70
    foundation matrix 79
    in-patient 71–3
    out-patient 70–1
    paranoia in 74
    projection in 73–4
    and psychosis 63–75
    psychotic phenomena in 66–70, 72
    resistance to work 68
    rules and rituals 67

theories and models 73–5
transference in 69, 81–5
guided discovery 124
guilt 193

hallucinations
    cognitive–behavioural interventions
        99–101, 126–7, 133–45
    command 126–7
    development of psychological
        interventions 131–3
    inadequacy of pharmacotherapy
        130–1
    somatic 127
Hawthorn Project
    aims 220–1
    clinical course 226–8
    impact on staff 233–4
    organisation 221–3
    outcomes 234–6
    patients 225
    research methods 228–30
    and social networks 228–34
    staff and training 223–5

idealisation 86
inductive formulation 121
inference chaining 122–3
inference level 156, 161, 165
    and research 157
institutions
    characteristic dynamics 215–18
    impact of Hawthorn Project 234
    interaction of sexual abuse and
        psychosis within 205–19
integration 197–8, 199–200, 204
    Arieti model 200–2
    failure of 15–16
    Finnish National Schizophrenia
        Project 238–53
    possibilities and problems 202–4
    within one therapy intervention 273

language 31–2, 46–7
  and aesthetic access to personality
    37–9, 43–4
  diachronic aspects 37
  dialectal emphasis 40
  dissolution of syntax 40–1
  metaphoric axis 43
  metonymic axis 43
  passionate syntax 41–3, 45
  phatic 34
  phenomenology 36–7
  and poetry 44–6
  and poiesis 39–40
  sexualisation 41
  synchronic aspects 37
  translocation of content and context
    33–6
long-stay patients, rehabilitation 244–5,
  249–50

malignant regression 173
Manchester Symptom Project 141–5
manic-depressive psychosis 21–5
meaning 255
  and narrative 258–9
mediation and borderline patients 85–6
Mental Health Act 1952 (Finland) 238
metaphor 43
metonym 43
moral management 5
multiple-density dialogue 41
Münchausen syndrome by proxy 169,
  177–8
myxoedema 3

named-nurse initiatives 216
narcissism 213
narrative 203, 255–8, 269–70
  competence 259
  and delusions 260–5, 268–9
  of illness 259–60
  implications 266–70

and psychopathology 260–5
and recovery 267–8
as source of meaning and
  understanding 258–9
National Health Service 235–6
  provision of psychotherapy services
    273–5
negotiation and borderline patients
  85–6
neurotic functioning and psychotic
functioning 51–3
Nordic Investigation of
  Psychotherapeutically Oriented
  Treatment for New Schizophrenics
  (NIPS) 20
normalising rationale 135

Othello syndrome 41

panic, prepsychotic 261
paranoia in groups 74
paranoid–schizoid functioning 15
paronomasia 34
passwords 35–6
pathological projective identification 16
personalisation 119
personality disorder 94
pharmacotherapy 13–14
  inadequacy 130–1
poetic precision 37
poetry 38
  terms, energies and processes 44–6
poiesis 38, 39–40, 44
  and passionate syntax 41–3
porphyria 3
postnatal depression 169, 175–7
power relationships and sexual abuse
  209–10
problem-solving (PS) 190–1
  evaluation 138–45
  in hallucinations 101
projection in groups 73–4

projective identification 17–18, 214
PS *see* problem-solving
psychiatric services, contribution of
 applied psychoanalytic psychotherapy
 60–1
psychoanalysis 5, 7, 13–14
 contribution to psychiatric services
  60–1
 in manic-depressive psychosis 21–5
 in schizophrenia 14–21
psychodynamic psychotherapy 13–14
 in manic-depressive psychosis 21–5
 in schizophrenia 14–21
psychosis 206–7
 characteristic dynamics 212–14
 concept of 171
 definition 63–4, 104
 endogenous 4
 and groups 63–75
 interaction with sexual abuse within
  institutions 205–19
 medical model 64
 predisposition to 53
 psychoanalytic development model 64
 psychogenic 3–4
 sociological model 64–5
 terminology 1–4
psychotherapy
 current views and practice 7–9
 development of use in psychosis 5–7
 provision of services within NHS
  273–5
 in schizophrenia 116
 within a complex care plan 272–3
psychotic anxieties 171–2
psychotic breakdown 172–3
psychotic character 26
psychotic functioning 172
 externalisation 61
 implications for assessment and
  treatment 53–9
 and neurotic functioning 51–3

psychotic phenomena 66
 in groups 66–70, 72
punishment 103–4, 131
Purpose in Life Test 264, 265

quality assurance in therapies 21
questioning
 circular 161
 reflexive 161

reality distortion 17–18
reality testing 100–1, 126
recovery and narrative 267–8
regression 173
 in groups 78–9
 psychotic 213
rehabilitation of long-stay patients
 244–5, 249–50
reinforcement 91, 131
 in antisocial behaviours 103–4
 in delusions 96, 98
 negative 103–4, 131
relapse prevention 107–10, 142–5, 181
resistance 224, 227
revictimisation
 in in-patient setting 206
 and sexual abuse 210
revolving-door syndrome 249
ritualised task performance in
 institutions 216
role rigidity in institutions 217

sadism 213
Salford Family Intervention Project
 133–4
Salford Symptom Project 138–41
scapegoating in institutions 217
schizophrenia
 antisocial behaviours 102–4
 cognitive–behavioural interventions
  95–110, 115–27, 133–45
 continuity with normality 117–18

development of psychological
   interventions 131–3
formulation 120, 121–2
history of concept 6
history taking 118–20
inadequacy of pharmacotherapy
   130–1
interpersonal theory 159–60
in mother and child 178–9
negative symptoms 104–6
positive symptoms 96–101
psychoanalytic and psychodynamic
   approaches 14–21
psychotherapy in 116
relapse 101
relapse prevention 107–10, 142–5
specific theory 17
and stigma 194
unitary theory 17
vulnerability/stress model 107, 115,
   119, 181–2
schizophrenogenic family/mother 160
selective abstraction 119
self-beliefs and sexual abuse 210
self-instructional training 98, 132
self-monitoring of hallucinations 99,
   132
semiology 159
sexual abuse 205–7
   and boundaries 208–9
   characteristic dynamics 207–12
   and countertransference 212
   interaction with psychosis within
      institutions 205–19
   and power relationships 209–10
   and problems with establishing
      trusting relationships 207–8
   and revictimisation 210
   and self-beliefs 210
   and sexualisation of therapeutic
      relationships 211
   and transference 211–12

shell shock 13
Social Functioning Scale 144–5
social interference 131
social networks 228–34
social skills training in schizophrenia
   105–6
Sopimusvuori Communities 244–5
speech *see* language
splitting in psychosis 214
staff
   impact of Hawthorn Project 233–4
   support for 218
stigma and schizophrenia 194
stimulus control 132
story-making *see* narrative
stress, psychological 3
subvocal exercises in hallucinations
   99
suicide
   cognitive–behavioural interventions
      125–6
   and failure of therapy 20
supportive therapy 202–3
syntax
   dislocation 45
   dissolution 40–1
   passionate 41–3, 45
syphilis 3
systemic treatment 8

therapeutic alliance 18, 185
   and trust 208
therapeutic community 169, 170, 173–4,
   244–5
therapeutic relationships, sexualisation
   211
time out 131
timing of intervention 202
token economy systems 89, 96,
   104–5
training in psychoanalytic and
   psychodynamic therapies 21

transference 224
  in groups 69, 81–5
  negative 227
  and sexual abuse 211–12
transference psychoses 16, 227
trauma and psychogenic psychosis 3–4
Turku Project 20

turmoil 261
Twenty Statement Test 225

unconscious 63–4, 65

vulnerability/stress model of
  schizophrenia 107, 115, 119, 181–2